# Management Consultancy for Innovation

This book provides a new perspective on innovation in consultancy firms. Focusing on how consultancy firms can innovate in the modern era, it exposes and discusses key drivers for innovation in the industry. These are broken down into five dimensions – or 'Poles' – relating to forms of capital (human capital, social capital, and three types of organizational capital) that consultancy firms can use in order to innovate, both for themselves and for their clients.

Readers of this book will not only gain insight into the 'innovative consultancy' from the perspective of each of these Poles. They will also discover how consultancy firms need to find the right way of connecting these Poles together in order to produce the desired innovation. Readers will learn about the dangers of misaligning the Poles, as well as implications of innovative consultancy for ethics, academic research in the field of consultancy, and for careers. In addition to the academic literature, the book draws from real-world examples, cases, and practice insights from various parts of the world.

This book will be of great use to those interested in pursuing a career in the consultancy industry, whether they are undergraduate and postgraduate Business and Management students, students not necessarily studying in business schools, or others seeking a career move into consultancy. It will also be valuable to seasoned consultants and managers of consultancy firms seeking new ideas on how to develop innovative capabilities in an increasingly competitive industry.

**Christopher Williams** is Reader in Management at Durham University Business School, UK. His publications include academic research in a range of journals, over 25 teaching cases, and the book *Venturing in International Firms: Contexts and Cases in a High-Tech World* (Routledge, 2018).

"This book provides well-researched, accessible and intelligent insights into the pressures on, and opportunities for, innovation in a complex and dynamic industry. These insights are supported by in-depth and multi-level international cases which will prove interesting to students, researchers and consultants themselves."

**Joe O'Mahoney**, *Professor of Management Consultancy,*
*Cardiff Business School, UK*

*"Management Consultancy for Innovation* is a fascinating examination of the consultancy industry and presents a powerful agenda for the 'innovative consultant' and the drivers of how consultancy firms can innovate. It is surprising that an industry worth billions of dollars, in which innovating solutions and insights to senior management problems are the core value proposition, has not received sufficiently deep investigation. Christopher Williams' book provides a detailed and example-laden analysis of how the consultancy firm can innovate, the challenges faced and ways forward."

**Mathew Hughes**, *Professor of Entrepreneurship and*
*Innovation, Loughborough University, UK*

"With *Management Consultancy for Innovation*, Christopher Williams invites the reader to stop and wonder: How much of our approach is really innovative and are we helping our clients to develop truly original ideas? By combining academic insight with examples from real-life business cases, this book offers a framework and inspiration to experiment with new solutions to boost long-term performance."

**Sophie Loquet**, *Management Consultant,*
*House of Performance, the Netherlands*

"Dr Chris Williams makes a welcome contribution to our understanding of the management consulting sector. This focused illumination builds on the increasingly well-charted broader landscape of consulting (organizations and practice). Chris' dual grasp of innovation and management consulting makes him ideally placed to offer insight into perspectives leading to client value plus organizational fitness and sustainability."

**Dr Simon Haslam**, *Chair of Academic Fellows, International*
*Council of Management Consulting Institutes, UK*

# Management Consultancy for Innovation

**Christopher Williams**

Routledge
Taylor & Francis Group

LONDON AND NEW YORK

First published 2020
by Routledge
2 Park Square, Milton Park, Abingdon, Oxon OX14 4RN

and by Routledge
52 Vanderbilt Avenue, New York, NY 10017

*Routledge is an imprint of the Taylor & Francis Group, an informa business*

© 2020 Christopher Williams

*British Library Cataloguing-in-Publication Data*
A catalogue record for this book is available from the British Library

*Library of Congress Cataloging-in-Publication Data*
A catalog record for this book has been requested

ISBN: 978-1-138-31278-4 (hbk)
ISBN: 978-1-138-31279-1 (pbk)
ISBN: 978-0-429-45801-9 (ebk)

Typeset in Bembo
by Apex CoVantage, LLC

For Bayley

# Contents

*List of figures* viii

*Preface* ix

Chapter 1  Introduction 1

Chapter 2  Pole 1: human capital 18

Chapter 3  Pole 2: social capital 34

Chapter 4  Pole 3: consultant virtualization 52

Chapter 5  Pole 4: disruption in the consultancy life-cycle 72

Chapter 6  Pole 5: reflective ability in consultancy 93

Chapter 7  Connecting the Poles to form the innovative consultancy 117

Chapter 8  Implications of the innovative consultancy 143

Chapter 9  Concluding remarks 156

*Appendix: cases of innovative consultancies* 159

*References* 214

*Index* 230

# Figures

1.1  A Uni-Dimensional View of Innovative Orientation
in Management Consultancy                                                    12
1.2  A Two-Dimensional (Internal–External) View of Innovative
Orientation in Management Consultancy                                        13
1.3  The Innovation Radar: Five Poles of Innovation in Management
Consultancy                                                                  15
1.4  The Inert Innovator in Management Consultancy                           16
1.5  The Enthusiastic Innovator in Management Consultancy                    16
2.1  Pole 1: A Focus on Human Capital                                        19
3.1  Pole 2: A Focus on Social Capital                                       35
4.1  Pole 3: A Focus on Consultant Virtualization                           53
5.1  Pole 4: A Focus on Life-Cycle Disruption                               73
6.1  Pole 5: A Focus on Reflective Ability                                   95
7.1  Two-Way Interaction #1: Human and Social Capital                       118
7.2  Two-Way Interaction #2: Human Capital and Reflective Ability           121
7.3  Two-Way Interaction #3: Social Capital and Consultant
Virtualization                                                               123
7.4  Two-Way Interaction #4: Life-Cycle Disruption and
Reflective Ability                                                           125
7.5  Two-Way Interaction #5: Life-Cycle Disruption in a Virtually
Organized Consultancy                                                        127
7.6  Three-Way Interaction #1: Virtually Organized Human
and Social Capital                                                           130
7.7  Three-Way Interaction #2: Human and Social Capital under
High Reflection                                                              133
7.8  Comparison of the Four Cases Using the Innovation Radar                 136

# Preface

I first came across management consultants while working in international firms in the 1990s and early 2000s. Sometimes they were brought into the team in which I was working to help with training and team development. Sometimes they were present in the corridors of power, helping the company on its strategy. Later, in London, I worked closely with one firm's own highly specialized consultants in a practice servicing global pharmaceutical clients. It was one of the most interesting episodes in my career. Since moving into business schools in 2007, I've met lots of business and management students wanting to pursue careers as management consultants. MBA programs can help students obtain a successful foothold in the consultancy industry by developing their knowledge *and* their skills. I've seen how highly experienced consultants share their experiences and reflect on their own career paths when they come to visit and engage with MBA students. My conclusion? Without a doubt, this is a fascinating and highly intriguing industry.

Management consultants always seemed to be different than the regular, general managers I met in organizations. They were somehow special; traveling to exotic places, working on a diverse range of projects for different clients, full of fresh insights and bright ideas, sometimes a bit aloof. And they could charge decent money for advising and guiding their clients on tricky issues and situations. Whether this 'special person' status is true or not (and there has been a fair amount of skepticism of consultants and suspicion about their true value[1]), what is for sure is that the consultancy industry is epic. It is large, it is complex, it is diverse, and it continues to grow. Consultancy.uk estimates the global consultancy industry at $277 billion (2018) and counting, with yearly growth at over 6 per cent in Asia Pacific, and 12 per cent in China.[2] And unlike sister industries such as accounting and the legal profession, there is less of an emphasis on professional association and formal regulation in terms of how the professionals involved (i.e., management consultants) deliver value (Von Nordenflycht, 2010). Of course, a consultant's work has to be accounted for, and it has to abide by the law. However, as O'Mahoney and Sturdy (2016) note, the consulting industry is a sector which is relatively new, concentrated and (comparatively) unconstrained by unions, institutions and the law.

(O'Mahoney and Sturdy, 2016: 261)

Management consultancy is also an industry in which boundaries surrounding the core activity (of providing advice and guidance) are continuously blurring (Sturdy, 2011). There are "alternatives to consultancy as a means of innovation, change management and legitimation" (Sturdy, 2011: 527). For example, large companies themselves often set up internal consultancy units (Hodges, 2017). The story of one of these is provided in the *iCon* case reproduced in this book (Chen, Tran and Williams, 2018). Elsewhere, influences on management decision making and change in organizations come through sources that are vastly different to the picture of a conventional consultant. Nevertheless, with these other sources we still see the act of consultancy occurring at the core. The *Hongxin Incubator* case (also reproduced in full in this book) is set in Xiamen in China and tells the story of how the leader of a highly successful business incubator not only offers management advice but is also influential in how that advice is actually implemented in practice. In other words, the core act of management consultancy is not exclusively the realm of external companies that position themselves as traditional consultancy outfits.

When an organization seeks some advice (we will refer to this organization as the 'client' throughout this book), it inevitably finds there are lots of competing entities queueing up outside to offer said advice. And this competition is becoming more and more intense. Gone are the days when management consultancy was only offered by a few large and influential business services firms such as McKinsey & Company. Today there are quite literally thousands upon thousands of small, independent consultancy firms and a myriad of other sources able to provide advice that can potentially compete for the attention of the same client. There are so many agents of management ideas (O'Mahoney and Sturdy, 2016) out there all bidding to be noticed by clients, and all wanting to stand out.

In order to do this, and, hopefully, grow their share of the industry, consultancy firms need to innovate. And they need to innovate like never before. We see this in the way the large consultancy firms restructure and develop new practice areas (Anand, Gardner and Morris, 2007; Christensen, Wang and Van Bever, 2013). But we also see it in the way non-traditional sources of consultancy seek new ways of attracting business (such as in the *Hongxin Incubator* case in this book). In O'Mahoney's (2011) study of management innovation in the UK consultancy industry, he finds 69 per cent of respondents believing innovation in the industry to have increased in the previous five years. A number of factors have driven this, including an increased demand for bespoke projects from clients as well as a need for consultancy firms to differentiate themselves because of increased competition on the supply side (O'Mahoney, 2013).

In my own experience with consultants, I have come to the conclusion that not all of them are innovative. Some try to be innovative and try to be disruptive. But when you really look into their thought processes and at what they're suggesting you soon realize that they're not really innovative at all![3] In these cases they seem to be applying the same model or framework or approach that they applied many times previously. However, others do seem to be innovative, coming up with new and creative solutions for their client, and helping their client with their own innovation agenda. In other words, we see a large variance in 'innovation' and 'innovativeness' amongst consultants and consultancy firms.

For a while now, I've been curious about what drives this variance. What makes some people more innovative than others? What makes some organizations more innovative than others? This book is about asking the question *what makes some consultancy firms more innovative than others?* In order to shed some light on this question it is necessary to understand the drivers of innovation in organizations and then to contextualize this into a consultancy setting. After all, consultancy firms don't have R&D departments in the traditional sense (Sundbo, 1997) and their innovations are typically not protected by patents (Semadeni and Anderson, 2010). We therefore need to understand what the literature has been saying on the question of innovation in management consultancy.

Unfortunately, there has not been much explicit attention in the texts paid to this question. There is no dedicated chapter or mention of innovation in the index of David Maister's (2003) best-selling work on *Managing the Professional Service Firm* (Simon & Schuster) for example. And this is a best-selling book! There are only two pages out of over 500 pages given in the index of the *Oxford Handbook of Management Consulting* (Oxford University Press) (Kipping and Clark, 2012) to innovation, and this only refers to future research on structuring consultancy firms. There are only two pages out of nearly 200 pages in the index of Margerison's (1988) *Managerial Consulting Skills: A Practical Guide* (Gower Publishing) and this only refers to an innovation case to illustrate role consultation.

In broad terms, scholars have lamented the lack of attention to consulting as a field of scholarly enquiry: "consulting, which has undeniable economic relevance . . . has not yet received significant attention from academic management scholars" (Canato and Giangreco, 2011: 240). And in terms of our focus in this book, scholars have recognized that more insights are needed on the links between consultancy and innovation. For example, Wright, Sturdy and Wylie (2012) state: "although there are many claims made of management consultancy, there remain few empirical studies documenting its consequences in terms of innovation" (659). Back, Parboteeah and Nam (2014) make the following comment in the context of emerging markets: "to our knowledge no study has directly investigated the link between management consultancy use and innovation in emerging markets" (391). And according to Crevani, Palm and Schilling (2011), who have a slightly broader perspective on business services firms: "there is a need to also look at the issues facing practitioners daily involved in attempts to foster innovation in service firms" (178). So, while the management consultancy industry is fascinating because of its size, complexity, diversity, and growth, what is particularly intriguing to me is the lack of *explicit* attention given to the question of innovation within firms in this sector.

This book aims to fill at least some of this gap and to provide students, researchers, and practitioners a fresh insight into management consultancy from the perspective of innovation. The book will attack the question of how consultancy firms (can) innovate in the modern era by exposing and debating key drivers – which I refer to as 'Poles' – for innovation in this particular industry. The first two of these Poles, so it could be said, 'state the obvious'. These relate to the importance of *human capital* (Pole 1) and *social capital* (Pole 2) in enabling consultants to come up with fundamentally new approaches and offerings for themselves and/or for their clients. While the logic of these two Poles might be obvious for many, the literature review and case examples used here do reveal some interesting nuances and peculiarities that make their inclusion as baseline arguments very worthwhile. The next three Poles are all forms of *organizational capital* commonly debated and used in the contemporary consultancy industry: virtual organization (Pole 3), life-cycle disruption (Pole 4), and reflective ability (Pole 5). Collectively, these five Poles relate to various forms of capital (human capital, social capital, organizational capital) that enable consultancy firms to be innovative, both for themselves (i.e., changing the way they do business) and for their clients (i.e., helping clients develop new products, services, and ways of working). We are therefore treating the topic of the 'innovative consultancy' as a multi-dimensional analysis and one that is heavily contextualized with an explicit focus on consultancy firms.

Chapter 1 is an Introduction. It discusses definitions and different perspectives on innovation, the issues of consultants innovating for clients versus innovating for themselves, and different themes in the literature on consultancy and innovation. Chapters 2 to 6 discuss each of the Poles in turn. In each of these chapters we will blend academic literature review with insights from the real-world of consultancy. Each of these chapters provides a background to the specific theme, and a discussion on the core theoretical message of why the Pole should be seen as having potential to drive innovative outcomes. Importantly, how this manifests itself in consultancy firms will be discussed. Each of these Pole chapters will draw on real-world examples and will include vignettes from practicing consultants from various parts of the world who have kindly volunteered to share their experiences for the purpose of this book. Four very different cases of innovative consultancies also are reproduced in full in the book, telling stories of the strategic innovation undertaken by consultancy firms in Canada, the US, Germany, and China. I chose these cases because they represent not only a diversity in the types of countries and consultancy firms, but also in terms of the scale and impact of the innovation they are pursuing. These are the Deloitte Dads initiative (Canada), Ergonomica Consulting and Solltram Hotels (US), iCon (innogy Consulting) (Germany), and Hongxin Entrepreneur Incubator (China).

In the *Deloitte Dads* case, a manager in the corporate strategy practice in the Toronto office of Deloitte spearheaded a new initiative for an inclusion and diversity group for fathers working in the organization. This builds on previous initiatives in inclusion and diversity and I see this as a case of incremental and internally-oriented organizational innovation.

In the *Ergonomica* case, the scale and impact of the innovation is slightly larger. Here, a small and niche consultancy firm based on the West Coast of the US was trying to find ways of winning new clients in the hotel industry to help them with energy efficiency. While the case describes the lead up to an ethical dilemma facing one of the consultants, the subsequent events[4] detail how the company had to find new ways of working following the fall-out from this ethical challenge. This involved the development of new quality assurance and control systems. This is incremental but with a bigger impact, but still internally focused.

Next, in the *iCon* case, the company had its origins as an internal consultancy unit for the German energy giant RWE. As a consequence of a carve out of innogy, a pure play energy retailer, from the group, the consultancy unit found itself with opportunities to sell to a new external client base. This is a much more radical proposition for the company, one that is clearly externally oriented and which will take the firm into new geographic territories as well.

Finally, in the *Hongxin Cloud Entrepreneurship* case, we see the most radical proposition within this set of four cases. Hongxin, a Chinese entrepreneurship incubator based in Xiamen, was expanding in size and influence. It had been involved in providing a management advisory service to established firms as well as incubation for new enterprises. Hongxin was considering moving into other locations in China using a web-based cloud platform that had not been tried and tested before. The organization had little experience in other locations and no experience with an Internet-based platform for interacting with clients.

In all of these cases of innovative consultancies, the focal organization is seen to embrace an innovative agenda in pursuit of long-term performance. But we see that the organizational system surrounding the key players differs markedly across the cases. We will discuss these cases throughout the book. Furthermore, insights from other published cases that I hope you find useful and are able to access and learn from are also given in each chapter. I encourage you to read these additional suggested cases and use them in discussions to expand your learning of the topic. I have found them to be extremely useful in class.

The book will then build on these five Pole chapters to discuss vital strategic leadership implications for building and managing the innovative consultancy. Chapter 7 leads the way here by discussing the leadership imperative of 'connecting the Poles'. It essentially argues that the innovative consultancy will never be truly realized without an appreciation of how the Poles are inter-linked and how they are inter-dependent on each other. Some of these connections are only implicitly recognized in the literature. What Chapter 7 does is explicitly bring the important connections to the fore. It provides a contingency argument that says bringing the Poles together *in the right way* (and perhaps only some of them, it does not have to be all of them, all of the time!) and *at the right time* (i.e., depending on the nature of the situation facing the consultancy) will determine effective innovative performance in the industry. In the penultimate chapter, Chapter 8, we discuss ethical considerations of the innovative consultancy, and also implications for research and careers in the field as a consequence of the perspective put forward here.

I hope that users of this book at undergraduate or postgraduate level will be interested not only in pursuing a career in the consultancy industry but also interested in the question of how they can contribute to innovation for their employers and their clients in this industry. The book can be used as a main reader for a module on 'Innovative Consultancy' or as a supplementary reader in modules that cover topics on management consulting, business services, and service innovation. Students ideally would have completed modules in strategy, organizational behavior and innovation, although this would not need to be a pre-requisite for reading or using this book. Many consultancy firms recruit from non-business and management faculties in higher education institutions and students in such non-business and management areas that want to learn about consultancy before entering the job market also will benefit from this book.

My gratitude goes out to Jeroen Brugman (the Netherlands) for his vignette linked to human capital, Folajimi Ashiru (Nigeria) for his on social capital, Claire Agutter (UK) for hers on virtual organization, Kamales Lardi (Switzerland) for hers on disruptive life-cycles, as well as one anonymous source who provided a vignette on reflective ability. Thanks also go to Ivey Publishing for permission to reproduce the four main cases, and to Carolyn Burns, Jonathan Chen, Simon Haslam, Martin Hogan, Kirsty Joshua, Andre Kik, Andrew Sutton, Sander van Triest, Maurice Wokke, and countless other inspirational consultants and analysts of consultancy who I have met in the last 20 years.

After reading this book and engaging in the ideas and material highlighted here, I sincerely hope you will be as fascinated and intrigued by the management consultancy industry as I am. I hope that you will be able to spot an innovative consultant or an innovative consultancy firm amidst the mass of advice-givers. I also hope that the ideas discussed will help you develop your own original thinking and new approaches whether you are a student of consultancy, a newly joined junior level staff member in an 'apprenticeship' mode within the industry, or a more senior experienced partner or independent consultant on the look-out for some new ideas.

Happy innovative consulting!

Chris Williams, Durham, Winter, 2018

## Notes

1 For instance, Wood (2002a: 8) highlights how "Gullible and inadequate managers are being persuaded to seek and adopt outside advice by the tactics of opportunists feeding off their insecurity, often with disastrous results". Winsborough and Chamorro-Premuzic (2013: 322) note: "consultants are quick to offer tools and methodologies that are scientifically dubious". Wood (2002a: 8) also points to the benefits consultants bring to client organizations, commenting on how many clients employ consultants on a regular basis.

2 "Consulting industry of Asia and Australia grows 6% to $50 billion," www.consultancy.uk/news/18819/consulting-industry-of-asia-and-australia-grows-6-to-50-billion, accessed 16 October 2018

3 Conversely, not all innovators are consultants. Trappist Monks have a long history of generating and developing transformative business ideas (Turak, 2013), but you will not see them advising in the boardrooms of S&P 500 firms very often! We will return to this point in the closing chapters.

4 The subsequent events for the Ergonomica case are summarized in Chapter 7 in the section on reflective ability and human and social capital.

# 1

# Introduction

## In search of the innovative consultant

Consultancy firms have certain characteristics that distinguish them from other firms. As professional services firms, they are high in knowledge intensity (Creplet, Dupouet, Kern, Mehmanpazir and Munier, 2001) (their output is dependent on a complex body of expertise and knowledge which they possess amongst their employees and routines, or have access to through their networks). And they have low capital intensity (you do not need a significant amount of non-human assets to start a consultancy firm, in the same way that you would for a manufacturing firm) (Von Nordenflycht, 2010). Other types of professional services firms also have a professionalized workforce, i.e., formally trained, regulated, and belonging to a professional body (e.g., lawyers and accountants), but management consultants are not seen in the same way as far as having a 'professional' status is concerned (Von Nordenflycht, 2010), even though many consultants will consider themselves to be part of a general professional class. According to Hitt, Bierman, Shimizu and Kochhar (2001), professional services firms – including management consultancies – contain people (i.e., professionals) who have a certain knowledge base gained through training and on-the-job experiences that allows them to deliver services to satisfy client needs and achieve performance for their firm.

Von Nordenflycht (2010) and Hitt, Bierman, Shimizu and Kochhar (2001) are highly cited and extremely insightful articles exposing characteristics of different types of professional services firms and, importantly, what determines performance in those firms. However, they do not mention innovation. And, as noted previously, there are also a number of textbooks on consultancy where we also see an absence of innovation explicitly covered, including the works of Maister (2003), Kipping and Clark (2012), and Margerison (1988).

Nevertheless, and echoing the tone of many writers on the topic of consultancy, Obeidat, Al-Suradi, Masa'deh and Tarhini (2016) state: "one of the main core competencies of consultancy firms is to provide their clients with the most recent and latest advice as well as to implement knowledge based on practical and scientific sources" (Obeidat, Al-Suradi, Masa'deh and Tarhini, 2016: 1215–1216). This emphasis on the 'most recent and latest' underlines how important it is for consultants to keep themselves up to date. It also puts a spotlight on the need for them to be able to innovate: to bring new ideas for products, services, and organizational change to their clients, and also to be able to bring such changes to their own organization when needed. Indeed, according to Poulfelt, Olson, Bhambri and Greiner (2017), consultancy firms continually need to change; their clients are in a constant evolutionary curve. Consultants need to be seen as credible advisors given the macro-environment turbulence and dynamism affecting their clients.

This applies to consultancy firms the world over. Srinivasan (2014), in a discussion of the growth of consultancy services in India, describes how clients may not have the ability to innovate for themselves, they may not even recognize the need to innovate in the first place. Consultancy firms can be used to inject creativity into uncreative clients in these types of countries, as much as they can in the developed markets. And within the global management consultancy industry, we have seen the emergence of smaller, entrepreneurial firms springing up and challenging the larger and older incumbents with fresh innovative approaches.

So does this mean academic writers and researchers have been somewhat unsighted and for some inexcusable reason overlooked the potentially rewarding study of innovation in management consultancy? No, not really. As we shall see, many researchers since the turn of the century have looked into innovation in management consultancy. These include Anand, Gardner, and Morris (2007), who examined how new practice areas form in management consultancy firms, Mors (2010), who illuminated the links between senior partners' personal social networks and their innovative performance, Semadeni and Anderson (2010), who researched the interesting question of how organization-level and offering-level factors combine to influence decisions in management consultancy firms when imitating the innovations of competitors, and Taminiau, Smit and De Lange (2009), who exposed the link between informal knowledge sharing and innovation in management consultancy. Others have shown an interest in innovation in other types of professional services firms, such as law firms. Malhotra, Smets and Morris (2016), for instance, looked at the links between changing career paths of professionals and innovation, finding that career path change (a shift from the 'up-or-out' mentality to one where new roles are created that give associates a better work–life balance) have a side effect of boosting innovation while benefiting the individuals concerned.

Overall, the important question of what determines innovation in management consultancy may have been overlooked by some researchers and writers on consultancy. However, where it has been taken on, it tends to be within very narrowly focused and constricted research frames. It can be argued that the literature on innovation in management consultancy is, indeed, rather scattered and fragmented.

Innovation, however, is a massive area of research, and, as we will see in the next section, it is a phenomenon in organizational life that can be looked at from many angles, and in all types of organizations, industries, and locations.

## Perspectives on innovation

While innovation may have been defined differently by different writers over the years, there is a strong consensus on what innovation is fundamentally about, namely the creating of something useful that has value derived from its novelty (Damanpour, 1991; Glynn, 1996). Baregheh, Rowley and Sambrook (2009) conduct a review of academic definitions of innovation, finding the word 'new' to appear 76 times in 60 definitions (Baregheh, Rowley and Sambrook, 2009: 1329). Novelty may be present in different ways, such as in terms of a new product, a new service, or a new way of doing things. It is important that this novelty can be encapsulated (or implemented) into a tangible deliverable (Evan, 1966) that creates economic value for the people or organizations producing it, and hopefully for the people or organizations using it. It is not just about an idea in someone's head. There is a process involved in creating something new and seeking to extract value from that change and newness. Baregheh, Rowley and Sambrook (2009: 1334) propose that "Innovation is the multi-stage process whereby organizations transform ideas into new/improved products, service or processes, in order to advance, compete and differentiate themselves successfully in their marketplace".

Various perspectives on innovation are found in the literature. These include the following: (1) the type of innovation, i.e., whether the innovation can be seen in terms of a tangible good, product or service (Bessant and Davies, 2007) vs. whether it relates to a process or a way of organizing production (Daft, 1978; Utterback and Abernathy, 1975); (2) the nature of innovation, i.e., whether the innovation is completely new and radical vs. whether it represents an incremental or improved state (Dewar and Dutton, 1986; Sundbo, 1997); (3) whether it affects the business system of the firm (i.e., the firm's existing range of products) vs. its managerial system (Damanpour and Aravind, 2012); (4) whether the innovation applies across a whole firm vs. a change that takes place and affects a unit within the firm (e.g., Tsai, 2001); (5) whether the innovation relates to core underlying technology vs. marketing innovation and improvements in the marketing mix (Naidoo, 2010); and (6) whether the innovation is based on exploitation or exploration (Jansen, Van Den Bosch and Volberda, 2006; March, 1991).

Abernathy and Clark (1985) present a 'transilience map' of innovation; a 2 × 2 map with technology production and markets/customer linkage as axes. Technology production ranges from entrenching existing competence to disrupting existing competence. Markets/customer linkage ranges from entrenching existing linkages to disrupting existing and creating new linkages. An aggressive (high) stance on both of these dimensions is *architectural* innovation. A passive (low) stance on both is *regular* innovation. Disrupting existing competence while entrenching existing customer linkages is *revolutionary* innovation. Conserving existing competences with newly created customer linkages is *niche creation*. Abernathy and Clark (1985) develop their model using insights from the US automotive industry.

Research shows how both *bottom-up* and *top-down* processes for innovation can exist in organizations (Daft, 1978). Top management and leaders may well be credited with directly driving innovation in many organizations, but they may also create an environment in which lower level organizational members can generate novelty and seek to turn their ideas into finished solutions. Evan (1966) had earlier noted in his trickle-up, trickle-down theory how lower-level organizational members may be more likely to contribute technical innovations. Daft's (1978) study was set in suburban high school districts in the US and found teachers to be the major source of technical ideas while administrative ideas came from higher levels in the hierarchy. Contingency matters: people will propose innovations related to their specific task domain.

Researchers have gone beyond a depiction of different forms that innovation may take; a large body of literature looks at determinants of innovation. Damanpour (1991), for instance, was one of the first studies to conduct a meta-analysis of determinants of organizational innovation. He examines 13 potential determinants of innovation and found strong and stable support for nine of them. These nine are the following: (1) *specialization* (specialists contain knowledge that can be used to generate new ideas), (2) *functional differentiation* (groups of professionals coalesce in units and innovations occur in these units), (3) *professionalism* (having workers with professional knowledge based on education and experience), (4) *centralization* (concentration of decision-making power having a negative effect on innovation), (5) *managerial attitude toward change* (having a conducive climate and organizational culture for innovation), (6) *technical knowledge resources* (allowing technical ideas to be understood and diffused), (7) *administrative intensity* (providing managerial support for – i.e., championing – innovation), (8) *slack resources* (providing funds for innovation and an ability to bear risk and absorb failure), and (9) *external and internal communication* (which facilitate knowledge flows from diverse external sources and helps cross-fertilize ideas internally) (Damanpour, 1991).

Brown and Duguid (1991) propose a 'communities-of-practice' explanation for innovation. This brings the unit of analysis for innovation down to a community level; communities being relatively small and comprising of individuals that have a shared focal point for their work. Over time, such communities change shape as the nature of their work unfolds and as they find new ways of solving problems and adapting to the challenges they face. They may challenge canonical knowledge[1] by narrating and discussing their shared experiences of solving problems: an intrinsically collaborative process. In Brown and Duguid's (1991) communities-of-practice view, communities offer a way for an organization to experiment and to create new knowledge that is not necessarily engrained into the organization's established ways of doing things. Such knowledge is highly tacit, i.e., cannot easily be written down and codified. Communities-of-practice, according to Brown and Duguid (1991: 51): "step outside the organization's inevitably limited core world view and simply try something new". Lee and Williams (2007) extend this in an examination of dispersed entrepreneurial dynamics in large international companies. Their depiction of 'communities-of-entrepreneurship' shows how dispersed actors come together in international companies in order to provide the genesis of a new idea or opportunity and how this may then proceed into development and legacy (a change to the canonical knowledge of the organization). Lee and Williams (2007) show how such communities-of-entrepreneurship differ from communities-of-practice in important ways, including the purpose of the community, the nature of its focal point, and where the community sources its members from. However, what these views do have in common – and therefore both emphasize – is the way innovative endeavor occurs in groups of people sharing some kind of focal point of interest, and how knowledge sharing and group learning go hand in hand through the innovation process.

In Miles, Snow, Meyer, and Coleman's (1978) classic work on organizational adaptation, the theme of innovation comes up in various guises as the authors describe the cycle of adaptation that all organizations – at some point in their history – need to go through. They develop a strategic typology of organizations: Defenders, Analyzers, and Prospectors. Defenders emphasize stability and seeking sales from a defined segment of the market for which they have limited offerings. They try to prevent competitors from entering this space and one way of doing this is to invest in making their production process as efficient as possible in order to keep prices low and competitive. In effect, while Defenders are narrowly focused and perhaps oblivious to the wider world of opportunities, they are innovators in their technological domain. Moving along the spectrum, Analyzers attempt to minimize risk while seeking to maximize their opportunity space in a balanced way. They aim to maintain their existing offerings to existing customers while contemplating new entrepreneurial opportunities – a 'duality' of purpose. They innovate in the sense that they develop new products and services once the viability of these new offerings has been established. Importantly, they face the complex task of integrating new innovations into the existing technological base in order to maintain their balanced approach. At the opposite end of the spectrum from Defenders one finds Prospectors. Prospectors need to innovate, not only in technological arenas but also in the administrative (organizational) system governing how the organization is run. They continually seek to identify and exploit new opportunities. They want to avoid a long-term commitment to any one technology or process. And they are faced by the administrative problem of how to coordinate numerous operations all conducting 'prospecting' activities.

Miles, Snow, Meyer and Coleman's (1978) strategic typology underlines how innovation is necessary in all types of organizations, not just in ones with an ostensibly high innovative or entrepreneurial orientation (Choi and Williams, 2016; Kraus, Rigtering, Hughes and Hosman, 2012; Lumpkin and Dess, 1996) such as the Prospector type. Entrepreneurial orientation in firms implies an innovative mindset and culture inside the organization. Firms can be classified on a continuum from 'passive' to 'aggressive' in terms of their entrepreneurial orientation (Choi and Williams, 2016; Kraus, Rigtering, Hughes and Hosman, 2012; Lumpkin and Dess, 1996). However, as Miles, Snow, Meyer and Coleman's (1978) work argues, at least some innovation will still be necessary even in the more 'passive' (Defender) type firms.

The phenomenon of innovation has been studied at different levels of analysis. Zheng (2010) highlight how the literature has focused at individual, team, organization, city, and national level. At an individual level, scholars argue that individual agents embody knowledge that is used and updated in innovative activity. As Glynn (1996) notes: "intelligence is manifested in individuals" (Glynn, 1996: 1082) – individuals possess the information processing capabilities needed to create useful novelty. At a team-level/sub-unit-level, individuals come together to annotate and refine creative ideas, searching for ways to evaluate and exploit them through their shared and collective knowledge (Brown and Duguid, 1991; Hirst, Van Knippenberg and Zhou, 2009). At an organizational-level, firms install administrative structures and control systems, organizational cultures and policies to promote innovative thinking across the different sub-units of the organization (Miles, Snow, Meyer and Coleman, 1978; Williams and van Triest, 2017). And at a network level, firms form part of inter-organizational networks and ecosystems that generate innovations. Dittrich, Duysters, and de Man (2007) examine the phenomenon at a network level using a case study of IBM's innovation networks and how these evolved in the 1990s as the firm sought to re-invent itself and move from mainframe computing into new areas of technology as well as advanced business services. A noteworthy finding from this study is how IBM's innovation networks changed over time, with partner firms entering and exiting the network, implying a strategic flexibility in managing networks when exploring new opportunities. Others study innovation at a country level, for instance, examining the national innovation systems of countries and how these systems influence overall innovativeness at a country level (e.g., Allard, Martinez and Williams, 2012).

Across these levels, the literature constantly tells us how innovation is an uncertain process. In March's (1991) seminal work on organizational learning (explorative and exploitative modes of learning), an explorative search for new possibilities involves variation and risk-taking, experimentation, and discovery. People engaging in these types of activities simply do not know what to expect; little can be predicted. In adapting existing systems and processes in an exploitative mode, firms may indeed gain temporary advantages and are able to deal with disruptions and challenges in the short-term, and they may do this based on knowledge that is less uncertain. However, an over-reliance on such an exploitative mode is likely to have long-term disadvantages. Firms that are able to both explore and exploit have become known as 'ambidextrous' organizations (Gibson and Birkinshaw, 2004; O'Reilly and Tushman, 2008). This organizational form is not a straightforward one to achieve. As argued by the innovator's dilemma (Christensen, 1997), the question of whether a firm should put a focus on exploration or exploitation when confronted by a disruptive force cannot easily be resolved. Innovation is fraught with uncertainty, not only in terms of 'entering the unknown' (and possibly the 'unknowable'), but also, as highlighted previously, because there are so many strategic choices that a firm can make about the type of innovative approach to adopt.

## Perspectives in the literature on innovation in consultancy

While the literature on innovation now goes back many decades (as evidenced by the dates of some of the citations in the previous section!), the literature on innovation specific to consultancy is much more recent. Without pre-empting any of the discussions that come later in the main chapters in this book, let's reflect on some of the main themes in this recent literature.

First and foremost, the management consultancy industry *does* innovate – let's be clear about this! While the innovations in management consultancy may not be protected by patents as much as they are in manufacturing, they can be protected by service marks (Semadeni and Anderson, 2010). And innovating for clients does not only have to be about grandiose new discoveries. It is often initiated through working with clients (O'Mahoney, 2011, 2013), diagnosing where change is needed in client organizations (Hodges, 2017), and finding new ways for clients to be resilient in daily operations (Williams and You, 2018). In the period 1989–1999, Semadeni and Anderson (2010) identified 557 service mark filings made by the largest consultancy firms in the US. While this might be a small number compared to typical volumes of patent filings by manufacturing firms, it is clear evidence that this industry is innovative, and it has been for decades. In O'Mahoney's (2011) study of management innovation in the UK consultancy industry, there was a 36 per cent increase in respondents reporting innovation within their consultancy (gauged by a new product or service being introduced). In general, innovation in consultancy has been on the rise for a while.

On the one hand, the literature highlights how knowledge-intensive service providers such as management consultants can act as co-producers and facilitators of innovation *for their clients* (e.g., Canato and Giangreco, 2011; den Hertog, 2000; Hipp and Grupp, 2005; Wood, 2002a). An example of this is the *Ergonomica* case reproduced in this book (Williams, 2017) where the consultancy firm is seeking to re-develop the way lighting is installed in the client's chain of hotels. Of course, this notion of 'helping the client become innovative' is important for us. If this were not feasible, we would have no story to tell! On the other hand, we also see a literature that shows how *consultancy firms themselves continually need to innovate* to stay relevant (Anand, Gardner and Morris, 2007; Christensen, Wang and Van Bever, 2013; Semadeni and Anderson, 2010). Examples in recent years have included new practice areas in management consultancy firms, such as new practice areas in the digital space.

Some of the inspiration on why and how the service provider should innovate will inevitably come through his or her relationships with clients (Amara, Landry and Doloreux, 2009; den Hertog, 2000; Hipp and Grupp, 2005; Mors, 2010; O'Mahoney, 2011; Shah, Rust, Parasuraman, Staelin and Day, 2006; Williams and You, 2018), but it is not the only source of creativity and novelty. Their internal organizational environment provides ample abundance of consultants who can be creative and embark on new initiatives for the consultancy firm (such as the Deloitte Dads initiative – Konrad and Shuh, 2013). So we see both sides of the coin here in terms of the locus for innovation: the client and the consultancy firm.

We find a large and growing literature on innovation in business services in general. Much of this is not consultancy specific, but it does lend some theory, insight, and ideas that we can find useful as we deal with the management consultancy space. For instance, many writers have highlighted customer involvement (e.g., Sundbo, 1997) – the need for business services firms to maintain good quality and embedded relationships with their customer base in order to learn about customer needs and how to come up with new ways of satisfying those needs. This is seen as a key area of theoretical and practical focus on the topic. As den Hertog (2000) notes: "feedback from clients can shape innovations in service firms, just as much as service firms can influence their customers' innovation" (den Hertog, 2000: 11). According to Hipp and Grupp (2005), integration with customers brings knowledge into the service provider to enable the service provider to learn about new opportunities and how to exploit them. However, Love, Roper, and Bryson (2011) look at how relationships with different types of external partners (not necessarily clients) have an 'encoding' function, i.e., external relationships between a service provider and external knowledge sources help transform explorative knowledge into tangible new offerings. This encoding function falls part way between explorative and exploitative parts of the innovation process in services firms and underscores how different external linkages matter not only for sourcing new knowledge, but also to be able to do something with that knowledge. While O'Mahoney (2013) finds the largest increase in the type of partner involved in the innovation process with consultancies to be that of clients, he also notes how other stakeholders are increasingly involved with consultancies in management innovation. This is also echoed in Sundbo's (1997: 446) finding that "Often customers provided the inspiration for new ideas, but it was employees or managers in the firm that develop them. Customers were not systematically involved until the testing of the prototype".

Crevani, Palm and Schilling (2011) review literature on innovation in services and note a tendency amongst academics to stress formalization of the innovation process. According to Crevani, Palm and Schilling (2011: 181): "This may include formal written plans for developing new services as well as a control structure, which supports a specific service innovation process". They note how some academic studies are vocal on the benefits of this approach. Their review also highlights collaborating in networks for innovation in services and actively involving clients in the process. It also underscores the importance of having an internal organizational culture conducive to innovation, i.e., one that fosters creativity and divergent thinking. What is noteworthy about Crevani, Palm, and Schilling's (2011) work is that they then ask practitioners what they think. Perhaps not surprisingly, the authors identify a number of gaps between what the academics say and what practitioners say. The emphasis amongst practitioners for innovation is in everyday operations in services, rather than being a formalized process (O'Mahoney, 2011, 2013). The practitioners also emphasize involving employees of the firm, not just an external focus on clients.

There is a somewhat smaller – but nevertheless growing – literature that specifically talks to innovation in management consultancy. As noted previously, this literature is still rather fragmented, and there have been calls for more work on this topic (Wright, Sturdy and Wylie, 2012). For example, in Sundbo's (1997) work, consultancy was one of the types of service organizations studied (he referred to this as 'C-type: Professional Organisations', a variant labelled 'collective professionals'). The use of the term 'professional' is interesting given Von Nordenflycht's (2010) assertion that consultancies are not professional in the same sense as accounting and legal firms. Sundbo's (1997) labeling is based on the looser definition that our management consultants are educated professionals. He talks about innovation being a collective task among these professionals and how an entrepreneurial culture will promote innovation. While this might be hard to manage, it posits a different approach to the client-driven approach for innovation in consultancy, and puts the emphasis firmly on the internal human capital inside the consultancy firm as a driver for creativity and novelty.

Perhaps counter to this, and partly reinforcing the same strand of thinking that Love, Roper, and Bryson (2011) and others have espoused relating to customer involvement in innovation, Mors (2010) examines how informal relationships with partners in large, international consultancy firms can be used to create knowledge and support the innovation process by those firms. One important difference is that Mors (2010) looks at both internal and external informal relationships, as well as local and global ones. She finds that dense networks amongst these different types of relationships matter specifically in heterogeneous environments because they allow for a diversity of knowledge to flow that will underpin a partner's ability to innovate. Similarly, Taminiau, Smit, and De Lange (2009) find informal knowledge sharing to be vital in helping consultants to innovate, a challenging topic for an individual whose main priority is often to work on one client project at a time, with a fairly narrow remit for that one client. Informal knowledge sharing, not only with clients, but with colleagues and superiors, happens in various situations such as lunches, dinners, drinks, and even carpooling! Meeting rooms and spaces can be designed to promote a positive climate for informal knowledge sharing in consultancy.

Semadeni and Anderson's (2010) study of imitation and innovation is based on large US management consultancy firms and draws from service mark data over a ten-year period between 1989 and 1999. One main, and highly relevant, finding is that these large consultancy firms tend to increase their imitation of a competitor when that competitor's level of organizational innovativeness, i.e., the collective innovative history of the competitor, increases. And, moreover, this effect is more pronounced when the level of innovativeness of the offering from their competitor is lower, i.e., the offering is based on concepts and ideas that were previously used. On one level, this finding underscores the importance of innovation in management consultancy; there will always be competitors out there who will find it relatively easy to imitate what you are doing and they will be especially keen (and able) to do this when you have a long track record of innovating, not necessarily because of your latest innovation. It also underscores a potential negative signaling effect of radical innovations in this industry – until the performance and market impact of any radical innovation is known, consultancy firms will be slow to adopt. This perhaps, is a sign of underlying conservatism in the industry, or at least a cautious attitude towards too many radical changes that may act to confuse existing clients.

Wood (2002b) asks a question which is the key concern for us: 'How may consultancies be innovative?' He outlines four basic ways in which consultancies act as agents of change for clients. (1) *Facilitators*: whereby the outsourcing of functions in the client to other companies is facilitated by the consultant, freeing up resources in the client to work in new ways in the core business. (2) *Conveyors*: whereby the consultancy acts as a 'messenger' responsible for bringing new insight (i.e., conveying) to the client something that originated in other sources, not necessarily from the consultancy firm itself. (3) *Adaptors*: whereby the consultancy helps guide the client in new directions, based on the specified needs of the client and their willingness to embark on innovation. And (4) *Initiators*: whereby the consultancy instigates change in the client organization, a more proactive mode of innovating likely also to have a technological as well as an organizational component.

The studies mentioned earlier on the topic of innovation in consultancy highlight a number of important points that form a platform for us in this book. Firstly, at a very basic level, they show that innovation in consultancy is rife, that it has been for a long time, but that the literature on the topic is much more recent than the traditional 'classical' literature on innovation. Secondly, it shows a significant literature on innovation in services, business services, and even professional services that can provide ideas and concepts to help us find answers to the question of innovation in management consultancy in particular. Thirdly, it shows that the smaller literature that does exist on innovation in management consultancy is fragmented. Each study appears to focus on one small part of the overall jigsaw puzzle. While there are some common themes, such as the role of customer involvement, experienced and trained staff, and having an organizational environment conducive to innovation, broadly speaking there is no one unifying theoretical base. There is no single view that addresses the specific case of innovation in firms in an industry that is worth hundreds of billions of dollars per year, that has been growing for decades, that is highly diverse and complex, and that clearly needs innovation as a way of competing.

## Our approach in this book

The literature on innovation in general, on innovation in business services, and on innovation in management consultancy in particular, collectively points to the fact that the antecedents to innovation in management consultancy will be multiple and diverse. No one single theoretical approach or group of conveniently selected variables that happen to fit nicely with a researcher's dataset will explain what we are trying to explain. Our focal phenomenon is one that cannot be predicted or explained by a capabilities-based approach (Barney, 1996; Peteraf, 1993) alone, or by a knowledge-based approach (Eisenhardt and Santos, 2002; Grant, 1996) alone, or by an external embeddedness approach (Moran, 2005; Uzzi, 1999) alone. It is hard to think of one single theoretical framework to guide what we are looking at. Indeed, this is reinforced by recent key works. Anand, Gardner, and Morris's (2007) work on practice emergence in large consultancy firms talks to the emergence of knowledge-based structures in these firms but the emerging theory touches on individuals' agency (i.e., of the practice's founder) and also political dynamics within the firm.

Can we – or more to the point, should we – assume a one dimensional strategic stance for consultancy firms considering the pursuit of innovation? This would be akin to the passive-aggressive continuum conceptualized in entrepreneurial orientation theory (Choi and Williams, 2016; Kraus, Rigtering, Hughes and Hosman, 2012; Lumpkin and Dess, 1996). Figure 1.1 represents this. The $y$ axis depicts a notional maximum range for innovative orientation of the consultancy firm, with 0 being completely un-innovative, and 1 being the highest level of innovation possible for that organization. Between time t and time t + 1, the firm has decided to move along this continuum in an upwards direction. Conversely, it is possible to move down this continuum too. Scholars have studied and debated what it means to have an innovative orientation as part of the strategic mindset of the firm. We can expect the firm at position 1 (at time t + 1) will have leadership supporting and providing resources and funding for innovative projects, a culture that supports experimentation, systems that support cross-boundary knowledge sharing and learning, and marketing teams that spearhead a market orientation that helps guide innovative work. This is all well and good. But the problem with it is that it does not help us decompose industry-specific dimensions and understand the interplay between those dimensions as we attempt to implement and manage an organization that we can call an 'innovative management consultancy'.

Having said that, the notion of a continuum is useful, and it is useful not in a uni-dimensional sense, but in recognition that there is more than one dimension at play. Let's consider two dimensions; the most obvious ones from our initial reading of the literature being an internal vs. external dimensional view. This would require us treating innovation in management consultancy as a two-dimensional internal-external

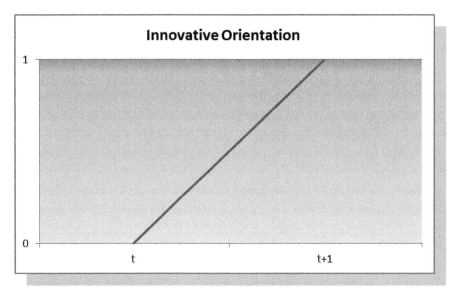

**Figure 1.1** A Uni-Dimensional View of Innovative Orientation in Management Consultancy

construct, with internal resources (namely, our consultants) working externally for a large part of their time (namely, with clients and possibly partners) and in doing so creating value through novelty, either for the consultancy firm itself or for the client (or both). Figure 1.2 is a representation of this. Imagine the $y$ axis as a representation of innovation in a management consultancy firm and four scenarios for our two dimensions. Scenario A is the least innovative. Scenario D is the most innovative. Firms may move between these scenarios in any direction over time. In scenario A, our firm is notionally low on both internal and external components, and it has the lowest innovative potential. In scenario B, the external component has increased (perhaps we are lucky enough to have all our consultants fully utilized with clients and innovating with them), but the internal component remains at rock-bottom. The firm's innovation has increased somewhat but has not reached full potential. In scenario C, the internal component has increased (perhaps we have recruited more trained staff) but the external component is low; again innovation only increases somewhat. It is in scenario D where both components have reached their full potential and where we are able to enjoy the maximum benefit in terms of innovation.

This, of course, is purely abstract and a conceptualization. However, it does take us a little bit further on from the rather top-level, 'strategic' and one-dimensional innovative orientation in Figure 1.1. Also, there is a large theoretical base of work behind Figure 1.2. On the internal side, when we talk about the education, training, and skills or our consultants, we are, of course, referring to our human capital, a cornerstone of resource-based theory of the firm (Barney, 1996; Peteraf, 1993). If our consultants are

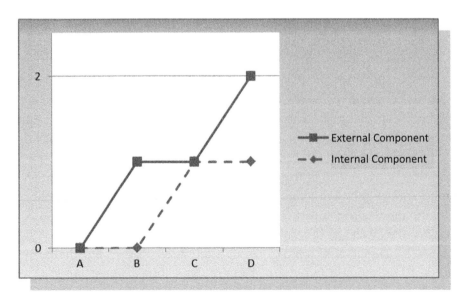

**Figure 1.2** A Two-Dimensional (Internal-External) View of Innovative Orientation in Management Consultancy

able to do things that are valuable, rare, inimitable, and non-substitutable, we will be able to achieve a sustained competitive advantage and produce innovations that will keep us ahead of the pack. And when we talk about the social network and embedment with clients in the external component, we have social capital (Burt, 2000; Moran, 2005; Uzzi, 1999) (and hopefully, trust [Maister, 2003]) with clients. External relationships can form the basis of our understanding of needs and how to evaluate solutions and exploit those needs through new offerings.

Nevertheless, there are multiple *industry-specific trends* that have taken place in the consulting segment of the business services industry (as well as more broadly in business services) that we simply have to consider when broaching the question of what drives innovation in management consultancy. As noted in the Preface, I concentrate on three of these trends in this book: the trend towards consultant virtualization, the trend towards life-cycle disruption, and the trend towards knowledge management and learning between consultants of the same firm, a factor that allows them collectively to reflect on their experiences. Consequently, in order to more fully understand the organizational determinants that are meaningful to our understanding of how to manage innovation in consultancy, we need to look at such organizational factors. The structure of the analysis in this book taps into three of the most salient features of the consultancy industry as ways of organizing, an aspect that we capture under the umbrella of 'organizational capital'. So we have the human capital aspect relating to the knowledge, experience, and skills of our consultants. We have the social capital aspect relating to the fact that our consultants are continuously engaged and embedded in relationships with clients and other actors. And we have the organizational capital aspect relating to how we organize our firm, run projects, and learn from each other.

We refer to these as the five Poles for innovation in management consultancy. The first two Poles, human and social capital, are well-established constructs and the corresponding chapters (Chapters 2 and 3) will discuss what they mean for the innovative consultancy. The next three Poles (consultant virtualization, life-cycle disruption, and reflective ability) are to be discussed as consultancy-relevant constructs that have emerged as forms of organizational capital in this industry through the competitive evolution of firms in the industry over a long period of time. What is interesting is that, in all of the five Poles, some research highlights positive effects on innovation, while some highlights negative effects. Yet others highlight contingency and moderating effects. We draw on these again in the final chapters where we discuss the challenge of 'connecting the Poles'.

Figure 1.3 depicts this approach as an 'Innovation Radar'. For the purposes of conceptual analysis and framing of literature and case material, we can consider each of these Poles as being a continuum in its own right. In theory, at least, any firm can be positioned as low or high on each of these dimensions. Figure 1.3 is a

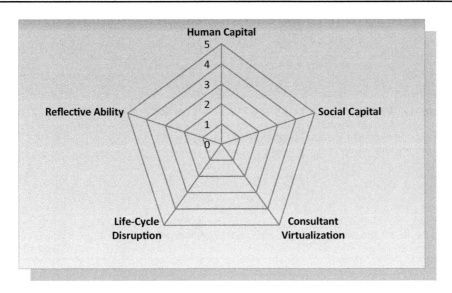

**Figure 1.3** The Innovation Radar: Five Poles of Innovation in Management Consultancy

blank canvas. There is no innovative consultant to be seen! It is a chessboard for our analysis, but with no pieces.

In Chapters 2 to 6 we will consider hypothetical situations of firms that are at a 'maximum' level on each of these Poles in turn, seeing what the literature says about why they might want to adopt an aggressive stance on each Pole and what this means for innovation. Again, for the sake of conceptual argumentation and to facilitate logical development, I simply put a scale of 0–5 on each of the Poles. If a firm has a value of 0 on the key dimensions of human and social capital, it probably is not a viable consultancy firm, or is at least in big danger. Perhaps you can think about and discuss how a firm can have a 0 level of human capital. Perhaps it is in an embryonic state of start-up. Similarly, how can a firm have a level of 0 on social capital? Again, perhaps it is yet to penetrate the market and find clients with which to build relationships. Or perhaps it was a small firm with a large dependency on one client, but that client has suddenly dumped the consultancy firm. If a firm has a value of 5 it has taken an aggressive stance on that Pole. It would have made a conscious effort to evaluate the costs and benefits of that stance, and would have allocated tangible resources to allow that stance to be implemented in practice.

In the final chapters of the book we will look at the phenomenon in a more integrative way. Research exists on the interactions between human, social, and different types of organizational capital. The implications of these interactions are relevant in our analysis because of the potential for heightened risks and uncertainty when we try to design a consultancy firm that will adopt an aggressive stance on all of the Poles at the same time. Figures 1.4 and 1.5 illustrate this.

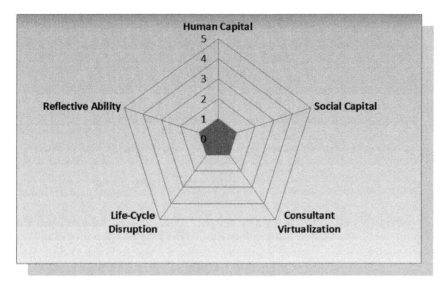

**Figure 1.4** The Inert Innovator in Management Consultancy

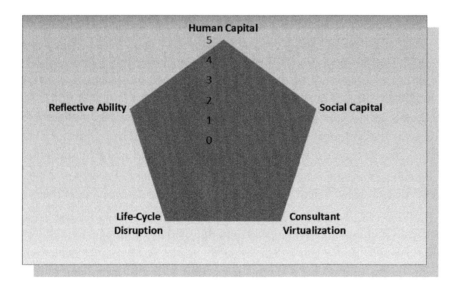

**Figure 1.5** The Enthusiastic Innovator in Management Consultancy

In Figure 1.4, our firm is highly passive, being low on all dimensions. The logic and argumentation of this book will assert that this type is inert: it is not a very innovative consultancy firm! In Figure 1.5, we see a highly aggressive consultancy firm, being high on all dimensions. I would refer to this as an 'enthusiastic innovator'. In this book we will assert that such a firm has the potential to leave a highly innovative footprint behind. But we need to be careful here and ask some important questions: in its enthusiasm to be highly aggressive on all five Poles, will it actually get in a muddle? In other words, is such a firm *too* enthusiastic to the point that innovation may actually suffer? How can a firm effectively manage high levels on all of these Poles simultaneously? Are there costs and risks associated with this constellation that need to be understood and managed?

The final chapters will examine this with reference to academic literature and case material. They will also discuss implications for ethical behavior in the industry as well as for careers in management consultancy and future research in the field. New ideas and suggestions for research will also be presented in the final chapter and some thoughts on what we can learn from this topic to help students with future careers in consultancy will be offered.

## Note

1 Knowledge that has been widely established, accepted, and taken for granted.

# 2

# Pole 1: human capital

## It's all about our people

This chapter will examine innovation in consultancy firms from the perspective of human capital. We will first look at the theory of human capital before examining why human capital is widely believed to have a positive impact on innovation. We will then look at the relationship between human capital and innovation in consultancy firms by reviewing academic literature on this topic, as well as reviewing case material and insights from practitioners. It goes without saying that the consultancy industry is a human capital–intensive one (Anand, Gardner and Morris, 2007; Hitt, Bierman, Shimizu and Kochhar, 2001; Maister, 2003; Von Nordenflycht, 2010; Wood, 2002a). Success in this industry is completely dependent on the knowledge and skills of the individuals within the industry who pitch themselves as consultants. Maister (2003) emphasizes how human capital in this industry goes beyond what consultants *know*, it also relates to their applied skills and what they *do* (winning trust with clients, listening effectively, making a convincing case with clients and so forth). So skills, training, and experience matter. And they matter to the proclivity of a management consultancy firm to be able to innovate for themselves or for their clients. Figure 2.1 schematizes our focus in this chapter. Let's assume, for the sake of discussion, a firm on our Innovation Radar with the maximum level of human capital possible, and let's – for now – turn a blind eye to the other Poles.

## Theory of human capital

The skills and knowledge that people have are a form of capital that has become known as *human capital* (Schultz, 1961). Human capital arises as a consequence of investment in education, training, and skills development (Becker, 1962; Schultz, 1961) and has certain distinctive features. These include the following: an inability to separate it from the person who has it, it can be seen as an ability (or abilities)

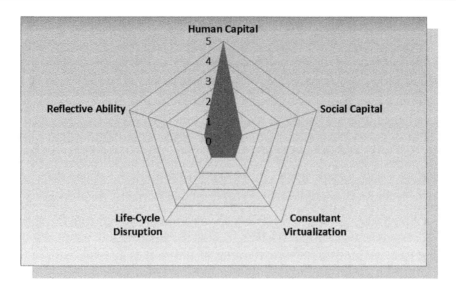

**Figure 2.1** Pole 1: A Focus on Human Capital

that are innate or that can be acquired, the fact that it is not directly visible, and that it has benefits to the individual who possesses it (Schultz, 1993). The theory proposes that investment in education leads to skills that are useful. These in turn can be sold in the form of a job contract (temporary or permanent) and can therefore be translated into income and wealth (Strober, 1990). Among the assertions made by human capital theory is that age is positively correlated with income because older people possess more on-the-job experience that is useful and valuable (Strober, 1990). Other assertions are that the quality of educational establishments in a country will determine the economic growth and development of the country, something highly salient for developing economies (Olaniyan and Okemakinde, 2008). Human capital theory is therefore seen as a supply-side theory. While it may not account for all of the variance in earnings, it does provide a baseline argument against which others can be built or tested (Strober, 1990).

At the economic level, investment in human capital is seen as being beneficial to productivity in an economy, to the modernization of an economy, to falling unemployment rates, and to economic growth (Becker, 1962; Schultz, 1993). Investment in human capital extends beyond pure education, it also includes investment in health, job search, information retrieval, migration, and in-service training (Blaug, 1976). In our analysis, we are interested in human capital at the organizational – or firm – level. At this level, the value and uniqueness of individuals' skills and capabilities provides a source of competitive advantage for the firm (Lepak and Snell, 1999). Investment in training in the firm leads to high stocks of human capital in the firm (Bontis and Fitz-enz, 2002). Scholars have noted how the Human Resource (HR) function of the firm has an important role to play in developing and retaining appropriate levels of human capital in the organization in order for the organization to be effective (Strober, 1990). Others have argued for a more encompassing 'human resource architecture' for the firm (Lepak and Snell, 1999). At its core, this consists of four basic employment modes, two of which are internal in nature (developing and acquiring human capital) and two of which are external in nature (contracting or alliancing for human capital) (Lepak and Snell, 1999). It follows that it is necessary to protect the transfer and leakage of the firm's valuable human capital to other firms (Lepak and Snell, 1999). After all, employers often pay for training for skills that are transferrable across employers (Booth and Bryan, 2005). It is also incumbent on a firm to invest in firm-specific training in addition to general training (Lepak and Snell, 1999).

Empirical studies have consistently shown links between investment in human capital by firms and competitive advantage for those firms. Hatch and Dyer (2004) investigate the inimitability of human capital in the semiconductor industry in the US, Asia, and Europe. By studying at the factory level in this industry, these authors find learning by doing performance is influenced by how the firm manages selection, development, and deployment of human capital. Learning by doing performance in this study relates to improving the yield performance of silicon wafers. Screening processes at the input side of human capital allow the firm to select individuals with the right aptitude and attitude. Investment in development of staff means that staff can participate in the task in a meaningful way. And deploying staff to explicit learning activities aimed at increasing knowledge in the firm leads to cost advantages. Williams and Lee (2016) investigate the interaction of human capital and HR processes in foreign subsidiaries of Korean firms (the subsidiaries were based in Europe) and find that higher levels of human capital in a subsidiary will be associated with knowledge outflows from the subsidiary to other units of the firm in the presence of formalized HR policies (i.e., well-designed performance evaluation procedures and incentives programs). Sparkes and Miyake's (2000) study of human resource development and knowledge assimilation in nine Japanese organizations in Mexico and Brazil is illustrative of how different approaches to on-the-job training are utilized by firms. Some formalize this investment, others do not. In Sparkes and Miyake's (2000) study it is found that firms that invest in on-the-job training and off-the-job training enjoyed advantages including lower employee turnover and higher knowledge assimilation. Collectively, these studies show that HR matters; it can activate human capital in the firm to becoming more valuable for the firm and through the development of socially complex tacit knowledge that is difficult for competitors to imitate.

# Human capital and innovation

Some scholars have studied the relationship between human capital and innovation at a national level. For instance, Williams and Allard (2018) find a positive association between the scientific and technical labor pool in a country and the extent of university-industry collaboration in R&D in the country. The availability of well-trained scientists and technologists in a country underpins the national technological competence of the country. Using data on firms in France over a six-year period, Gallié and Legros (2012) show a positive impact of training on patenting performance. This effect holds for different aspects of training, including the following: training hours per employee, access rate to training, and training expenditure per employee. These authors make the point that training is goal oriented, and that the decision to invest in human capital happens because of the firm's goals with respect to innovation. Analyzing data from Finland, Simonen and McCann (2008) show that labor acquired from the same sub-region as the firm can have a negative impact on innovation, while labor acquired from outside the sub-region of the firm – as long as it is sourced from the same technological industry – will have a positive impact on innovation. These studies point to the importance of relevance of training and experience as inputs to drive innovation in the firm.

According to Bozeman, Dietz, and Gaughan (2001) scientists and technologists possess three types of skills that comprise their human capital and that make them a valuable source of innovation in an economy. These are cognitive skills, substantive scientific and technical knowledge, and contextual skills. Cognitive skills relate to cognitive abilities such as mathematical reasoning and ability to synthesize knowledge, largely independent of context. Substantive knowledge refers to knowledge obtained through formal scientific education. Contextual skills are those gained by 'doing'; they are tacit in nature and define the craft of the scientist. Davidsson and Honig (2003) identify three aspects of human capital that have a positive impact on nascent entrepreneur status in an economy. These are years of education, years of work experience, and previous start-up experience. These broadly fit with Bozeman, Dietz and Gaughan's (2001) categorization: years of education (cognitive and substantive), experience of work, and start-ups (context experience). Davidsson and Honig (2003) show how tacit and explicit human capital at the individual-level are factors that lead to both opportunity discovery and the decision to becoming an entrepreneur. The higher the level of education, the more likely an individual will discover opportunities they want to pursue. Higher human capital gives individuals the confidence to take risks.

At the firm level, numerous studies highlight a positive association between human capital in the firm and innovation by the firm. Acs and Audretsch (1987) find human capital to have a positive impact on innovation and that this effect is virtually identical in large firms and small firms. In Baldwin and Johnson's (1995) study of training and innovation in small- and medium-sized enterprises (SMEs) in Canada, it is found that firms with a higher emphasis on innovation will invest more heavily in training. Human capital development is highly complementary to innovation and what these authors refer to as 'technological advance'. Training is a way of upgrading the skills of employees and is associated with all of the four types of innovation strategy identified in their data (general innovator, passive adaptor, R&D-driven innovator, and outward-oriented innovator).

In their study of 150 Spanish firms, Bornay-Barrachina, la Rosa-Navarro, López-Cabrales, and Valle-Cabrera (2012) confirm a direct effect of human capital on innovation across three operationalizations of innovation: new products, improved products, and radicalness. They draw on Subramaniam and Youndt's (2005) measure of human capital that reflects skills, expertise, and knowledge levels within the employee base. However, Bornay-Barrachina, la Rosa-Navarro, López-Cabrales and Valle-Cabrera (2012) also show important indirect effects of human capital on innovation: firms that underinvest can still achieve high levels of innovative outcomes if they have high levels of human capital. Other work also highlights indirect effects. Chen and Huang (2009), for example, show how strategic HR practices in the firm lead to innovation performance of the firm when mediated by knowledge management capacity. Strategic HR practices, which include staffing (selectivity in hiring), participation (allowing employees to make decisions) and compensation (links between performance and reward) as well as formal training, all have their effect on innovation in the firm because of the firm's ability to manage the knowledge that is generated through the application of the firm's human capital. This study suggests how knowledge management capacity and human capital development go hand-in-hand in order for a firm to optimize its innovative potential.

De Winne and Sels (2010) use a sample of start-ups (<49 employees) in Belgium to show the importance of human capital and Human Resource Management (HRM) as determinants of innovation. While the level of human capital and the number of HR practices in these small and young firms is a significant predictor of innovative output, there is also an important interaction effect whereby the impact of human capital on innovative output is amplified as the number of HR practices increases. D'Este, Rentocchini and Vega-Jurado (2014) examine how human capital can lower the barriers (or impediments) to innovation in firms in Spain. They find human capital to have a significant effect on reducing two types of barriers, namely knowledge barriers and market-related barriers. Knowledge barriers concern aspects such as lacking qualified personnel and information. Market barriers include presence of incumbents with market power as well as there being uncertainty over demand. Similarly, in Japan, Kato, Okamuro, and Honjo (2015) identify how founders' human capital positively impacts innovation outcomes in start-ups. Interestingly, they show how founders' *specific* human capital directly impacts innovation outputs. Specific human capital relates to founders' prior experience in innovation and patenting, as opposed to more general educational background (i.e., *generic* human capital). Marvel and Lumpkin (2007) also look at how specific and generic human capital impact innovative outcomes, seeking to understand the degree of radicalness in the innovation. They find depth of experience and formal education (measures of general human capital) to have positive impacts on radicalness, while technology experience (specific human capital) also has a positive impact. Interestingly, experience on ways to serve markets (also specific human capital) has a negative impact on radicalness. This highlights the possibility that firms will be more radical in their innovation efforts if they do not have the answers about how to service new markets. Overall, there are multiple dimensions of the human capital construct and these may impact innovation outcomes in different ways.

## Consultancy and innovation through a human capital lens

The previous sections looked at the theory of human capital and its implications for innovation. As was noted, the links between human capital and innovation have been examined in a number of empirical settings, both in terms of geography and industry. We now turn our attention towards human capital and innovation in professional services, and in management consulting in particular. We find a number of important studies and insights in this field.

In Hitt, Bierman, Shimizu, and Kochhar's (2001) seminal work on the effects of human capital in professional services, the authors take a resource-based view, arguing that human capital constitutes the dominant resource in these types of firms. Fieldwork on a sample of 93 law firms reveals a curvilinear relationship with firm performance, captured as return on sales. With low levels of increases in human capital, performance initially drops. But as human capital then continues to increase, performance turns positive. The initial 'cost' of human capital is attributable to high compensation for graduate lawyers compared to their marginal productivity. While this study does not set about explaining innovation per se, it is a noteworthy point that human capital has a cost and that this may be reflected in outcomes. It is also interesting in the Hitt, Bierman, Shimizu, and Kochhar (2001) study that human capital exhibits a positive bi-variate correlation with clients in new geographical markets. As Hitt, Bierman, Shimizu, and Kochhar (2001: 20) note: "As firms diversify into new geographical markets, their motives and outcomes may vary". This is likely to require an innovative mindset and innovative capabilities on the part of the professional services provider, and it is no coincidence that there is a positive correlation between human capital in the provider and new geographical markets amongst the client base.

Christensen, Wang, and Van Bever (2013) use the case of McKinsey & Company to highlight how management consultancy firms pursue strategic innovation on the back of their human capital. Interestingly, the perspective of disruption in the consulting industry puts a spotlight on how business model innovation in the industry will require new types and uses of human capital to be created. The company innovated in its business model in 2007 and created a new practice area with its McKinsey Solutions practice. This was an innovation for McKinsey & Company as it was "not grounded in deploying human capital" (Christensen, Wang and Van Bever, 2013: 3) in the traditional sense. Installing analytics and 'hard' solutions at clients for relatively quick wins and potentially smaller revenues was a departure for McKinsey & Company. However, a different type of human capital would be necessary for this. Christensen, Wang, and Van Bever (2013) argue that this disruption has been part of a wider shift in the industry to modularization.

Christensen, Wang, and Van Bever (2013) is not the only article to put a spotlight on new practice emergence within consultancy firms. Anand, Gardner, and Morris (2007) conduct one of the first substantial research projects on how new practice areas emerge in professional services firms. They use a qualitative, case-based approach, initially using four cases of new practice area generation in management consultancy firms. A second phase validates the findings using a larger sample of 25 more cases. Seeking to answer the question about what determines the generation of new practice areas within management consultancy firms, Anand, Gardner, and Morris (2007) identify four elements: *socialized agency* (actions taken by consultants to boost their career prospects through their 'ownership' of the new practice area), *differentiated expertise* (a defined and distinctive base of knowledge that constitutes the new practice area), *defensible turf* (a 'persuasion' capability to convince others of the need for the new practice area), and *organizational support* (including resources and personnel). While not presented explicitly in human capital terms in the article, all four of these generative aspects have their roots in human capital. Here we see strong links between different facets of human capital and organizational innovation in consulting.

Bessant and Rush (1995) highlight the role played by consultants in facilitating technology transfer and enabling innovative use of new technology for clients. Consultants are able to fill the capability gaps that organizations suffer from in key areas, such as these: recognition of requirements for technology, exploration of technological options, comparison of options, selection of the 'best' option, and help with acquisition (which includes negotiation) and implementation and operation of the technology (Bessant and Rush, 1995). In a similar vein, Czarnitzki and Spielkamp (2003: 2) highlight the role of business services organizations as "providers, users, originators and intermediary institutions of the transfer of tech-nological and non-technological innovation" in the knowledge economy. These authors concentrate on the German context and the national innovation system in Germany, a country that traditionally relied on a strong manufacturing base (and innovation within the manufacturing base). They highlight how this has changed over time, as – consistent with other advanced nations – employment in business and technical services has grown. Their study highlights the impor-tance of the development of human capital in the country during this process of industrial change. Czarnitzki and Spielkamp (2003: 12) note how "know-how-intensive services . . . demands highly skilled workers". They argue how scientists and highly skilled workers are not only useful in bringing new knowledge into a company, they are also vital in putting the new know-how to use. Den Hertog (2000) goes beyond the pure technology-transfer role of consultants and describes five ways in which a business services provider can innovate: *supplier-dominated innovation* (following a technology-push approach to the client), *innovation within services* (when the service provider innovates for itself), *client-led innovation* (the ser-vices firm responding to the well-defined needs of the client), *innovation through services* (influencing the process of innovation within the client), and *paradigmatic innovations* (truly revolutionary innovations affecting a complete value chain). Den Hertog (2000) notes how specialized knowledge and expertise within the services provider will allow it to operate in any of these modes of innovation with clients. Tether and Tajar (2008) show how specialist consultancy firms can be engaged by clients to assist them in their innovation activities. This can range from operating as an informal source of information to a fully fledged co-operative arrangement. Tether and Tajar (2008) find services firms are more likely to use external consul-tants to assist in innovative activity.

An important point made in these studies (Bessant and Rush, 1995; Czarnitzki and Spielkamp, 2003; den Hertog, 2000; Tether and Tajar, 2008) is that knowledge about new technology and the process of innovation is a vital asset that the consul-tant needs to have if they are to act as an intermediary in technology transfer and innovation for their clients. This in itself requires education and the ability to locate sources of new knowledge on behalf of the consultant. In other words, human capital matters as consultants assist clients in their identification and adoption of new technology.

To this end, HR policy and knowledge management policy within the con-sultancy firm are essential to get right. Indeed, Baldwin and Johnson (1995) find that professional workers are more likely to receive formal training. Boxall and Steeneveld (1999) highlight how professional services firms need to adopt simi-lar strategic HR policies – strategic management 'recipes' that emerge over time (456) – in order to remain competitive as credible members of the industry. Their study focuses on engineering consultancies in New Zealand. One side of this is to allow them to attract and retain talented human capital, and this is partly secured through the offer of potential ownership, a form of 'institutional glue' (Boxall and Steeneveld, 1999: 459) found in the professional services industry.

Obeidat, Al-Suradi, Masa'deh, and Tarhini (2016) examine how knowledge management processes influence innovation in consultancy firms in Jordan. A consultant's knowledge is *the* foundation stone of their individual human capital, and how they acquire and manage this knowledge can be seen as a broader firm level capability that will influence how the consultant helps clients innovate. Prusak (2001) argues how knowledge management (in the firm) extends the idea of human capital (at the level of the individual) and offers a way for firms to organize themselves to benefit from their collective human capital. The first of Obeidat, Al-Suradi, Masa'deh, and Tarhini's (2016) hypotheses concerns knowledge management *processes*, including the acquisition, sharing and utilization of knowledge. These processes typically are ones that are under the control of the firm; they are owned and formalized by the firm. The authors find a statistically significant and positive effect between all three of these processes and the consultancy firm's ability to innovate for its clients. The result shows how acquisition and recombination of knowledge by consultants in the firm is a vital capability within the human capital base of the firm. New and innovative ideas for clients can only be generated when consultants are able to access and combine new sources of knowledge with existing knowledge. As noted by Obeidat, Al-Suradi, Masa'deh, and Tarhini (2016: 1231): "hiring new employees for acquiring new knowledge has undoubtedly a fruitful benefit for innovation, as new employees might bring new ways of thinking and can stimulate the creation of new ideas that will encourage innovation".

## Practice insight

The following practice insight was kindly provided by Netherlands-based consultant Jeroen Brugman.

### Using my skills and training to help a client reduce cost of compliance

During my Executive Master at Nyenrode Business University in the Netherlands, I wanted to research the use of process mining technology for risk management purposes. I had found out about process mining while studying on my Executive Master's in Finance and Control program and was curious to see how it could be used in practice. At the time I was doing an assignment for a data-driven company and I spotted an opportunity to use a specific process mining technology called

Disco to help the company evaluate whether the internal controls they had been using in operations were effective.

One of the problems facing large companies with sophisticated and complex IT systems is how to access and make sense of data held deeply inside those systems. Process mining helps because it allows a way of accessing and analyzing this 'hard to access' data in order to shed light on how efficiently an organization is performing. However, these tools don't operate automatically; consultants need to be skilled in how to set them up, use them, and interpret the results.

With management's permission, I researched the use of process mining to give insight into the effectiveness of the organization's internal controls. If the exercise worked, the organization could reduce the cost of compliance. I trained myself up in Disco and I retrieved an event log from the organization's SAP system as a source of data. I was able to analyze the control effectiveness of a segregation of duties implemented in a key process. This control had only been implemented recently. Through my training and use of the tool I was able to show a 'before' and 'after' picture. From this I was able to visualize the process improvement and also the improved efficiency of the process. My analysis showed there was less rework in the new situation and the new process also improved compliance with SOx.[1] I had demonstrated the tool was able to analyze processes locked deeply inside client IT systems and how it could be used more broadly to reduce the cost of compliance.

When I presented my findings, I was somewhat surprised that senior management were not that enthusiastic about using the tool beyond this proof of concept exercise. It seemed odd to me that, in a company driven by a data culture, my initiative was not embraced. I had expected a different reaction. In the finance department where this experiment with process mining took place there was still a lot of manual work and not a lot of effort on automating processes. Because the investment into the uses for the tool can be large, not just monetary but also time-wise, support by senior management is crucial.

Nevertheless, I felt I had contributed to the organization's thinking on process efficiency and compliance and I later found out that other similar organizations had started adopting the approach. The experience taught me how my own investment in education and training can lead to my own attempts to innovate for client organizations.

## Case reflections on the theme of human capital

There are a number of published cases showing clear links between human capital and innovation in consultancy settings. In the cases highlighted in this chapter, these links are a conspicuous theme, principally relating to innovations taking place within client organizations.

The case of Tommasi Motorcycles in Japan (Hicks and Lehmberg, 2012) describes a situation where an Italian motorcycle manufacturer encounters performance issues in Japan. These issues were not visible to the country manager in Japan who was an Italian expat on a fixed-term rotation. However, the company had hired an external consultancy to help with the implementation of a Customer Relationship Management (CRM) system globally. The consultants engaged to do this in Japan soon identified a range of 'soft' organizational issues (i.e., not IT or 'hard' data issues relating to the system itself). These softer organizational issues had their roots in understanding the cultural context and ways of doing business through dealerships in Japan. The two external consultants who identified these issues were not Japanese but possessed human capital in the form of language skills and cultural competence (they were fluent in Japanese and had lived there for a number of years), on top of their IT implementation skills. It was this human capital that enabled them to identify the issue, bring it to the attention of the country manager, and thereby lay the foundation for a new organizational approach in the subsidiary for collaborative working with dealers in Japan. Without this human capital, it is likely that no change would have happened and under-performance in the client would have continued.

In the case of Campbell Management Consulting (Erskine and Cruji, 2010), a fresh-out-of-business-school MBA graduate took on a project at an automobile manufacturer in Ontario, Canada. The goal of the project was to establish whether efficiency savings could be made for the client in the area of waste removal from the shop floor. The particular skill that the consultant possessed was in conducting time studies in an assembly plant setting. The consultant also had skill in designing a sampling approach for data collection and for extrapolating the data collected in order to make an informed calculation that could help the client make an important decision in how to make a key change to its assembly operations. This change would achieve higher levels of efficiency and competitiveness. The consultant also demonstrated skills in dealing with a number of obstacles to data collection that he encountered when being physically present on the shop floor.

The case of Ergonomica Consulting (Williams, 2017) (reproduced in this book) shows the efforts of a consultant at Ergonomica Consulting to win a deal at a key client for the installation of new energy efficient lighting systems across its portfolio of hotels. An initial pilot project appeared to show the desired benefit for the client. The consultant's expertise in green projects and her understanding of large volumes of complex data was central to the potential for innovation in lighting systems as part of a strategic upgrading of client assets. Without the application of this specific form of human capital for the client, the client's innovation strategy would not have even considered the lighting systems. Nevertheless, the case hinges on a crucial decision point as the consultant realizes a mistake made in one of her spreadsheets may have led to overestimating the benefit to the client. The case therefore also highlights how a lack of human capital – in this case the ability to check and verify complex calculations as early as possible in the consultancy assignment – can lead to the possibility that a client would decide not to proceed with an innovation.

Digging deeper, however, we can expect that these situations are ones that would likely also lead to innovation within the consulting organization itself. In the case of Tommasi, the consultancy firm could (and should) review internally to see if similar issues were arising amongst clients in different countries around the world. This could lead to the genesis of a new practice area that would be based on its cultural competence, not just on its IT implementation competence. For Campbell Management Consulting, the application of the consultant's human capital to the automotive assembly project could lead to a formalization of a way of conducting time studies in this kind of setting – a new tool he could use on future assignments. For Ergonomica Consulting, the case illustrates how the company might harness distributed forms of human capital across different consultants with related expertise in order to avoid the type of situation that arose.

## Implications

Human capital has huge implications for consultants and consultancy firms that want to innovative for themselves and for their clients. What consultants know and how they apply their knowledge to the problems they and their clients face is a cornerstone of innovation in management consultancy. This knowledge will derive from formal training and education, as well as 'on-the-job' experience. There are various reasons why human capital matters for innovation in management consultancy, and the literature review and case examples discussed provide insights into these reasons. I offer four points of reflection on this.

Firstly, greater levels of human capital will allow consultants to be clear about why innovation is required in any given situation. In client engagements, if an innovative approach is to be proposed to a client, the client may be exposed to new levels of risk and uncertainty they had not previously anticipated. In order to not put the client in a worse situation than they were in before they engaged the consultant, the consultant must be clear about the reasons for an innovative approach. Human capital helps in answering the 'why' question because it allows the consultant to use a wealth of experience across a range of clients and client projects in justifying an innovative approach for a specific client. Greater levels of human capital will be associated with greater insights into what worked well and what worked less well in innovative projects in the past; even better when this experience was firsthand experience gained by the consultant and not simply secondhand 'word of mouth'.

An experienced and well-trained consultant will be able to clearly articulate the consequences of NOT pursuing an innovative response in a way that is credible in the eyes of the client.

Secondly, human capital will allow the consultant to answer the question about timing – i.e., 'when' an innovation is required. Is the client ready for an innovation? Is the consultancy firm ready for an innovation? Perhaps organizational, leadership, or system changes need to be completed first. Perhaps the results of other projects need to be reviewed and harnessed before any major-scale innovation is even started. The timing of innovative work will play an important role in its eventual success. Greater levels of human capital will allow the consultant to answer the question of whether an innovation is required urgently or whether it is something that should be considered for 6 or 12 months into the future, or perhaps not at all given prevailing conditions. Human capital will allow the consultant to appreciate levels of absorptive capacity in the client organization (and/or the consultancy firm) needed for innovation. In other words, the consultant will be better able to appreciate the learning context surrounding the innovation and anticipate any barriers to learning that might negatively impact the implementation of an innovative project.

Thirdly, human capital will allow the consultant to determine the 'where' question with an innovation. Should the innovation be confined to one part of the client organization, such as one functional unit or group, or perhaps just one overseas subsidiary, or should it be something that is contemplated as an organization-wide response. We see this question arising in the case of Tommasi Motorcycles (Hicks and Lehmberg, 2012), where the consultants could potentially suggest to their own headquarters that a new approach needs to be taken towards the client globally, rather than just in Japan. This is a question of scope of innovation. It is important because the greater the scope, the greater the underlying risks and impact of failure. Human capital in the consultancy firm will allow this question to be better addressed convincingly. This echoes the previous two points. Prior experience of what has worked well and what has worked less well (i.e., learning from failure of previous innovation efforts) will allow better judgements about the scope of new innovative activities.

Fourthly, human capital will allow for a better assessment of 'what type' of innovation is required, whether it be for the client or for the consultancy firm. As noted earlier, innovation comes in all kinds of shapes and sizes (product vs. process; radical vs. incremental; organizational system vs. business system; firm-level vs. unit-level; technology vs. marketing). So, on top of the thinking needed to determine the 'why', 'when', and 'where' of innovative proposals, it is absolutely necessary for the consultant to be able to articulate what type of innovation is required. This also has major implications for both client and consultant as levels of risk and associated costs (financial and reputational) will differ according to the type of innovation proposed. Risks are likely to be lower with incremental approaches. But in other cases, the risks will be higher. For instance, with a product-based manufacturing client where the consultant recommends a major strategic innovation by moving into services, the capability gaps and associated stretch would make the potential costs and risks higher. The consultant would need to provide clear and sound justification for this.

For these reasons, consultancy firms need to appreciate the strong links between human capital and innovation in consultancy. Training in order to develop human capital in the innovative consultancy will matter. So will the selection and recruitment of expert and experienced individuals who have the skills appropriate for innovating. And measures need to be taken to ensure suitably qualified and skilled individuals do not leave the organization: retention matters. Because of the combined needs for training, selection and recruitment, and retention, HRM systems that are appropriate for continually developing innovative consultants will need to be conceived, implemented, monitored, and changed as necessary. Depending on the size and scale of the consultancy organization, both central HR managers and line managers in distinct practice areas of the consultancy firm will need to be involved in making sure that these HRM systems are appropriately specified, receiving suitable investment and are fit for purpose.

In addition to this, the HR function needs to address the question of how the role of the consultant as functional specialist vs. the role of the consultant as generalist plays out in forming the innovative consultancy. There may be certain situations in which the specialist skills and experience of the consultant[2] will need to be brought to bear on the question of how to justify an innovative response to a challenge facing a client or a consultancy firm. In other words, the consultant is trusted to innovate in a niche area precisely because of his or her skills in that niche area. In other situations, more generalist skills may matter. One could argue that the range of general skills possessed by the consultants in the Tommasi case will allow them to provide a new proposal for leading a change program across the client globally. These skills include language, social and cultural competence skills, IT (specifically CRM systems), and skills in stakeholder management and communication with key stakeholders.

## Summary and learning points

In this chapter on Pole 1: human capital, we have seen the following:

- How academic literature and empirical research show strong positive effects between human capital and innovation in general terms and how this applies in the field of management consultancy.

- Consultants' training, skills and experience to be the primary sources of their value to their employer and their clients.
- That human capital in a consultancy firm is associated with its absorptive capacity – its ability to make sense of new information and knowledge and to use this as a basis for new commercial endeavors.
- That human capital is relevant when we consider a consultant innovating on behalf of a client as well as innovating for their own consultancy firm as the firm drives its own change agenda.
- How cases based on real-world situations facing consultancy firms of various sizes and located across different countries all highlight the need for training, skills, and experience to underpin the process of innovation in management consultancy.
- How a broad range of abilities and skills, some hard (e.g., technical skills) and some soft (e.g., presentation skills and persuasion), are needed to help answer the simultaneous questions of 'why', 'when', 'where', and 'what type' when it comes to contemplating, planning and carrying out innovation in a consultancy setting.
- That practice emergence (the formation of new practice areas) in consultancy firms promotes the creation of new bases of human capital in the firm.
- How the literature highlights the management of human capital as something that is under the control of the firm; there is a vital role for HR policy to attract, nurture, utilize and retain human capital for innovation in management consultancy.

## Notes

1 Sarbanes–Oxley Act (2002).
2 E.g., specific human capital in certain computer systems and high-technology, or in energy-efficiency projects (in the *Ergonomica* case in this book) or in specific industrial verticals such as oil and gas (see the Pay Zone case, reference at the end of the chapter).

## Suggested additional cases for analyzing human capital and innovation in consulting

Andreu, R., Lara, E. and Sieber, S., 2004. 'Knowledge management at CAP Gemini, Ernst & Young', *IESE Publishing* (product number: IES133).

Batra, S. and Puri, S., 2015. 'GCS consulting: Should corporate or personal interests come first?' *Ivey Publishing* (product number: 9B15M042).

Geok, W.B. and Buche, I., 2008. 'Tata Consultancy Services of India (A): Human capital management as competitive strategy', *Asian Business Case Centre* (product number: ABCC-2008-004A).

Hicks, J. and Lehmberg, D., 2012. 'Collision course: Selling European high performance motorcycles in Japan', *Ivey Publishing* (product number: 9B12M025).

Munro, M. and Huff, S.L., 2008. 'Pay Zone consulting: A global virtual organization', *Ivey Publishing* (product number: 9B08C004).

Prashar, S., Kodwani, A.D. and Kumar, M., 2017. 'Deloitte and KPMG: The war for talent', *Ivey Publishing* (product number: 9B17C023).

Su, N. and Pirani, N., 2014. 'Transforming the business service portfolio at Global Consultancy', *Ivey Publishing* (product number: 9B14E001).

# 3

# Pole 2: social capital

## It's all about our relationships with clients (. . . and others)

This chapter examines innovation in consultancy firms from the perspective of social capital with clients (. . . and others). Some scholars have referred to 'client capital' as a discrete form of social capital with clients (Swart, 2006). We will stick with the term 'social capital' for analytical purposes in this chapter. Adler and Kwon (2002) summarize social capital as an umbrella term for a range of constructs based on social relations between people. In contrast to the human capital logic of the previous chapter, the social capital logic in our analysis will hinge on the maxim: "It's not what you know, it's who you know" (Woolcock and Narayan, 2000: 225). The baseline logic is that external stakeholder engagement, including client involvement and customer centricity matter for 'dual value creation', i.e., the achieving of benefits for the client and the service provider (Shah, Rust, Parasuraman, Staelin and Day, 2006). And this involvement does not happen through Morse code signals; it happens because of complex and meaningful relationships with clients and other stakeholders (O'Mahoney, 2013). We will start with a brief overview of the concept of social capital before exploring what this means for innovation and then move on to the question of how social capital can impact innovation in a management consulting context. Cases and examples will then shed more light on this perspective before we discuss key implications of social capital for innovation in consultancy.

In a similar way that human capital plays a fundamentally central role in the consultancy industry, social capital also is a core aspect of the industry; without social capital with clients (. . . and others), consultancy firms will not be able to operate at all. Unsurprisingly, there is a whole section in the *Oxford Handbook of Management Consulting* (Oxford University Press) (Kipping and Clark, 2012) dedicated to "consultants and their clients", highlighting the importance of the client-consultant relationship. Maister (2003: Chapter 6) points out how listening to clients provides a deep understanding of client problems, of their wants and needs. New opportunities and prospects can be pursued with clients when the consultant is an effective listener. This has an important socialized aspect; consultants interact socially with

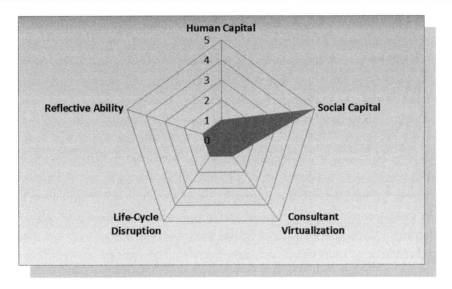

**Figure 3.1** Pole 2: A Focus on Social Capital

representatives from client organizations in order to expand their knowledge of the client (Anand, Gardner and Morris, 2007; Mors, 2010; Taminiau, Smit and De Lange, 2009; Tether and Tajar, 2008). They meet clients face to face in both formal and informal settings. And through this socialization they become exposed to the opportunities for consultancy work for the client. Maister (2003: 61) highlights the link between this socialized listening and innovation:

> Listening – soliciting clients' evaluation of current services and getting them to describe their unfilled needs – has two interrelated purposes: (a) improving the competitiveness of current services and (b) identifying opportunities to develop new services.

Figure 3.1 schematizes our focus for the second Pole in this chapter. As in the last chapter, let's downplay the role of the other Poles for now, and focus our attention on a firm that has achieved the maximum level of social capital possible. Why would a consultancy firm do this, and is it a good thing for innovation?

## Theory of social capital

The core argument of social capital theory is that value resides in social connections and inter-connected networks amongst people (Burt, 2000, 2001). There are two network mechanisms that facilitate this value: structural holes (a structural hole is a gap between two individuals) and network closure (or dense and strong connections between individuals) (Burt, 2000, 2001). The argument goes that being in a position within a social network where the transfer of information between parts of the network is under the control of the individual will put the individual in a valuable position. For instance, being a 'broker' between two or more sub-networks and effectively filling the structural hole will allow the broker to gain access to new sources of information. When a network is closed and the individual is strongly interconnected can also create social capital and value through denseness (Bourdieu, 1989). However, there is debate on this (Flap, 2002). For instance, when there are strong ties between parts of the network (Granovetter, 1983) novel information might be less (or not) forthcoming and such a position would have less value. Overall, and unlike the theory of human capital which is concerned with the expertise, skills and abilities of individuals and how those can be applied in ways that create value, theory of social capital refers to how value can be obtained through social connections with others.

There are a number of well-known outcomes of social capital, including these: influencing job search and career success, effectiveness of teams across different units of large organizations, facilitating entrepreneurship and start-ups, strengthening supplier relationships and learning between organizations (Adler and Kwon, 2002). Social capital allows an 'appropriability' (Coleman, 1988), meaning that social connections can be used in beneficial ways for more than one purpose. It supports goodwill and trust between individuals. The position of the individual within a structure of social relations influences the extent to which social capital is a resource available to the individual for useful purpose (Adler and Kwon, 2002).

The literature sees social capital as a resource embedded in social networks (Lin, 2008). This resource can be accessed and utilized through the ties that an individual has with others in those networks. Lin (2008) makes a key point that social networks and social capital are not interchangeable terms. Social networks allow access and mobilization of resources embedded in the network, but the value that can be gained from these resources, i.e., social capital, is not the same as the network itself. Similarly, Portes (1998) emphasizes how the construct of social capital is a fundamental concept in the field of sociology: there are positive consequences for the individual *and* the community through involvement and participation in groups. Social capital should be thought of as a non-monetary form of capital that is desired amongst the 'recipients' and provided by 'donors' who are themselves motivated to provide the privileged access and benefit for others. Flap (2002) argues that social capital can be seen in terms of the number people ready or prepared to help an individual, the extent to which they are actually ready to help, and the nature of the resource at the end of a tie in the network. In this way, social capital adds to the value of other forms of capital (such as human capital) embodied in an individual.

Social capital comprises the "expected future benefits derived . . . from connections with other persons" (Flap, 2002: 37). Tsai and Ghoshal (1998: 465) see social capital as encompassing "many aspects of a social context, such as social ties, trusting relations, and value systems that facilitate actions of individuals located within that context".

Various studies have empirically examined the effects of social capital on organizational outcomes. Overall, social capital is seen to be a source of sustainable competitive advantage in firms (Bolino, Turnley and Bloodgood, 2002; Nahapiet and Ghoshal, 2000). Bolino, Turnley, and Bloodgood (2002) argue for a reciprocal relationship between citizenship behavior (comprising loyalty, obedience, functional participation, social participation, and advocacy participation) and social capital (structural, relational, and cognitive dimensions). Social capital stimulates additional citizenship behaviors amongst employees. Strong interpersonal connections between employees who know each other well and like and trust each other mean employees "behave in ways that support the group's or organization's social structure"(Bolino, Turnley and Bloodgood, 2002: 516). Florin, Lubatkin, and Schulze (2003), in a study of 275 initial public offerings (IPOs), find social capital to positively influence the organization's ability to accumulate finance before going public as well as to boost the venture's productivity immediately after going public. The central argument for these direct effects is the reduction in time and investment to gather relevant information and knowledge in order to build and sustain a competitive advantage. Florin, Lubatkin, and Schulze (2003) operationalize social resources as the sum of business relationships with Fortune 1000 companies, personal relationships at director level (directors with other board memberships), and underwriters subscribing to the IPO. These social resources have positive effects on financial capital at the time of the IPO, as well as return on sales after the IPO (but not sales growth). Seibert, Kraimer, and Liden (2001) use a sample of 448 employees to show how social capital is related to career success when mediated by what they refer to as network benefits including access to information, access to resources, and career sponsorship. Thus, different aspects of social capital interact to provide value to an individual's career path.

Woolcock and Narayan (2000) review the concept of social capital in terms of its implications for economic development, highlighting local community and civil society (a communitarian view of social capital), intercommunity connectivity within and between organizations (a network view), the role of political and legal actors (an institutional view), and synergistic actions between citizens and governments in society (a synergy view). Importantly, Woolcock and Narayan (2000) raise the prospect of social capital as a double-edged sword, something that can lead to positive economic development or negative economic development depending on the fit between type of social capital and nature of the nation state.

## Social capital and innovation

Social capital has a beneficial impact on innovation in firms when it allows access to a variety of information sources that can be used during inventive and creative activities. Amara and Landry (2005) find that greater levels of novelty are present in firm innovations when firms use a wide variety of information sources. In a study of knowledge-intensive business service firms, Amara, Landry, and Doloreux (2009) find very strong ties between the firm and clients to be positively linked to product innovation but negatively linked to process innovation. Shah, Rust, Parasuraman, Staelin, and Day (2006) argue that customer centricity involves a relationship-orientation rather than a transaction-orientation and this creates value not only for the customer, but also for the service provider itself; it is about 'dual value creation' (115). Williams, Colovic, and Zhu (2016) find that, for Chinese firms, knowledge of foreign markets and customers has a positive impact on innovative performance of the firm, but this effect is amplified when that foreign market knowledge is sourced from a wide breadth of countries, as opposed to a narrow breadth of countries. Laursen, Masciarelli, and Prencipe (2012) find that firms that are situated in geographic locations characterized by a high degree of social capital will invest more in innovation and will generate higher levels of innovative output. Physical co-location in networks can matter because new information is forthcoming in a timely manner. Tacit knowledge exchanges are made possible through face-to-face exchanges and 'fine-grained' information flows. These types of studies all support the argument that innovation is a process that requires access to new sources of knowledge and an ability to combine new knowledge with the existing knowledge of the firm.

In a study of manufacturing firms, Landry, Amara, and Lamari (2002) explore two inter-related questions that reflect innovation as a two-stage process of (1) a decision to innovate, and (2) a decision of how much to innovate. The questions are therefore these: whether social capital determines innovation (i.e., a yes/no answer) and to what extent it determines innovation. Findings reveal two types of social capital impacting the decision to innovate: participation assets (participation in meetings, associations, and networks) and relational assets (an index of personal acquaintances involved in innovation). Contrary to prediction, trust assets (reciprocal trust with a range of external agencies) are not found to impact the propensity to innovate. Results indicate a positive change in the participation assets index increases the likelihood of innovation. For relational assets, a same level of change leads to a greater likelihood of innovation. In terms of radicalness of innovation, participation assets do not matter, while relational assets do. Contrary to prediction, trust assets are not significant. Interestingly, and somewhat expected, is that use of a research network (public research organizations, technology transfer organizations, universities and community colleges) for information has a positive bearing on radicalness of innovation.

Davidsson and Honig (2003) identify three aspects of social capital that positively impact nascent entrepreneur status (discovery of opportunity) and performance outcomes (exploitation of opportunity). In terms of discovery, parents being in business, encouragement by friends or family, and close friends or neighbors being in business are found to be strong predictors. In terms of successful exploitation, being a member of a business network is a positive and significant predictor of success. These results suggest bridging ties (weak ties) become more important than bonding ties (strong ties) for new entrepreneurs as time passes. Weak ties are seen to contain valuable and specific knowledge not possessed by the close network of the entrepreneur, emphasizing how "successful entrepreneurship is a social game" (Davidsson and Honig, 2003: 323).

Social capital can also be beneficial for innovation because it allows trust to form between partners. This then facilitates risk-taking and innovative behaviors. Ahuja (2000) studies links between collaborative networks and innovation output (measured as patent counts) in 97 firms in the chemicals industry over a ten-year period. His study finds strong support for the hypotheses that direct and indirect ties in inter-organizational networks are predictors of innovation. Indirect ties between firms in a technology network allow spillovers of knowledge that contribute to the innovative efforts of firms. Ahuja (2000) makes an important point in distinguishing the differences between direct and indirect ties. Direct ties are sources of resources and information, while indirect ties are mainly sources of information. Also: "unlike direct ties, indirect ties entail relatively low or no maintenance costs for the firm" (Ahuja, 2000: 448). Ahuja (2000) also finds a moderating effect of direct ties on the relationship between indirect ties and innovation output; the higher the level of direct ties, the weaker the influence of indirect ties on innovation will be. Finally, a negative effect of structural holes is identified, with the implication that trust and cohesiveness among inter-firm partners in a network outweighs the concern (and need) for informational diversity that networks with structural holes will bring.

Supporting this, Panayides and Lun (2009) find a positive association between trust and innovation between firms in supply chains. Supply chain relationships built on trust are argued to underpin innovativeness in the relationships between the firms involved because trust reduces opportunism and allows high quality interactions (valuable insights) and tacit knowledge to be exchanged. Investments in innovations in supply chains are examples of asset-specific investments, not easily applied in other contexts. Using a questionnaire survey of UK-based manufacturers and their suppliers, the study shows a positive link between trust and innovation. Rost (2011) also identifies a positive impact of strong ties on innovations. In her study on the German automotive industry she shows that weak ties between firms will not have an impact on the creation of innovation (i.e., patents) unless strong ties are in place. Strong ties, on the other hand, will lead to the creation of innovation without weak ties necessarily being in place.

Zheng (2010) conducts a literature review of empirical work on the relationship between social capital and innovation. The result shows strong support for positive effects for structural and relational social capital on innovation, often moderated by contextual factors such as the nature of ties and intellectual capital. The cognitive aspect of social capital is not found to have strong support in the literature. Indeed, the cognitive dimension is argued to be a constituent of relational social capital.

In their seminal work on the effects of social capital on innovation within the context of one large international firm, Tsai and Ghoshal (1998) find both structural and relational aspects of social capital to have positive effects on product innovation within the firm. They sample 15 business units within one, large electronics company and test a model that proposes structural, relational, and cognitive dimensions of social capital will impact resource exchange and combination in the firm. The latter will then lead to value creation in terms of new product innovations. They find structural social capital (weak, social interaction ties) and relational social capital (strong, trustworthy ties) to have positive direct effects on resource exchange and combination and the latter then has a positive impact on product innovation. Tsai and Ghoshal's (1998) work is important because it shows the impact of structural and relational forms of social capital on the resource exchange that is needed within a social network in order for actors in the network to innovate.

Similarly, Yli-Renko, Autio, and Sapienza (2001) use a social capital perspective to study determinants and consequences of knowledge acquisition in a range of new ventures in the UK. They show how social interaction and network ties with clients have positive impacts on knowledge acquisition. This then has a positive impact on new product development. Interestingly, relationship quality in Yli-Renko, Autio, and Sapienza's (2001) study negatively impacts knowledge acquisition, suggesting that weak ties with clients are more conducive to innovativeness than strong ties. Put differently, structural connections allowing frequent interactions matter more than 'overembeddedness' with clients (Yli-Renko, Autio and Sapienza, 2001: 607), which can insulate firms from useful data sources.

In a related literature, scholars have shown how government policies that promote social capital between firms can be good for innovation performance amongst those firms. Cooke and Wills (1999), for instance, in a study of SMEs in Denmark, Ireland, and Wales, describe how European Union (EU)–funded programs led to impacts of social capital in terms of improving know-how and innovation commercialization. This study highlights how policy intervention matters. It enables SMEs to enhance their innovation output through linkage to new networks, synergy with government policy and integration (embedment in SME networks).

## Consultancy and innovation through a social capital lens

Den Hertog's (2000) work on co-production of innovation in knowledge intensive business services (KIBS) brings attention to the symbiotic relationships between service providers and their clients in working together in the generation of innovation (see also Amara, Landry and Doloreux, 2009). Den Hertog (2000) puts a major emphasis on the direct social interactions between supplier and client and on the implications that these interactions have for knowledge exchanges that underpin the innovation process. An example is the difference between explicit and tacit forms of knowledge flows between provider and client. At the client interface, an explicit flow may entail the client reading certain documentation from the supplier, while a tacit knowledge flow may entail the supplier sharing a 'feeling' with an internal designer on what an appealing website might look like. While a number of other examples are provided by den Hertog (2000), perhaps the most important point made relates to the author's prediction of flexible boundaries between external and internal KIBS staff, co-operation at these boundaries being the key to innovation.

Taminiau, Smit, and De Lange (2009) explore innovation in consulting from the perspective of various knowledge sharing mechanisms. Through interviews with 29 consultants in the Netherlands they show how consultants are under pressure to be as utilized as possible in order to achieve rewards and how this can be an obstacle to innovating because it takes time away from creative (non-billable) endeavor (note: we will cover this in more detail in Chapter 6 on reflective ability). Out of the various possible knowledge sharing modes (codified, formal, informal), Taminiau, Smit, and De Lange (2009) show how informal knowledge sharing between consultants plays a pivotal role in the process of creating an innovative service in consultancy. At the heart of this is the close social networks amongst consultants and between consultants and clients.

In Mors's (2010) study of innovation in a global consultancy firm, informal relationships between senior partners and various constituencies for knowledge sourcing (internal, external, local and global) are argued to be useful for providing heterogeneity and stimulation for consultants' innovative behaviors. Mors (2010) argues how the integration of diverse information through these ties is important in the innovative process in consultancy firms. Heterogeneity increases as ties move from internal to external; it also increases as ties move from local to global. Findings from a dataset of 1,449 informal relationships of 79 senior partners indicate innovation performance is negatively impacted by density of ties between the partner's local environment (internal) and the global environment (internal). Findings also show a positive impact on innovation performance of density of ties between the partner's local environment (internal) and global environment (external) and ties between global environment (internal) and global environment (external). Collectively, these results show how social capital matters for innovation in consulting: network structure of individual senior partners influences how they innovate. Of particular importance in this study is the identification of context as a moderating influence between network structure and innovation performance. In homogeneous contexts, senior partners seek low density open networks for the knowledge needed for innovation. In heterogeneous contexts, senior partners benefit from dense networks and close interactions that help in the interpretation and integration of new information.

In Anand, Gardner, and Morris's (2007) work on practice emergence in professional service firms, four generative elements are identified: socialized agency, differentiated expertise, defensible turf, and organizational support. Arguably, we can discern the construct of social capital at play within all of these concepts. Within socialized agency, personal brand building and attracting of clients to the offerings of the practice area is possible because of the partner's socialized efforts internal and external to the firm. Within differentiated expertise, knowledge, and input from client assignments matter and this is possible because of social encounters with clients over a period of time. For defensible turf, a degree of persuasion (i.e., through social interaction) with other partners is needed, as is the leveraging of strong client relationships. And for organizational support, the developing of juniors in the firm, and the cross-selling of the new practice with long-standing clients are both activities that require deep social interaction.

Back, Parboteeah, and Nam (2014) show an interesting effect of the use of consultants by firms in emerging markets. Based on a survey of 1,330 businesses in nine emerging markets, the authors show that the use of management consultants is a predictor of innovation inputs by those firms (this captured in terms of R&D expenditure) but not innovation outputs. The challenges of innovating in 'catch-up' economies can be partially dealt with through the use of external consultants to fill knowledge and information voids. Consultants also legitimize the innovation efforts of client firms. The effect is more pronounced in countries with low institutional levels compared with higher institutional levels (a proxy for this being the country's level of intellectual property rights). While not explicitly stated in Back, Parboteeah, and Nam's (2014) work, the mechanisms by which external consultants 'fill' institutional voids in a country in order to allow client firms in the country to take risks with higher levels of R&D investment will undoubtedly involve the consultants drawing on their social capital during projects with clients. They themselves will need to understand the specific areas of deficiency in a country's institutional environment and will need to share this knowledge through their social interactions with clients.

Hughes, Ireland, and Morgan's (2007) work on stimulating dynamic value creation includes a case of a UK-based IT consultancy where the managing director makes a strong point about "working closely with . . . business to improve our [product] offering" (Hughes, Ireland and Morgan, 2007: 166). External networking is seen as a prominent way of gaining experience and learning that could be used to develop and improve the service offering and indeed, the same quoted managing director seems to be critical of the incubator in which the firm was based; its management could have done more to promote external networking proactively. According to Hughes, Ireland, and Morgan (2007: 165): "by forging close, interactive ties, firms can leverage knowledge and resources which help them not only achieve parity with established competitors but also develop new ways of overcoming competitive threats".

Sturdy, Clark, Fincham, and Handley (2009) examine boundaries in consultant-client arrangements; the notion of 'boundary' being one that, arguably, lies at the heart of the discussion of social network between a consultant and a client. These authors are critical of what they see as a rather dichotomous (or 'polarized') view of the role of the consultant in knowledge transformation, i.e., either as innovator (bringing new knowledge to client organizations) or as a legitimator (legitimating pre-existing client knowledge). Sturdy, Clark, Fincham, and Handley (2009) point to the fact that boundaries in general have become less formal and more dynamic and prone to flux. They can also be symbolic, a quality that "emotionally separates, unites or alienates" (Sturdy, Clark, Fincham and Handley, 2009: 631). Boundaries can be physical (e.g., defined by technology or infrastructure), cultural (defined by cognition or the emotions of belonging), or political (defined by power and dependency relations). Consultants do not necessarily have to adopt a role as innovator or legitimator given the fact that (1) boundaries have a complexity defined by these different aspects and (2) they can change over time as projects progress. A consultant's role in enabling knowledge flow will be contingent on the nature of the project and the condition of the various boundaries at any point in time.

In Tether and Tajar's (2008) study, openness was found to be a consistent and significant predictor of use of specialist knowledge providers (such as consultancies) by firms in their innovation activities. The finding suggests external consultancies are used to complement the range of information (and information sources) available to firms through their own social network. Compared with private research organizations and the public science base, a higher proportion of consultancies has strong and weak ties with firms, indicative of the role of social capital between consultants and clients that seek to compete on the basis of innovation.

Looking beyond social capital with clients, the literature notes how consultancy firms are an integral part of the wider knowledge management industry, interlinking with other knowledge-intensive institutions such as business schools, business support organizations, and academic centers (Hidalgo and Albors, 2008; Love,

Roper and Bryson, 2011). Consultancy firms view themselves as developers of innovation management techniques and use innovation management techniques such as business plan development, project management, corporate intranet, and benchmarking with various goals in mind. These include knowledge management, increasing flexibility and efficiency, and facilitating teamwork. They also are used to support relationships with suppliers and to make client relationships more effective. Hidalgo and Albors (2008) also highlight how specific tools and techniques, which have been 'routinized' by the consultancy firm, are used to support the broader social networks in which the firm participates.

In Hargadon and Sutton's (1997) ethnographic study of innovation in a product design consultancy (IDEO, Palo Alto), the importance of network position and constant learning from other organizational entities in the wider network are emphasized. In addition, the use of routines within the firm that make an explicit and deliberate attempt to bring knowledge from different sources together in new ways is emphasized. Such 'routinization' of activity within the firm's social network is designed explicitly with client innovation in mind and puts the consultancy firm in a position of knowledge broker. This role is responsible for accessing, acquiring, storing, and retrieving knowledge from widely differing sources (e.g., from different industries) in order to design new solutions for clients based on combinations of ideas.

Love, Roper, and Bryson (2011) examine external linkages with different types of partners and emphasize how these have an 'encoding' function. This refers to linkages between a service provider and its external partners that allow externally sourced ideas to be transformed into tangible, marketed innovations. Falling in-between explorative and exploitative phases of the innovation process (March, 1991), this encoding function allows the service provider to make sense of – and actually use – newly acquired external knowledge in order to create new offerings, and then command sales from those offerings. There is a range of interesting aspects to Love, Roper, and Bryson's (2011) study. Perhaps at the top of the list is the fact that they look at a broader conceptualization of external connectivity for innovation, i.e., not just towards clients but also to other types of partners including suppliers, competitors, and universities. Their analysis using the UK Community Innovation Survey (CIS) data indicates interaction with customers is most important for external knowledge sourcing for new service ideas, while interaction with commercial labs and public research bodies is most useful for the knowledge transformation stage. Finally, interaction with professional industry associations is most important for exploiting innovation. While these results may be country specific and we must be careful not to generalize, they do highlight the fact that while social capital with clients may be important in the explorative phases of innovation, consultancy firms will need to look beyond these stakeholders in later stages of the innovation process.

## Practice insight

The following practice insight was kindly provided by UK-based Folajimi Ashiru of Durham University Business School, UK.

### Using a partnering model for a new social enterprise in Nigeria

Imagine a country where only 62 per cent of pregnant women have had HIV counseling and testing (Dauda, 2012). And of those tested, almost a third did not return for their results. Yet, the timely administering of long available drugs can sharply reduce transmission of the virus to newborns. With a population of approximately 198 million people (NPC, 2018), Nigeria is the largest country in Africa and accounts for 47 per cent of West Africa's population. Nigeria is also the second largest economy in sub-Saharan Africa and accounts for 41 per cent of the region's GDP.

HIV/AIDS was first reported in Nigeria in 1986 (Dauda, 2012), two years after the first case was reported in the US. For several years, the central focus of the AIDS campaign had been the provision of anti-retroviral drugs and creating the necessary testing and monitoring facilities. It has brought life-saving treatment to millions of people. But there are millions with the disease untreated. Out of 33.3M persons living with HIV/AIDS globally in 2009, 22.5M were living in sub-Saharan Africa, with 5 per cent prevalence, 1.8M new infections, and 1.3M deaths (UNAIDS, 2010). Nigeria was the second most affected country in 2009 (UNGASS, 2010). Nigeria has been in the grip of a growing HIV/AIDS epidemic with a national infection rate of 5 per cent since 2003 (Hilhorst, van Liere, Ode and de Koning, 2006).

Nigeria sought to tackle the HIV/AIDS menace via its National Agency for the Control of AIDS (NACA). A key component of NACA's strategy was to expand its reach via less stigmatized media; information can help in effective prevention and treatment of the disease.

Funding was a major concern as the main source of finance was from foreign donors such as the Global Fund (Switzerland), the President's Emergency Plan for AIDS Relief (PEPFAR) (US), and the UK Government's Department for International Development (DFID). The Nigerian government was barely able to provide 5 per cent of total funding required for HIV/AIDS annual intervention. The shortage of funding meant most of the intervention funding was directed towards anti-retroviral drugs. There was still a need to overcome the stigmatization by improved communication.

NACA had to come up with alternative strategies. They invited various partner organizations and I represented my bank as a financial partner and advisor. At a round table summit we met to discuss the issue and a call center idea was put forward. The recommendation was that a call center would enable the general public to get professional and up-to-date advice about HIV/AIDS. Since it would not be a face-to-face interaction, the fear of stigmatization would be reduced. People who were shy or ashamed would open up more. Ultimately, the more information in the hands of people, the more they would be able to use that information. The logic was that the more informed people are, the more the HIV/AIDS epidemic would reduce. This call center idea seemed like a novel idea but the challenge was twofold: raising funds and carrying out the implementation. All funds approved for NACA had already been assigned to other projects. Although there was a possibility NACA might be able to raise funding by lobbying or seeking assistance from companies, support was not assured.

My bank had actually been seeking for a way to win the business account of NACA but there had been so many inhibiting factors that made it nearly impossible to achieve this. So this was my chance to actively participate in an innovative social program that would help alleviate the social stigma and reverse the HIV/AIDS prevalence in Nigeria. Of course there was the added benefit of establishing a banking relationship with NACA, an account I had actively sought out for about 18 months.

To enable us to raise the required funding for the project, I designed a charity activity plan which involved raising financing on a voluntary basis from a wide range of empathetic clients of the bank. The plan was to appeal to clients' moral sense of compassion. I needed to draw on the bank's existing social capital. After the approval by the bank's management and board, in partnership with NACA, we designed communication materials asking for donations towards the objective of reversing the HIV/AIDS epidemic. This communication was done electronically as well as physical delivery of letters through account officers (the bank had over two million accounts and each individual account was looked after by dedicated account officers). The project plan also included a charity walk event for creating awareness for HIV/AIDS.

The charity walk event was a success. Staff including all executive management, customers, NACA officials, and many members of the public joined the event. The funds raised were used to equip the call center. This was an innovative solution and over 3,000 people contributed towards the initiative. As a result, the bank initiated a yearly staff voluntary charity activity and different social projects are now identified and supported.

The call center is always extremely busy and has provided an outlet for free expression and an avenue to obtain professional help. The success of this initiative would not have been possible without tapping into our wider social capital and getting all stakeholders involved and committed. My commitment initially was drawn from my objective to ensure my bank raises its financing base by attracting funding sources that can provide core liquidity. However, this commitment was strengthened by networking with other stakeholders who described the incredible work being undertaking in the health and humanitarian sector, some of which was critical to help resolve near hopeless situations.

## Case reflections on the theme of social capital

The relationship between social capital and innovation in consultancy is described in a number of published cases. The two following cases portray quite different situations in terms of social ties and the value of social capital to innovation.

In the case of A Consultant's Comeuppance (Buday, 2003), there had been a long-standing and strong relationship between the head of the financial services practice at the consultancy firm and the head of the retail banking unit at the client. The relationship was indeed a valuable one having earned tens of millions of dollars in fees in the past decade. These two people attend baseball games together and were familiar with each other's family members. There were strong bonds between the two companies and this was centered on the relationship between the two individuals.

However, the arrival of a new CEO at the client brought about a re-assessment of the nature of the relationship. The new CEO was skeptical of the value that external consultants could bring and was embarking on a new cost-cutting exercise across the bank. In effect, this meant all consultants were required to re-sell their value to the client. They were given, quite literally, a handful of days to prepare and deliver a pitch to the client. The days of a strong and cozy relationship between consultant and client were over.

A central issue at the core of this situation – which is an all too familiar situation in the consulting industry – is the lack of immediate transparency that client and consultant could have on the value provided by the relationship. All the new CEO could see was a multi-million dollar cost over a ten-year period. But there was no evidence in the case that the consultant was able to immediately and confidently produce an audited and trustworthy (perhaps independent) report to attest to the value derived from this investment. The client's intervention made the consultancy firm realize the dangers of an over-committed relationship and that a new and fresh approach would now be needed. By challenging, or even breaking, the relationship the consultancy firm was forced – albeit in a short space of time – to demonstrate its value and come up with some new approaches to deal with the client's predicament, i.e., to innovate. Absent the intervention by the CEO, the status quo and strong bond could – one may argue – inhibit innovation both within the consultancy firm and for the client.

In the case of Robertson and Davies Management Consultants – Toronto Office (Ma and Saigaonkar, 2010), the promotion prospects of a relatively new recruit were dealt a blow by the organization as the partners decided the individual was not ready for promotion, despite achieving excellent results with clients and being highly sought-after and valued by clients in a short period of six months. The central issue was that the individual had been so tied up delivering for clients that he had avoided internal contact and socialization opportunities within the consultancy itself. Senior members of the promotion panel considered his efforts at assimilation into the consultancy to have been very weak. This created the impression that he was not aligned with the company's values and culture. He worked late and was attentive to the needs of his clients, but he had not managed to establish a trustworthy relationship with his peers.

At the heart of the issue – from an innovation angle – is the fact that the consultant has some very useful industry experience in telecommunications and clearly is beginning to establish himself with clients. But he has not built strong ties with his colleagues. His knowledge is likely to stay confined to himself. His colleagues might not trust him if it came to working on new innovative products and services. Indeed, partners perceive him not to be a cultural fit at all within the company.

His absence of strong ties within the organization might encourage us to consider the extent to which he has developed weak ties. The literature on weak ties, as highlighted earlier, indicates a strong link to innovative capability. Many weak ties could mean a diversity of knowledge and information in the hands of the central node and this could be beneficial for creative endeavor. However, here too, we see little evidence of any weak ties. If anything, the individual has developed his ties solely with his clients, and possibly with his line manager. He has not made any efforts to seek out perspectives and insights from others within the consultancy firm. His internal social capital is under-developed and he has little chance of becoming a source of innovation for the firm.

## Implications

In the previous chapter on the relationship between human capital and innovation in consultancy, we argued that skills and experience will allow consultants to determine answers to key questions relating to 'why', 'when', 'where', and 'what type' when considering innovation. Social capital, as discussed in the present chapter, puts a new slant on this. Without doubt, good and healthy relationships between consultant and client, and between consultant and other stakeholders, will allow answers to these questions to be formulated. Social capital will allow the experiences of others to be shared with a focal consultant. Importantly, it will allow for tacit knowledge to flow to the consultant, knowledge that is not available in written form and which can be used to great effect because it deals with the nuances of the process of formulating an innovative response. To this end, social capital augments human capital. It allows the consultant to refine his or her thinking relating to these specific questions.

However, social capital presents an opportunity to offer something extra as far as innovative responses by the consultant are concerned. In some situations, the consultant themselves is able to actually carry out the implementation of an innovation. In these cases, the innovation is likely to be narrow in scope, incremental in nature, and something that lies squarely within the skillset and experience (and motivation) of the consultant. For most innovation projects a range of people become involved in setting the implementation agenda. Ideas become annotated over time as risks and uncertainty are discussed and ways of dealing with them are agreed. More people then become involved in the building of prototypes or piloting and testing of initial versions of the innovation. This applies to service and process innovations, as much as it does to product innovations. For radical innovations with a large scope, higher numbers of people will be involved over a lengthy period of time, some providing expertise and advice, others being gatekeepers to resource pools needed to push the innovation forward.

Social capital, therefore, allows the 'how' question for innovation (i.e., the issue of what actually needs to be done to implement the innovation in the target context) to be addressed. Ties with various stakeholders within and outside client and consultant organizations allow new resources to be included in the innovation process. These may include third parties contributing particular technology and capabilities so that the innovation can materialize. This extends also to other stakeholders such as government officials and regulators in situations in which regulatory approvals are required. Social capital allows for these additional organizations to be identified and for the identities of the units and individuals in these organizations to be isolated. They provide a basis for contact that will help in determining the cost and feasibility of any proposed innovation, as well as offering ideas and suggestions on what is possible and what will not work. Social capital during implementation matters for the successful outcome and learning from innovation projects, and for trustworthy relationships to be established that may form the basis for additional innovation projects in the future.

Our review of the social capital argument, and evidence from cases and stories such as the Nigerian HIV/AIDS social enterprise, point to a potentially powerful role for social capital on top of the human capital argument. However, there are some important differences from this review of social capital logic compared to our review of human capital logic. The social capital logic is arguably more complex given the different forms of social capital (i.e., strong vs. weak ties, and structural vs. relational vs. cognitive social capital). With human capital we see a more tightly defined construct with conceptual overlap between constructs such as 'skills', 'experience', 'expertise', and 'know-how'. At a base level, these constructs all talk to the ability of the consultant to innovate. With social capital, the question opens out into how the consultant can use others (through social networks) to conceive new innovation and implement new innovation. The focus is less about the consultant, and more about the consultant's contacts. In particular, it allows us to assess how a consultancy firm can use different types of social capital in different situations in order to fulfil the promise of innovating for clients or for their own organization. In addition to the different types of ties, a consultant operating in a consultancy firm of any size (theoretically at least, with more than one employee) will be living and working in an social 'duality' where one part of the social network is internal to the firm, and one part is external (predominantly clients, but also other stakeholders such as other consultants and contacts in other firms, regulators, universities, and technology providers). What role these two parts of the combined network play in formulating and progressing an innovative initiative will need to be determined by the consultant. Early and exploratory work may be client-led and kept 'secret' in order to provide maximum protection from competitors. Alternatively, path-breaking work with clients might be a trigger for upgrading the broader service offerings of the consultancy firm (we will discuss this in greater depth in Chapter 6 on reflective ability). What is undisputed is that relational skills help consultants to recognize opportunities and develop new innovative solutions. The contingencies under which consultants use different types of social capital need to be clearly understood.

## Summary and learning points

In this chapter on Pole 2: social capital, we have seen the following:

- How theory of social capital provides different views on how social structures and relationships influence creativity and innovation, one main debate being the influence of strong ties vs. that of weak ties.
- How academic literature and empirical research show strong positive effects between different forms of social capital and innovation in consultancy.
- That the main source of this innovative potential is the consultant's involvement with clients, this providing knowledge of where new opportunities lie, knowledge about how to evaluate those opportunities, as well as ideas about how they may be exploited.
- That social capital can also be formed with non-client organizations, including universities, research centers, governmental organizations, and other business services suppliers.

- How informal socialization has an especially important role to play in innovation in consultancy.
- How social capital can provide an explanation for how consultants innovate on behalf of or for a client as well as whether and how they innovate for their own consultancy firm.
- Numerous cases and real-world situations in various types of advisory organizations highlighting the role of social capital in underpinning innovativeness.
- While different forms of social capital can help answer the questions of 'why', 'when', 'where', and 'what type' of innovation to adopt in a consultancy setting, it also has a potent effect on answering the 'how' question.

## Suggested additional cases for analyzing social capital and innovation in consulting

Eccles, R.G., Narayandas, D. and Rossano, P., 2013. 'Innovation at the Boston Consulting Group', *Harvard Business School* (product number: 9-313-137).

Frydman, F., Arnaudo, G., Rena, C. and Berger, G., 2003. 'Alliances that build alliances: McKinsey-Ashoka and the fundacion compromiso', *Social Enterprise Knowledge Network* (product number: SKE024).

Hicks, J. and Lehmberg, D., 2012. 'Collision course: Selling European high performance motorcycles in Japan', *Ivey Publishing* (product number: 9B12M025).

Li, X., Williams, C. and Mu, Z., 2014. 'Hongxin Entrepreneur Incubator: Expanding the cloud', *Ivey Publishing* (product number: 9B14M113).

Williams, C., 2017. 'Ergonomica Consulting and Solltram Hotels: An ethical dilemma', *Ivey Publishing* (product number: 9B17M153).

# 4

# Pole 3: consultant virtualization

## It's all about working from anywhere

This chapter examines innovation in consultancy firms from the perspective of virtual organization. Virtual organization is *a way of organizing work*. It is based on using advanced information and communication technology (ICT) that allows people to work from remote locations, not physically co-located, with people communicating and coordinating using computer-based systems. The phenomenon is not new, and the academic attention on all things virtual really took off in the 1990s (e.g., Boudreau, Loch, Robey and Straud, 1998; DeSanctis and Monge, 1999; Jarvenpaa and Leidner, 1999); a reflection of what was happening in organizations at the time. Organizations were seeking new ways of competing by allowing what became known as 'telecommuting' (Kurland and Egan, 1999) and using emerging ICT to tap into globally distributed resources.

Importantly for us, virtual organization is increasingly used to foster innovation (Harvey and Griffith, 2007). And it has become commonplace in consultancy, with many consultants working from remote locations, even from home on a regular basis when they are not required in the office or at a client site. This has helped save costs for employers and boosted the benefits of flexible working and work–life balance in an industry that traditionally required consultants to be away from home and travelling for lengthy periods. According to Bergiel, Bergiel, and Balsmeier (2008: 106): "because virtual teams are diverse and heterogeneous, these teams are much more powerful and effective structures compared to traditional team structures influenced by time and place. Diversity helps engender creativity and originality among virtual team members".

As a way of organizing, virtual organization is a form of organizational capital. Organizational capital refers to practices and modes of control that support the functioning of the firm (Acs and Fitzroy, 1989). Organizational capital is seen as the firm's set of productive information; an asset that determines the limits of what a firm can do (Prescott and Visscher, 1980). It affects employee "citizenship efforts" involving investment in improvement to productivity and worker well-being (Tomer, 1998). In our analysis we conceptualize organizational capital as being a firm-specific good embodied in both the organization of production (i.e., the organization of consultancy work) and the relationship of employees (i.e., consultants) to tasks (i.e., innovating on behalf of clients or the consultancy firm itself) (Atkeson and Kehoe, 2005).

As a way of organizing that harnesses value for the consultancy firm, virtual organization is different to the constructs of human capital and social capital discussed in the previous two chapters. The maxim for this Pole could be taken from Boudreau, Loch, Robey and Straud (1998): "Virtual organizations . . . allow individual employees to perform their work in a variety of locations: home, car, office, or on airplanes" (Boudreau, Loch, Robey and Straud, 1998: 122). We will start with a definition and exploration of the concept of virtual organization before discussing its relationship with innovation and, then, its use for innovation in management consulting. As in the other chapters, cases and examples will be used to shed more light on how virtual organization might (or might not) encourage innovation in a consultancy setting.

Figure 4.1 provides a schematic for our focus on Pole 3 in this chapter. Again, as we review the literature here, try and imagine a firm that has a maximum level of consultant virtualization, i.e., having all of its consultants working from a remote location (if that is possible) and let's consider the ramifications of this for innovation.

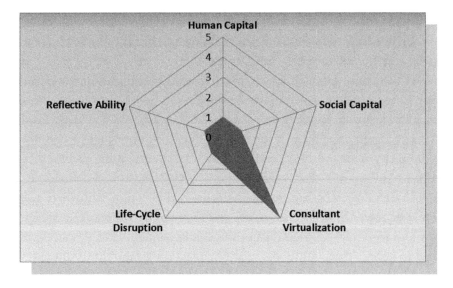

**Figure 4.1** Pole 3: A Focus on Consultant Virtualization

## Exploring virtual organization

Boudreau, Loch, Robey, and Straud (1998) describe three characteristics of a virtual organization: (1) dependence on a federation of alliances between organizations (i.e., the virtual organization is a network; Kasper-Fuehrer and Ashkanasy, 2003; Larsen and McInerney, 2002) with the organizations working together through contractual or other means (such as equity ownership); (2) spatial and temporal dependence, according to Boudreau, Loch, Robey, and Straud (1998: 122) being "able to overcome vast spatial and temporal barriers by linking together geographically remote resources"; and (3) flexibility, with parts of the organization changing over time (i.e., nodes being formed, reformed or disbanded) according to changing environmental conditions. According to Jarvenpaa and Leidner (1999) *global* virtual teams: (1) have no common past or future, (2) are culturally diverse and geographically dispersed, and (3) communicate electronically. While there are clear similarities between these definitions, it is important to emphasize that virtual organizational forms do not have to be international and spanning national borders. It is the characteristic of being geographically dispersed that is important (DeSanctis and Monge, 1999). However, as a consequence of globalizing forces (such as the emergence of accessible lower cost, highly trained human capital in countries like India) they often are highly international and consequently comprised of individuals who are culturally and linguistically diverse and not likely to get to meet face-to-face.

Importantly, it is ICT that underpins virtuality, with different types of technologies being used for different purposes. Boudreau, Loch, Robey and Straud (1998) describe these purposes in terms of "needs" and categorize them into three components: the need for the virtual organization to be efficient, the need for it to be responsive, and the need for it to support learning.

But is ICT the only pre-requisite for making virtual organization work? Research has also pointed out how collaboration amongst the people involved is needed to make virtual organizations effective (Cohen and Mankin, 1999). People need to be able to come together at short notice, be willing and motivated to communicate using computer-mediated tools, and to have a 'win-win' mindset when tackling problems. According to Cohen and Mankin (1999: 2), a team is defined as "a collection of individuals who are interdependent in their tasks, who share responsibility for outcomes, who see themselves and are seen by others as an intact social entity . . . and who manage their relationships across organizational boundaries". So, we have the notion that within a virtual organization a number of discrete virtual teams may be at work each with its own focal point (normally a specific project or assignment for a client). While virtual teams will be organized on a virtual basis and may therefore constitute a virtual organization, it is quite common for virtual organization to be applied to a larger number of teams, i.e., there is not a 1:1 mapping between a virtual organization and a virtual team.

At the level of the virtual team, a significant literature has emerged. Again, a common theme has been how collaboration is developed and maintained. Jarvenpaa and Leidner (1999) examine the relationship between communication and trust in virtual teams, using data from email archives and questionnaires in university settings around the world. Importantly, they show that, despite the members of the teams never meeting face to face, there are mechanisms by which trust is formed. Trust is a potential issue when people and activities are organized virtually not only because of a lack of face-to-face meeting opportunity while the team is in operation, but also because of the lack of past and future association. One of the participants in Larsen and McInerney's (2002: 454) work on virtual organizations is reported as saying they had: "difficulty trusting someone I don't know, someone whose work I have never seen before". This arises because virtual organizations are temporary (project-based) forms (Kasper-Fuehrer and Ashkanasy, 2003). However, Jarvenpaa and Leidner (1999) show how it is possible to establish *and maintain* trustworthy relationships between distributed team members, despite their virtual setting and their cultural and geographic distances. At the core of this is the ability to manage "the uncertainty, complexity, and expectations of the virtual environment" (Jarvenpaa and Leidner, 1999: 809–810). Trust is not seen in terms of the traditional socially oriented trust found in co-located teams. Instead it is seen in terms of *swift trust*, i.e., trust that appears to be in place despite the team members not having any previous experience of working together (Kasper-Fuehrer and Ashkanasy, 2003). Not all teams in Jarvenpaa and Leidner's (1999) study exhibit swift trust from the start, but those that do show confidence and optimism and are not skeptical about what they have to achieve. Importantly, those teams that exhibit swift trust are able to solve problems and operate more effectively than those that lack trust. Communications between team members that have a social aspect (as well as a task aspect) appear to be linked to high-performing virtual teams.

DeSanctis and Monge (1999) describe the relationships amongst individuals in virtual organizations as tenuous. Relationships are more likely to be contractual than based on ownership (see the Practice Insight segment below on the UK-based eConsultancy Scopism, where none of the eConsultants are actual employees of the firm). Work can be dynamically allocated across people in different locations and this highlights the very flexible nature of the virtual organization. Boundaries become permeable (Stough, Eom and Buckenmyer, 2000) and while this may be an asset in terms of responding to changes in the organization's environment, there may be downsides to this because of pressures on communication and the need to continuously establish swift trust in discrete project teams. Electronically mediated communication takes a preeminent position in virtual organizations, although this leads to an inherent tension in the model: there is a need to have richer communication with a social content (Jarvenpaa and Leidner, 1999) as well as more formal communication with a transactional content.

Gallivan (2001) provides a counter-point to the argument on trust in virtual organizations. He studies open source software (OSS) projects as a form of virtual organization and finds that other control mechanisms are at play in determining the effective performance of virtually organized projects. These relate to practices that are explicit forms of control, namely controlling people in terms of efficiency, predictability, and calculability of processes. In other words, there is a set of control mechanisms that is possible to deploy in virtual organizations that go beyond trust. This is also reinforced by Markus and Agres's (2000) work. They comment that open source projects are often tightly disciplined through governance mechanisms that are put in place to avoid what potentially could be chaotic consequences. Virtual organizations work when they are self-governed through membership management, rules that allow members to adapt, monitoring mechanisms, reputation as a control mechanism, and shared values and norms (Markus and Agres, 2000). According to this view, trust may be more implicit, and is not as relevant as other literature (e.g., Jarvenpaa and Leidner, 1999) suggests. In many ways, Gallivan (2001: 278) is doubtful of the role of trust in these settings, describing it, for instance, as a "lofty ideal".

In addition to these discussions on communication, trust, and control mechanisms in virtual organizations, scholars have also examined the nature of the information infrastructure that is needed to support them (Strader, Lin and Shaw, 1998). Clearly, as a network of knowledge workers and distributed information processing units, a virtual organization will be an enormous 'processor' of information and 'creator' of knowledge. The potential for chaos in how this information and knowledge are generated, stored, and utilized is arguably a lot higher than in tightly constrained hierarchical organizational forms. Strader, Lin, and Shaw (1998) propose an information infrastructure framework for understanding informational needs throughout the life-cycle of virtual organization. This perspective is interesting because it explicitly highlights the fact that virtual organizations can come and go. The phases identified are *identification* (of opportunity), *formation* (related to partner identification, selection, and formation), *operation* (the main business function performed by the virtual organization), and *termination* (ultimately involving asset dispersal once the mission of the virtual organization has been fulfilled). There are clearly different informational needs at different phases of this life-cycle, with one example put forward by the authors being the use of the Internet in the early phases, and an Intranet in the latter phases.

## Virtual organization and innovation

There are many reasons to think that organizing virtually will allow firms to innovate. Firstly, virtual organizations are able to draw on and utilize resources beyond that of any one hierarchically integrated organization (Gallivan, 2001). Secondly, they are flexible and adaptable forms, able to change in nature very quickly as circumstances change (Bergiel, Bergiel and Balsmeier, 2008; Mowshowitz, 1997a). Thirdly, when they are international in nature, they will contain sub-units (and people) from many different locations and cultures. This will bring diversity into the organization and this can be used as a basis of creativity and innovation (Harvey and Griffith, 2007). Fourthly, communications, by virtue of the fact that they are electronically mediated, will be fast. This speed of communication will underpin speed of response, an essential quality of virtual organizations that seek to exploit new opportunities (Stough, Eom and Buckenmyer, 2000). This means that relevant knowledge that is needed to help the organization make progress on an innovative idea or project can – in theory – be brought to the attention of those that need it without any undue bureaucracy. Fifthly, virtual organizations are themselves seen as an innovative form (Kasper-Fuehrer and Ashkanasy, 2003; Mowshowitz, 1997a; Stough, Eom and Buckenmyer, 2000), challenging the traditional way of organizing for value creation. The constituent parts will therefore inherit the characteristics of this innovative form, and will have a propensity to act and behave in innovative ways.

Larsen and McInerney (2002) report on a teaching exercise where groups of students spread across four distributed universities were asked to develop information products (a white paper). This highlights the innovative potential of virtual organizations. Firstly, they can be used as a basis for learning – a key component in innovation (Brown and Duguid, 1991). Secondly, they allow newly identified opportunities to be evaluated and exploited. Indeed, as noted by Larsen and McInerney (2002: 449): "Some researchers see virtual organizations as a response to opportunities in the marketplace. When such opportunities arise, virtual organizations are created quickly to take advantage of the opportunities by creating unique and innovative solutions".

Mowshowitz (1997a) argues that virtual organization is an innovative approach to organization that lends itself to satisfying requirements. The management of tasks in a virtual organization involves the analysis of abstract requirements, the tracking of ways to satisfy those requirements, ways of allocating 'satisfiers' to the requirements, and ways to make this allocation procedure optimal (Mowshowitz, 1997a: 375). This can be seen as a naturally innovative process of 'switching' between 'satisfiers', a notion that puts creative capability at the core of virtual organization. Furthermore, the mechanism for deploying this creative capability within a virtual organization is something that is seen to be reviewed and continually enhanced. This makes sense in terms of its alignment with the definitions of virtual organization given earlier and found in various articles on the topic (Boudreau, Loch, Robey and Straud, 1998; DeSanctis and Monge, 1999; Jarvenpaa and Leidner, 1999). If the virtual organization is to be adaptable (through switching of satisfiers) to changing needs and flexible enough to deal with various and changing scenarios, the heuristics engine at the heart of the virtual organization will need to undergo continual rejuvenation. Mowshowitz (1997a) shows how this principle can be applied to a wide range of industrial settings, including automobile manufacture, tax management, and investment management.

A counter-argument is put by Chesbrough and Teece (1996). According to these authors, centralized and hierarchical organizational forms actually have advantages over distributed, virtual organizational firms because they allow for control of the innovation process. The virtual form is unstable and may result in certain members of the network benefitting from joint innovation, while others do not benefit. While the incentives to take risks and innovate may be higher in decentralized virtual organizations, the ability to control and manage conflict is higher in non-virtual, hierarchically integrated organizations (Chesbrough and Teece, 1996). The authors make the point that the way in which organizational form influences innovation will depend on the type of innovation. In particular, they distinguish between autonomous and systemic innovations. Autonomous innovations are ones that can be pursued independently from other innovations, while systemic innovations require a fundamental change to the product system (Chesbrough and Teece, 1996). It is autonomous innovations that are better suited to being developed in virtual organizations. Firstly, virtual organizations are efficient at codified knowledge exchange and this type of knowledge is useful for autonomous innovations that need to be integrated into other – already existing – components. Secondly, systemic innovations require higher amounts of new and complex knowledge, mostly of a tacit nature, and this is better coordinated and protected within the hierarchical control of one organization.

In a similar vein, Gibson and Gibbs (2006) examine the differential effects of the four characteristics of virtuality on innovation (see also Bergiel, Bergiel and Balsmeier, 2008; Kirkman, Rosen, Gibson, Tesluk and McPherson, 2002). These are *geographic dispersion, electronic dependence, structural dynamism*, and *national diversity*. They provide reasons – using established literature – to suggest that these four characteristics can actually hinder innovation rather than support it. Geographic dispersion can prevent external communication, mutual support, and speed of innovation. Electronic dependence can reduce opportunities for improvisation and subtle control. Structural dynamism can create uncertainty that makes it difficult to handle the political (power relations) side of innovation while also being more difficult to plan. National diversity in members can make it difficult to communicate, resolve conflicts and develop a shared vision (Gibson and Gibbs, 2006; Kirkman, Rosen, Gibson, Tesluk and McPherson, 2002). Through a dual methods study firstly involving interviews with a variety of teams in different industries and then a questionnaire survey of aerospace design teams, Gibson and Gibbs (2006) find broad support with some interesting nuances. Firstly, the interview data indicates a strong *negative association* between innovation and three out of the four characteristics of virtuality: geographic dispersion, electronic dependence, and national diversity. A regression analysis of questionnaire data also supports the core argument, showing negative direct effects on innovation for all four characteristics. However, the regression analysis also reveals that when there is a psychologically safe communication climate in the team, the negative direct effects of the four characteristics are less pronounced, indicating that this will be an "important facilitator of innovation in teams by helping them overcome the challenges posed by virtuality" (Gibson and Gibbs, 2006: 484).

Despite these concerns in the literature on the ability of virtual organization to drive innovation, a number of studies have shown how virtual organizations can be managed in order to provide a viable basis for innovating. Bergiel, Bergiel, and Balsmeier (2008) highlight the importance of various factors working in unison: trust, communications, leadership, goal-setting, and technology. Jarle Gressgård (2011), for instance, develops a conceptual model from a literature review showing how shared understanding and knowledge development (in broad terms, two areas of concern for Gibson and Gibbs [2006]) can be created through new and changing forms of human interaction such as through text and social media. Lin (2011), using data from 86 information and electronics companies in Taiwan, shows how virtual organization is associated with organizational innovation, where organizational innovation is captured in terms of both product and process innovation. Virtual organization has a positive direct effect on product and process innovation, and it also positively moderates the relationship between employee creativity and innovation. As noted by Lin (2011: 250): "Firms with highly virtualized structure not only possess a high degree of organizational innovation and employee creativity, but also strengthen the relationship between creativity and innovation. Creativity and innovation co-develop in the same direction when firms are highly virtualized".

According to Ojasalo (2008), product development in a virtual setting allows a greater freedom for individuals to innovate than within a physically co-located setting, and this is indeed seen as a principal advantage of a virtual mode of organization as far as innovation is concerned. However, Ojasalo (2008) does acknowledge the difficulty of managing innovation virtually and that an explicit attempt needs to be made to maintain personal and informal contact. In Ojasalo's (2008) view, virtual organization is a central part of a 'free' approach to the management of innovation in networks, a form in which trust takes precedent and, while hierarchy is avoided, there is still a central coordinating authority to oversee and manage issucs as they arise. Sawhney and Prandelli (2000) point out how communities of firms can engage in collaborative innovation, emphasizing explicitly how virtual organization can still act to support a sense of community and focus between organizations that are physically distant. Virtual spaces are supported with technologies such as Extranets (external web-enabled spaces for member organizations to interact on problem-solving and innovation). In Sawhney and Prandelli's (2000) study, the cases of Caterpillar and Fiat receive special mention as these organizations set up external virtual spaces for suppliers to collaborate, exchanging files and design know-how. The point is made that it is not only on the supply-side that this is seen; firms commonly organize virtually on the demand-side. This is seen in multiple industries and countries.

Verona, Prandelli, and Sawhney (2006) place an emphasis on the role of virtual knowledge brokers in distributed innovation networks. Virtual knowledge brokers play a pivotal role in facilitating knowledge flows in virtually organized environments. Importantly, they are seen as neutral members of the network. This perceived neutrality is critical because it allows them to be trusted by members of the networks, including customers. They can therefore receive and package customer knowledge in a way that makes it immediately useful to connected firms. The consequence is that any organization within a virtual setting will engage in knowledge exchange both directly with other actors, as well as in a mediated way through virtual knowledge brokers who themselves adopt a high network orientation (Verona, Prandelli and Sawhney, 2006). Wi, Oh, and Jung (2011) provide an approach on how to form a virtual team for new product development. They divide the virtual team formation problem into two parts: the challenge of forecasting members' performance and the challenge of selecting members who are able to satisfy the specific project requirements. Social network analysis is used to measure collaboration ability (communication, coordination, and cooperation) and, this, along with knowledge of the individual member determines overall capability in a virtual team setting. The virtual team manager was selected as the member with the highest score in terms of knowledge and collaborative capabilities. The key point about Wi, Oh, and Jung's (2011) approach is that it is possible to take a scientific and methodical approach to determining how virtual teams are formed, this exercise being necessary to enhance the chances of success and overcoming any problems of virtuality through appropriate design and governance choices.

## Consultancy and innovation in a virtual context

While virtual organizations yield great benefits for participants, and have the potential – when managed correctly – to provide a potent basis for innovating when compared to hierarchically integrated organizations, the question for us is whether this is the case in the domain of management consultancy. If consultants (and clients) are organized on a virtual basis, will this mean greater levels of innovativeness, both in terms of innovative outcomes for clients, as well as for the consultancy firms themselves?

De Vries (2006) explores theory of service innovation from a networked perspective, explicitly incorporating virtual organization into his discussion. Drawing on the work of Mowshowitz (1997b), De Vries (2006) argues that innovation in service industries is supported by virtual organization because of the dynamic switching capability of virtual organization: "Both the requests and services change over time. To accommodate the dynamic character of virtual organizing, the assignment of services to requests must be dynamic, which is referred to as switching and is seen as the basic difference between traditional ways of organizing and the virtual approach" (De Vries, 2006: 1041). De Vries's (2006) theory extends previous conceptualizations of service innovation (Gallouj and Weinstein, 1997) by accounting for the fact that a client organization co-produces with at least one provider (but eventually any number of provider organizations) and can dynamically switch between them as it seeks to satisfy its emergent and changing requirements. This also incorporates the idea that service providers themselves may interact in order to co-produce for a given client. De Vries (2006) uses examples from five cases in the Netherlands to illustrate the ways in which the capability and technology vectors from a client and multiple providers interact and change to yield innovative outcomes.

Hislop's (2002) study of the role of the client in innovation involving external consultancy firms acknowledges that the knowledge underpinning the innovation process is distributed across organizations. The temporary nature of project teams in consultancy has become part of "organisational life" (Hislop, 2002: 665). In the examples provided by Hislop (2002), pre-existing social relations are seen as highly pertinent to deciding which consultants a client firm would use for innovation. He describes swift trust (as highlighted earlier, seen as a way for temporary virtual teams to become productive quickly and overcome the hazards of virtuality) as a "precarious form of trust" (Hislop, 2002: 665). Hislop's analysis suggests that a more conventional view of embedded social relations instigated by the client organization is a way of reducing dependence on swift trust. This means pre-existing and known contacts are used within these networks – they provide reputational advantages as well as a shared understanding of the type of practices that are known to work across organizational boundaries. Hislop (2002) does point out how, in the cases he uses, there is some degree of difference in terms of the autonomy given by the client to the consultant during the innovation – this impacting the extent of customization in outcomes.

Huang and Newell (2003) examine the process of knowledge integration in innovative cross-functional projects in different industries. All four of the cases studied led to some form of process innovation. Two of the four cases studied used external consultants, and these two cases also had internal steering committees as a primary governance mechanism. It is noteworthy that in only one of the four cases (and indeed, it was one of the cases where external consultants were not used), there had been a history of virtual teamwork. In this instance, the previously established virtual team had provided a basis of experience and knowledge that benefited the project in question.

There are some interesting insights from Huang and Newell's (2003) and Hislop's (2002) studies. Firstly, not all cross-functional and large-scale innovation projects that will transform the way a client organization operates will use virtual teams. Indeed, if they have been used in the past then they may provide the basis for useful knowledge and insight that can help the innovation process. However, their use may not be as prevalent as one might be led to believe from the copious literature on virtual organization. Secondly, traditional – or conventional – forms of trust, developed through previously co-located projects, can form the basis for trust before any virtual organization is established. Over a long period of time, virtual organizations may be used interchangeably with co-located forms, and at times that fit with the nature of the innovation and the overall goals of the projects.

Jünemann and Lloyd (2003) assess virtual organization for consultants, putting an emphasis on the communication issues of virtuality and the challenges for management in ensuring effective communications across time and space in teams where members do not meet face to face, do not use technology extensively, and do not have a propensity for boundary crossing. Jünemann and Lloyd (2003) identify specific competences for leaders and team members in virtual teams. This echoes related literature that puts an emphasis on special leadership capability in a virtual setting in order to manage the increased complexity (Bergiel, Bergiel and Balsmeier, 2008). Leadership competences include selecting and using collaboration technology, networking across boundaries, leading in a cross-cultural environment, building and maintaining trust, developing and adapting processes to meet team demands, coaching and managing performance, and developing and transitioning team members. Perhaps more interesting for our discussion, however, is Jünemann and Lloyd's (2003) observation that consultants can play a key role in helping client organizations deal with the challenges of virtual organization and in developing these types of competences in clients. In other words, virtual organization is not only an opportunity for consultants because of potential advantages that can accrue to the consultant as a consequence of the consultant adopting this organizational form. It can also present an opportunity for the consultant to assist clients grappling with virtual organization. The types of requirements for consulting skills to meet this opportunity include analysis skills in a virtual setting (i.e., without face-to-face client contact), project management skills using collaborative technology, inter-personal skills (including cross-cultural communication) in virtual settings, knowledge of team management and technology in virtual settings, and even enthusiasm for technology-based communication (Jünemann and Lloyd's, 2003).

McKinlay (2002) critically assesses managerialist approaches to knowledge management by drawing on insights from three knowledge management projects in a global pharmaceutical company. One of the projects involved a major external consultancy firm and aimed to develop a new knowledge management system for the pharmaceutical company. This project, referred to as 'Warehouse' in McKinlay's (2002) study, aimed to integrate social and technical aspects of knowledge into a formalized corporate-wide system based on groupware and a centralized database. The knowledge management product was, in essence, a platform to support virtual organization through horizontal communications globally. The role of the external consultancy firm in building this system is a key feature of the case. The main client undoubtedly would not have been able to design and implement the groupware solution on its own. As part of McKinlay's critique the groupware solution is described as creating new political dynamics into the client organization. For instance, users would be giving up their expertise (and their power) by capturing their knowledge onto the system. And users of the system would be exhibiting 'weakness' (a sign of inexperience) by needing to draw on the system for their work (McKinlay, 2002: 81). The implementation of a system to support this kind of virtualization in the client is an innovation central to the client's corporate strategy, but one that can marginalize and sub-ordinate the dispersed employees who are required to contribute and use the system.

In a similar vein, Swan, Newell, Scarbrough, and Hislop (1999) are critical of an emphasis on technology over social process when setting up a virtual organization. Any lack of attention to the social processes required for innovation can mean 'electronic fences' are reinforced rather than dismantled (Swan, Newell, Scarbrough and Hislop, 1999: 267). They use case examples from banking and specialist equipment handling manufacturing to illustrate this point. In both cases, external consultants were used. The outcome was successful for the manufacturing firm, and less successful for the bank. In the case of the bank, Swan, Newell, Scarbrough, and Hislop (1999: 267) note:

There were countless examples where project teams had spent time and money on developing an application for their particular intranet only to find later that another group had done something very similar which they could have used instead. For example, a number of the intranet projects had used a particular firm of consultants and in each case there had been problems with the relationship and the service provided by this consultancy. However, given that there was limited (no) communication across the intranet projects, the same mistakes with this consultancy continued to be made. Reinvention, then, was extremely common in an innovation initiative specifically aimed at preventing such reinvention! Further, expertise was not shared across functional specialisms within the bank, especially business management and IT.

These types of problems did not occur for the manufacturing client where a common business information system was implemented, with external consultant support. Key features of the project included senior management involvement, human resource function involvement at an early stage, a close partnership with the external consultant, acknowledgement of the role of pre-existing communities of practice, regular face-to-face meetings during the project set-up phase at a central location, and distributed teams across geographies responsible for implementation. Importantly, this project accounted for the social process side to launching an effective system to support networked communities that are able to innovate through virtual organization, and of close cooperation and collaboration with an external consultant through centrally coordinated activity.

Williams and Cothrel (2000) highlight the role of consultants working in technology companies in setting up online communities that support innovation in software. In Williams and Cothrel's (2000) study, the Java community is centered on Sun Microsystems's Java Center Organization, covering 15 countries and over a 1,000 members at the time of the study. The Java Center Organization plays host to the community which focuses on complex software development involving Java and involves internal and external membership. While this example is a virtual organization that promotes the application of a particular software technology, it is described in a way that has important parallels with management consultancy. It is, in effect, a virtually organized consulting practice with Sun's "authority and expertise" at its heart (Williams and Cothrel, 2000: 88). Consultants access others' expertise, acknowledging their own knowledge deficits by definition. Their virtual collaboration allows them to specialize and reinforce the community. Williams and Cothrel (2000) put forward three key capabilities for creating and sustaining online communities: *member development* (identifying and retaining appropriately trained and 'savvy' members through online *and* offline mechanisms), *asset management* (monitoring and managing tangible and intangible assets of the community and having a person or persons responsible for this function), and *community relations* (norms and guidelines to moderate online behavior and deal with conflicts as they arise).

# Practice insight

The following practice insight was kindly provided by UK-based Claire Agutter, Director, Scopism Limited.

## Challenging traditional consultancy with a virtual model

There are many aspects of 'traditional' consultancy engagements that lead to frustration for both client and consultant. In today's workplace, it's very rare for someone to be engaged in the same task for the whole working day, and plans change at the last minute.

For clients, this often means they don't feel they are fully utilizing their consultants, or an urgent meeting means they are not able to dedicate the time they need to be working with them while they are on site. This means they are not getting value for the money they are investing. For consultants, they might feel they have to 'look busy' when in fact they are waiting for client input. This can lead to low morale and frustration that they are not delivering the results they should be – as well as losing them potential repeat business.

Agile ways of working being adopted in many organizations focus on short 'sprints' of work, followed by reflection and adjustment. This also isn't aligned to the traditional model of consultants on site for a solid block of time and then little contact or input afterwards.

At Scopism, we've created a virtual model of 'eConsultancy'. This allows clients to engage with consultants in a way that meets their needs and doesn't require them to fill every hour of the working day with them. For example, a person who is new in a role could have a weekly support session for a few hours with an eConsultant to help him or her shape his or her new tasks and provide objective support. A client who has a project that's in crisis could get a targeted intervention to help him or her get back on track. eConsultancy engagements can range from a few hours to a few years – depending on what is required.

eConsultancy also allows clients to engage with someone anywhere in the world – if you're in the UK, digital connectivity means it shouldn't matter if your idea consultant is on the other side of the world.

Developing the eConsultancy model has required us to examine the best ways to work. We are still experimenting with the best tools to support the service, including how to talk, how to share documentation and how to schedule time together. eConsultant sessions can, for example, be recorded so they can be used again later. Trust is a key factor, so the profile of our eConsultants internationally and on social media must be good.

## Case reflections on the theme of virtual organization

The case of Pay Zone Consulting: A Global Virtual Organization (Munro and Huff, 2008) concerns a small-sized, boutique consultancy firm specializing in information management projects for the oil and gas exploration and production sector. The solutions they provided were innovative and cutting-edge. There were only five principal consultants located in Canada, the UK, and various (and changing) locations, including Kazakhstan. There were no physical offices. The company drew on software developers and contractors on a project-by-project basis, many of these working from home. There are some particularly interesting features about this case. Firstly, the way the virtual organization has allowed the consultants to build an innovative response for clients in the industry while at the same time allowing the consultants to achieve their desired level of work-life balance is a noteworthy point. However, this set-up and balance between work and lifestyle would not have been possible without the prior experience and training of the partners over the course of many years in physical co-located settings with clients. Secondly, the success of the virtual organization form for this consultancy meant that ongoing strategic decisions needed to be made relating to how to take the business forward: how to recruit and develop new consultants as future partners who want to – and are able to – work effectively within this type of organizational form. Or, alternatively, the partners might decide that selling the company while the going is good could be a viable and lucrative way forward. These points highlight some of the themes in the academic literature on virtual organizations, including the potential for them to be temporary – the expertise used to make them work being derived from other types of organizational forms in the past, and hard decisions that might be required to bring the virtual organization to a natural closure at some point in the future once it has fulfilled its mission.

In the case on Hongxin Entrepreneur Incubator: Expanding the Cloud ( Li, Williams and Mu, 2014), entrepreneur Qiang Li, founder of the Hongxin Entrepreneur Incubator in Xiamen, China, is pondering over how to expand his particular model of business incubation to other locations in China. A central feature of the case is how an online platform can be used to support the services that Hongxin has provided in the Xiamen locale. Qiang Li's success with Hongxin in Xiamen may be attributed to his other skills, experience and even his philosophy that had been guided by Taoist values. He had been personally involved in a consulting capacity to member organizations, getting to know their founders and leaders and meeting them in social settings in Xiamen. This close contact had been a central part of his (and Hongxin's) journey with the member organizations, which often involved an equity investment. His advice and help with implementation of change and organizational development programs within these organizations had been a critical success factor. The challenge is that, while this co-located model had worked to incredible effect in the home base of Xiamen, how could a virtual organization support this across a country as vast and disparate as China? The idea is that a growth of virtual organization ('expanding the cloud') into more provinces in China would yield a growth in the number of member organizations, especially member organizations with international connections and interests. Clearly, this is a tall order and, arguably, a challenge to the previous business model that had built success on the basis of working in close proximity with members. An interesting feature of the case is how the incubator is preparing for this next phase of growth. As shown in Exhibit 1 of the case (the organization chart), a separate organizational unit had been created in order to spearhead the virtual organization. This unit contained an investment bank, a policy and consulting department, an entrepreneurship investment department, a coach and consulting department, an entrepreneurship finance department, and a marketing department. In other words, the coaching, consulting and advising that Qiang Li originally had done himself would now be functions that would be engrained into a virtual organization.

The case on Knowledge Management at Cap Gemini Ernst & Young (Andreu, Lara and Sieber, 2004) is an interesting example of how a large, global management consultancy firm implements virtual organization to great effect. Prior to a merger with Cap Gemini, Ernst & Young had recognized the importance of knowledge management and had set up four units to underpin knowledge management globally: an innovation center in Boston, a transformation unit based in Dallas but with 100 people around the world, a technological division centered in Virginia, and a center for business knowledge, centralized in Cleveland but with multiple local sub-units around the world. Out of these four units, the transformational unit was the one that was set up as a virtual organization. It was responsible for process reengineering, IT projects, and organizational change, amongst other roles; a highly innovative unit. Ernst & Young had its own intranet to support virtual teamwork and collaboration – this was called EY/KnowledgeWeb and, according to the case, allowed its entire workforce of consultants to access thousands of knowledge sources internally. For external sources, the company had set up a system called EYInfo-Link to access similarly large numbers of external information sources. Lotus Notes was used as an underlying technology platform. Ernst & Young was keen to foster social connections and teamwork, i.e., to focus on people and not just technology and process within the virtual network. Pre-merger, Cap Gemini also had its own approach to virtual collaboration, with a large number of forums for international teams to share ideas and knowledge. Virtual organization played a central role in integrating and developing the knowledge management architecture for the company post-merger. An interesting feature is the continuation of Cap Gemini's corporate university as CGE&Y's university and how this offered distance learning and virtual training. Other features include the use of virtual rooms for account teams working on specific accounts and virtual rooms for specific sector and service lines.

## Implications

The phenomenon of virtual organization raises some important questions for innovation in management consultancy. The literature shows how virtual organization is seen as an innovative form of organizing in itself, a way of generating organizational capital that has value for organizations. But just because this way of organizing is innovative, do we necessarily expect outcomes to be more innovative than they would be in a non-virtualized/co-located setting? After all, there are certain costs and downsides of virtual organization highlighted in the literature. If not acknowledged, monitored, and managed, these can lead to a virtual arrangement that will disappoint. The presence of these costs and downsides lies at the heart of any debate about the use of virtual organization for innovation in management consultancy. While cases such as Pay Zone and CGE&Y have strong links with innovative outcomes, researchers have placed important question marks on the whole viability and feasibility of virtual organization (Chesbrough and Teece, 1996; Gibson and Gibbs, 2006; Kirkman, Rosen, Gibson, Tesluk and McPherson, 2002).

In order for consultancy firms to be creative and original, and to create new knowledge and learning that can be used for innovation – either for themselves or for their clients – there is no doubt that the deployment of virtual organization is an option. It has the potential to bring many benefits to the process of innovating. These include, firstly, linking and integrating the knowledge and perspectives of a diverse set of people in disparate locations around the world. This follows a logic that diversity is good for creativity; there is a wider set of experience and multiple perspectives that can help the consultancy firm to be innovative. There is a bigger search space for opportunities and for potential solutions to opportunities. Secondly, the use of the latest IT and communications technologies for storing, sharing, sorting, and manipulating diverse sets of complex data over large distances is a characteristic of the virtual organization that can help innovation within consultancy. Organizations that need to identify – and even develop – the latest technology for this purpose will have a latent innovative orientation and awareness of the value of knowledge management for innovation. This technological layer will support the sharing of knowledge of opportunities and solutions much faster and to a wider set of individuals than a co-located organization ever could. Thirdly, as noted in much of the literature, virtual organization can be used selectively in time. Virtual teams can be set up and then disbanded after they have delivered to their principal objective. In this way virtual organization can be used as part of a wider system of innovating and creating knowledge in and across organizations. Related to this, inherent flexibility within a virtual organization will lend itself to innovation. This is not just about individual members in far-flung places having a nice work-life balance. It relates to the ability of those leading the virtual organization to introduce new members and 'cut' ties with existing members as circumstances change over time. These features are well suited to the explorative and uncertain nature of innovation in consultancy.

However, the drawbacks do need to be managed through a deliberate effort made by the leaders of the virtual organization. Chesbrough and Teece (1996) argue that the use of hierarchical control is beneficial for managing the complex flows of tacit knowledge. Gibson and Gibbs (2006) argue that there are fundamental problems with geographic dispersion, electronic dependence, structural dynamism, and national diversity in members (see also Kirkman, Rosen, Gibson, Tesluk and McPherson, 2002). The implication of this is that it should not be assumed that simply by establishing an organizational form with these characteristics, useful innovations for consultancy firms or clients will prevail. Managing the technical infrastructure is only one side of the coin; the other is managing the human social processes that are always needed during collaborative innovation efforts. So the virtual organization in consultancy still needs assistance, support and help through an alert managerial capability to encourage social processes and trust. The literature does provide some ideas on how the benefits of virtual organization can be maximized while the drawbacks minimized. This is both a leadership and a managerial challenge.

After reviewing the literature and the cases I offer five additional points. Firstly, there needs to be *purpose*: the purpose of virtual organization needs to be defined and communicated to all concerned, including the type of innovation that the virtual organization is expected to yield. Secondly, there has to be appropriate *knowledge management infrastructure*; the choice of IT and communications technologies needs to be made upfront and reviewed on a regular basis with respect to the purpose of the virtual organization. Thirdly, *duration* must be made clear – how long the virtual organization is expected to last, and this of course should also be reviewed as circumstances unfold. Fourthly, *membership choices* need to be made with some consideration to the innovative outcomes that are expected. This speaks to the level of diversity within the virtual organization and the extent to which diversity is expected to matter to innovative outcomes. Again, this needs to be reviewed on an ongoing basis and the leadership should be prepared to cut out members and introduce new members as and when required. Finally, a *virtual mentality* needs to be developed and nurtured across the virtual organization. If members are motivated and have the demonstrated capability to work on innovation projects within a virtual setting, there is a higher likelihood that the consultancy firm can yield innovative outcomes as a consequence. Put alternatively, members who do not have the proclivity or ability to work on innovation projects virtually will need to be reconsidered as potential contributors. Selection and training will be useful in the consultancy firm to develop a mentality for virtuality both within the firm itself, as well as with clients.

## Summary and learning points

In this chapter on Pole 3: consultant virtualization, we have seen the following:

- How virtual organization can be seen as a form of organizational capital that adds particular value to consultants because it can provide a basis for innovating, both for a client and for the consultancy firm itself.
- How the virtual organization itself can be seen as an innovative form of organizing, implying that consultants adopting this form may already have a strong innovative orientation.
- How scholars have identified a range of challenges and potential costs to virtual organization and that it is possible to challenge the notion that the key characteristics of virtual organization (i.e., geographic dispersion, electronic dependence, structural dynamism, and national diversity) will always lead to innovative outcomes.
- Why it is important for a consultancy that sets up a virtual organization in order to promote innovation will need to address these challenges and pay particular attention to the governance and management of the virtual community such that social processes underpinning innovation are encouraged and not stifled.
- That some individuals might be more able and open to working in a virtual organization than others, this putting an onus on those setting up a virtual project to screen and select people appropriately.
- How real-world cases of virtual organization in consultancy provide insight into the motivation, challenges and outcomes of this organizational form.
- How this form of organizing is present in all types of countries; we see it in the West as well as in newly emergent economies such as China.

## Suggested additional cases for analyzing virtual organization and innovation in consulting

Andreu, R., Lara, E. and Sieber, S., 2004. 'Knowledge management at CAP Gemini, Ernst & Young', *IESE Publishing* (product number: IES133).

Eccles, R.G., Narayandas, D. and Rossano, P., 2013. 'Innovation at the Boston Consulting Group', *Harvard Business School* (product number: 9-313-137).

Farhoomand, A.F. and Ng, P., 2002. 'PricewaterhouseCoopers knowledgecurve and the spinning off of PwC consulting', *Centre for Asian Business Cases* (product number: HKU221).

Li, X., Williams, C. and Mu, Z., 2014. 'Hongxin Entrepreneur Incubator: Expanding the cloud', *Ivey Publishing* (product number: 9B14M113).

Munro, M. and Huff, S.L., 2008. 'Pay Zone consulting: A global virtual organization', *Ivey Publishing* (product number: 9B08C004).

# 5

# Pole 4: disruption in the consultancy life-cycle

## It's all about how we execute client projects

This chapter will examine innovation in consultancy firms from the perspective of life-cycle disruption. We will examine literature and cases on life-cycle approaches and explore why thinking ahead of time about how to approach the life-cycle in individual client engagements is important. At one end of the spectrum, consultants can use a traditional, stepwise approach to solving client problems. This typically draws on conventional and well-established project management techniques for which there are plenty of resources available. At the other end of the spectrum, consultants have been disrupting the linear nature of the traditional life-cycle and finding new ways to organize and mobilize resources to meet client needs. Indeed, a shift towards modular approaches in consulting was reported in Denmark in the mid-1990s (Sundbo, 1997). Furthermore, O'Mahoney (2011) reports only 21 per cent of his consultancy firm respondents as having a formal innovation process. Consultants have been acting as a disruptive force for a while, not only for clients, but also for themselves.

The concept of disruption implies a disturbance or a re-arranging of activities within a process. As this chapter will point out, this is not necessarily a bad thing. Both client and consultant can benefit by using various approaches that disrupt any traditional or assumed way of working. We will review key academic literature on life-cycle disruption, how and why this might be useful for stimulating further innovation, and how this manifests itself in advanced business services such as management consulting. Cases and real-world insights on this topic will also illuminate our thinking here.

Because life-cycle disruption in the field of management consultancy relates to how to organize project work for clients over time, it can be seen as a form of organizational capital. As discussed in the opening section of the previous chapter on

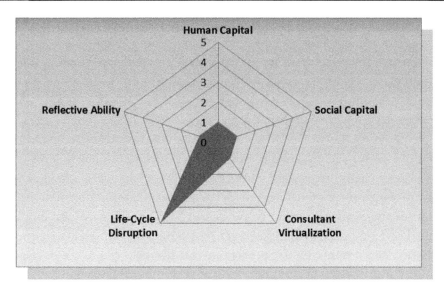

**Figure 5.1** Pole 4: A Focus on Life-Cycle Disruption

virtual organization, organizational capital relates to practices and modes of control that support the functioning of the firm (Acs and Fitzroy, 1989), delimiting what a firm can do (Prescott and Visscher, 1980). How we organize service encounters has a direct bearing on innovation in services (Yu and Sangiorgi, 2018). Should a consultancy firm be able to disrupt traditional life-cycle approaches in terms of how it delivers work to clients, it will possess a form of organizational capital that can be of value. Further, if the disruptive approach itself leads to new innovations (either directly for the client or for the consultancy firm), then the organizational capital would have been realized in the form of innovative yield. The purpose of this chapter is to explore this issue and the potential upsides and downsides of a disruptive approach.

Figure 5.1 is a schematic for Pole 4. A firm that has the maximum level of life-cycle disruption is what we need to envisage now. Let's try to understand the implications of this and why this variable has become so important for consultancy firms.

## Exploring life-cycle disruption: the shift from hard to soft paradigm

Client assignments in consultancy are discrete projects that require management. This process of management is seen as a capability (Crawford, 2006). It is a capability that can lead to successful outcomes as well as unsuccessful outcomes (Söderlund, 2011; Williams, 2005). This extends to the ability of managers to learn from projects, a task that is seen as critical but often poorly implemented in practice (Williams, 2004).

It has been argued that there are fundamentally two different paradigms in project management: a hard paradigm and a soft paradigm (Pollack, 2007). A paradigm refers to a "commonly shared set of assumptions, values and concepts within a community" (Pollack, 2007: 266, quoting Kuhn, 1962) – it refers to the way a group of people perceives the world. When used in the context of project management, we can think about the community of project managers and stakeholders with an interest in how client projects are set up, executed, and closed. In a hard paradigm, there is an emphasis on predefined goals, control, structure, and quantitative measures. This is a rationalist perspective (Williams, 2005). A soft paradigm emphasizes ill-defined or ambiguous goals, learning, social processes, and qualitative measures (Crawford, 2006). Pollack (2007) points out that the field of project management traditionally had developed along the lines of a hard paradigm; complex scenarios being reduced to simpler, discrete entities in a mechanistic way. However, there has been growing criticism of – and discontent with – the hard paradigm, particularly in messy project situations (Pidd, 2004). The hard paradigm might be well-suited to rather uncomplicated and stable situations where things can be forecast and predetermined, but it is not suitable in all situations, especially those that are more complex and ambiguous. Almost all project failures are rooted in issues that are human in nature (Posner, 1987) or where goals change throughout the life-cycle of the project. Projects commonly need to be re-interpreted during execution, this requiring participative learning and effective stakeholder engagement as well as tools and techniques that allow problems to be restructured rather than solved. This restructuring is a key feature of the soft paradigm.

Koskela and Howell (2002) argue for an explicit theory of project management, noting how professions need theories, it is what distinguishes them from skilled crafts. Drawing from the PMBOK Guide (Project Management Body of Knowledge) as well as from the project management literature, they argue that a theory of project management needs to cater for a theory of project and a theory of management. When studying the project, theory needs to cater for transformation, flow (how to turn inputs into outputs), and value generation. When studying management (of projects), theory needs to cater for planning, execution, and controlling in a way that links theory and practice.

In many ways, Koskela and Howell's (2002) argument is disruptive in nature and reinforces Pollack's (2007) points about the need to move away from an exclusively hard paradigm to a soft paradigm in project management. The reality of practice is almost always set in a context of human behavior and activity and the world is continually presenting complex and global project problems to be addressed for which the hard paradigm will suffer. These sentiments are also echoed by others. Winter,

Smith, Morris and Cicmil (2006) report on a UK funded two-year research program aimed at "Rethinking Project Management", with the main findings in five areas: *project complexity*, *social processes*, *value creation*, *project conceptualization*, and *practitioner development*. In common with Koskela and Howell (2002), they see "no single theoretical base from which to explain and guide the management of projects" (Winter, Smith, Morris, and Cicmil, 2006: 640). If there *was* a dominant model, it was from the hard paradigm. They also note how the problems facing project managers (and academics studying project management) have become more socially complex and challenging for the hard paradigm. That said, they do report that the 'textbook' classical life-cycle approach does not need to be dispensed with, it just needs to be enriched (Winter, Smith, Morris, and Cicmil, 2006: 641). There needs to be theory for the social processes side of practice, one that sheds light on human action and interaction, and stakeholder relations. Further, a focus on value creation in project management needs to be made, along with a conceptualization of projects being multidisciplinary, not always pre-defined and open to renegotiation. These are all aspects of the soft paradigm and the implication for practitioners is to become effective learners (we will talk more on this issue in the next chapter.)

Williams (2005) points to the need to move on from the hard paradigm in project management because of the tendency for project overruns. The traditional approach might even make project problems worse rather than deal with them. He states that "for projects that are complex, uncertain, and time-limited, conventional methods might be inappropriate, and aspects of newer methodologies in which the project 'emerges' rather than being fully preplanned might be more appropriate" (Williams, 2005: 497). Projects typically overrun because of a compounding effect of (1) their *structural complexity* – the size or number of elements in the project; (2) their *uncertainty* – not being clear about project goals or how to achieve project goals; and (3) *tight time constraints*. Williams (2005) notes how the software industry has led the way for developing alternative methods such as the agile methods (Lycett, Macredie, Patel and Paul, 2003) which cater for the uncertainty of ill-defined and changing requirements. According to Lycett, Macredie, Patel and Paul (2003):

> Agile development emphasizes the human or crafted aspects of software development over the engineering aspects – individuals and interactions over processes and tools, working software over comprehensive documentation, customer collaboration over contract negotiation, and responding to change over following a plan.
>
> (79)

In line with this and with Koskela and Howell (2002), Williams (2005) also notes the importance of understanding the characteristics of projects and of finding the most appropriate balance between traditional and flexible approaches depending on those characteristics.

Cicmil and Hodgson (2006) are critical of traditional ways of theorizing about project management and defining project performance. They highlight how projects should be seen as 'social arrangements' and project management as a 'social practice'. They reinforce the emerging questioning of the belief system surrounding traditional, functionalist approaches to managing projects. Project management needs to cater for the political side of resistance to change in organizations, to focus on who is included in the social construction of projects (Crawford, 2006), and even the management of meaning and legitimization of projects. Cicmil and Hodgson (2006) summarize with a point that a critical view of project management will require us to

> reexamine the currently dominant imperative of performativity in relation to how this shapes the development of the body of knowledge and best practice in the field (particularly related to "critical factors for project success") and illuminate the importance of considering other indicators of "project success" beyond time, cost, and quality performance, to encompass environment, health and safety, economy, and ethics.
>
> (119)

While they do not refer to disruption per se, clearly a change in thinking about core purposes of projects and how they should be managed constitutes a disruptive force in the academic literature on project management.

Söderlund (2011) conducts a literature review of more than 300 articles in the field of project management and presents a categorization of the main schools of thought in the field. There are seven schools of thought (please see Table 2 in Söderlund, 2011): *Optimization School* (quantitative and logical, rooted in management science), *Factor School* (understanding project performance and outcomes, rooted in a diverse literature), *Contingency School* (how to fit projects to a complex environment, rooted in organizational theory), *Behavior School* (understanding behaviors, learning and emotions, rooted in organizational behavior), *Governance School* (emphasizing governance, bureaucracy and control, rooted in transaction cost and principal agent theory), *Relationship School* (emphasizing project networks, international projects, social capital, and stakeholders, rooted in industrial marketing and economic geography), and *Decision School* (emphasizing information, project assessment, and risk, rooted in political science and psychology). Looking at this list of 'schools of thought' we can broadly discern a split between the hard and soft paradigms as described by Pollack (2007) and others. The Optimization School, Governance School, and Decision School align with the hard paradigm. The Behavior School and Relational School seem to align with the soft paradigm.

Perhaps somewhere in the middle are the Factor and Contingency Schools, schools of thought that seek to understand both what project managers need to do to achieve desired outcomes and recognizing that these decisions around designing and organizing projects are influenced by the nature of the challenge.

Svejvig and Andersen (2015) also conduct a structured literature review but theirs is on a particular subset of the project management literature, namely the *rethinking* project management (RPM) literature. They find and review a total of 74 articles in the RPM field dating back to the early 1980s. This is a field that has grown particularly since 2006 (Svejvig and Andersen, 2015: 285). While classical project management (the hard paradigm) is characterized by executability, simplicity, temporarity, linearity, controllability, and instrumentality, the RPM field (a growing shift into the soft paradigm) is characterized by learnability, multiplicity, temporarity, complexity, uncertainty, and sociability (Svejvig and Andersen, 2015: 280). The result is six categories of work within the RPM field: *Contextualization* (thinking beyond isolated projects and putting projects in a broader organizational and strategic context), *Social and Political Aspects* (focusing on social and political processes rather than tools and procedures), *Rethinking Practice* (concerning alternative methods, perspectives, and approaches used by practitioners), *Complexity and Uncertainty* (how to understand increasing complexity and the likelihood that intended outcomes will not remain relevant), the *Actuality of Projects* (emphasizing what actually happens in projects, a project-as-practice approach), and *Broader Conceptualization* (a focus on new and emerging perspectives on project management). Contrasted with Söderlund's (2011) review, Svejvig and Andersen's (2015) work undoubtedly has a stronger emphasis on the soft paradigm. Elements of the soft paradigm appear in all of their six categories. This is possibly due to the biased sample of their review; they delimit their review on work that by definition challenges the mainstream in project management. However, what is noteworthy is that the RPM body – at the time of their review – was itself sizeable (74 articles). When one also considers that at least two of the categories in Söderlund's (2011) review (which was not delimited by an RPM definition) fall under the soft paradigm, one can get a picture of the importance of challenging traditional project management approaches to deal effectively with projects in an increasingly complex and uncertain world.

## Life-cycle disruption and innovation

It might be seductive to think that innovative projects, i.e., those that produce a new product, technology, service, or way of doing things, will require non-standard project management practices across the life-cycle of the project. But is this really the case? And what are these project management practices for innovative projects?

Research strongly suggests that the management system surrounding a project matters for the innovative potential of the project. Miller and Floricel (2004) show how firms that outperform in terms of performance are ones that adapt capabilities and practices appropriately. By 'appropriately', Miller and Floricel (2004) refer to innovation 'games' that firms compete in; it is important to understand the game in order to adopt the right policies and practices. Eight games are identified: races to the patent and regulatory offices, customized high-tech craft, delivering safe science-based products, asset-specific problem solving, systems design and consulting services, R, D, and E products and services, delivering workable solutions in packs, and battles for architectures. The influences on innovation (i.e., whether the game is influenced by regulators, the science and technology community, customers, competitors) differ by game. As a result, there are distinct capabilities and practices that are associated with success in each game, networking and influence over standards being important in asset-specific problem solving games and policies for entrepreneurship and corporate venturing in games for battles for architectures being notable examples. The key point here is that it is important for those managing the life-cycle of an innovation project to be aware of the type of game the firm is competing in, who the main external influencers are and then selecting the most appropriate organizational form and practices.

In a similar vein, Besner and Hobbs (2008) compare project management practices between innovative and non-innovative projects. Analysis of 91 practices shows there are some factors that discriminate between high- and low-performing innovative projects, including participation of the project or program manager at the front end, availability of competent staff and enhancing project definition. Innovative projects are found to have a wider range of practices than non-innovative ones, and they have more interfaces with other systems and projects. This is a reflection of the greater level of complexity in innovative projects. Ten tools are identified as having a higher level of usage in innovative projects: concurrent engineering, requirements analysis, configuration review, work breakdown structure, a database for cost estimating, team development plan, stakeholder analysis, monitoring critical success factors, quality plan, and updated business case at key milestones (gates) (Besner and Hobbs, 2008). Overall, results suggest a maturity in project management capability is needed for innovative projects as well as the need for project managers to be aware of how innovative a project or program is expected to be *before and during* its execution. Without this awareness it will be difficult to assess which tools and practices should be deployed.

When it comes to project management for innovation and the life-cycle of work that surrounds producing new products or services, various empirical studies are relevant. Westerman, McFarlan, and Iansiti (2006) highlight the role of contingency theory in understanding how to organize and 'design' a system for the mobilization of resources and tasks aimed at producing innovation. In the early stages of an innovation project, there will be greater uncertainty and more unknowns. Looser, more flexible and organic structures are required in this stage (Burns and Stalker, 1961); they are better suited to variation. But the strategic contingencies that determine an optimal organizational design for innovation will change over the innovation's life-cycle. Later on, particularly as the new product or service enters the commercialization phase, explorative designs are less optimal and a greater emphasis on efficiency is needed. Using a paired case method, Westerman, McFarlan, and Iansiti (2006) show the dynamic nature of the contingencies surrounding innovation projects and argue that there is no single, optimal design. Instead, the contingencies that managers face in innovation projects are often conflicting, forcing them to "choose designs that optimize for one contingency while addressing the other to the fullest extent possible, given their firms' particular contexts and capabilities" (Westerman, McFarlan and Iansiti, 2006: 237). They show how firms use a decentralized approach during explorative phases – where decision rights are allocated to remote units or lower level employees – but then re-integrating those units as and when required. A key capability in the innovation life-cycle is this switching between organizational design forms over time as contingencies change.

Kapsali (2011) advocates systems thinking in understanding project management for innovation. Systems thinking emphasizes the social as well as the technical, incorporating insights from the individual as well as the collective levels. It acts as a counter to reductionist and cause-effect thinking, allowing for synthesis and indeterminism. It is therefore well-suited for understanding contingencies and ways that organizations can adapt to different situations over the life-cycle of an innovation project. Kapsali (2011) makes the point that project management in innovation should allow the organization to cope with the unfolding situation, rather than just measuring it in a closed, hard paradigmatic manner. Her work is based on multiple case studies within EU innovation deployment programs in healthcare. Results show highest performing projects are the ones that deal with change during the life-cycle of the project; plans are emergent and specific to the situation. The 'soft' systems approach in these cases involves continuous planning (staying focused on goals but allowing the project manager to decide on courses of action), active boundary management (formal and informal communications with all stakeholders, and not necessarily standardized reports), and flexible task control.

Lévárdy and Browning (2009) make the point that any assumptions made about how to use resources and perform tasks during a new product development project are often challenged once the project is underway. New information comes to light once the product development project has started that may fundamentally challenge the project assumptions. This echoes the point made by Westerman, McFarlan, and Iansiti (2006) in terms of contingencies that change as innovation projects progress over time. Lévárdy and Browning (2009) put forward an agile approach they call adaptive product development process (APDP) based on the principles of complex adaptive systems (CASs). A CAS has "independent but connect agents that collectively adapt and self-organize, causing the overall behavior of the system to emerge over time" (Lévárdy and Browning, 2009: 604). They underline how pre-specifying activities in a rigid way in advance is not appropriate for innovation that is highly uncertain and in which learning (including trial and error learning) occurs over time. It is necessary for projects to adapt (and be adaptable) in time. Options can include delaying, abandoning, contracting, expanding, switching, or improving a project (Huchzermeier and Loch, 1996). Also possible are trial and error, and selectionism: pursuing several options and later choosing the best one. Lévárdy and Browning's (2009) APDP model does not support the idea of a pre-specified path through the life-cycle of an innovation project, but rather the need to generate a process space where there are a number of possible paths or options at any one point in time. The available paths at any point are determined by the current state of the project and are influenced by time, cost, performance, risk, and value.

According to Winter and Szczepanek (2008), all projects should be seen as value creating processes. In contrast to the traditional view of projects as being about temporary production, projects need to be seen as being about mobilizing clients "to create their own value from the project or programme's various offerings" (Winter and Szczepanek, 2008: 96). Drawing on Normann's (2001) work on value creation, this sees project management as a way of co-creating new value with clients. While the previous focus had been on the first-level relationship between the project and its client, the new focus needs to be on a second-level relationship between the client and the client's client (to be precise, Winter and Szczepanek [2008] use the term 'customer'). This is essentially a value focus requiring strategic thinking of the broader value system in which the project is embedded on behalf of those running the project(s). Project management then needs to think carefully about how a project creates new value for multiple stakeholders and enables clients to create their own value for their clients.

In Koria's (2009) research, the case of the recovery program in Sri Lanka following the 2004 tsunami is used to show how large and complex projects can have an innovative dimension, particularly in terms of administrative innovation (i.e., the adoption of novelty into the structures and processes of the organization). Koria (2009) is critical of the matrix structure used to manage the recovery program; this was exacerbated by internal and external political tensions within and surrounding the project. The consequence was delays getting individual recovery projects started, a lack of willingness to share project management resources, and even a lack of trust between participating agencies. Koria (2009) concludes that innovative HR policies are needed in this type of large and complex program, especially to attract and retain the type of talent that can assist in learning and knowledge sharing across projects. At the program level, handling political issues and ambiguity is needed, as well as flexibility to handle new and changing circumstances.

The setting up of an organizational system around project management is a deliberate and intentional activity that itself can be seen as innovative. For example, O'Leary and Williams (2008) describe the case of two project and program management Centres of Excellence (CoEs) set up in a UK government department. The one that was set up to directly intervene in ongoing projects (this was a "central 'hit team'" [O'Leary and Williams, 2008: 560] – an innovative approach) yielded the highest impact on project performance. The experience of the managers in this CoE and their mandate to influence day-to-day activities of projects are seen as important success factors. Furthermore, this intervention ability mattered more to performance than the introduction of best practice structured approaches.

Staying on the theme of centralized project management offices (PMOs),[1] Darling and Whitty (2016) argue that practices within these central coordination units for projects will vary widely depending on the type of organization and the industrial setting. PMOs are interesting organizational forms in their own right that have evolved over time. Most recently they are seen as central repositories for knowledge, tools, and methods (echoing the CoEs in O'Leary and Williams's [2008] study). Darling and Whitty (2016) chart the history of PMOs from 1805 to the present day, noting how PMOs have evolved into units where an holistic view of projects and their impact can be taken, and where connections to the power structure of the organization are tight. There is some skepticism of PMOs, including from senior management in organizations; they are caught in the political tensions of the organization and can be difficult to measure and sometimes not easy to justify.

Cunha and Moura (2014) note that while PMOs take many different forms, they are essentially there to support "alignment and systematic management of projects, programs, and portfolios to achieve strategic organizational objectives" (Cunha and Moura, 2014: 41). The PMO has come about as a discrete organizational unit by virtue of the increasing complexity of projects. They undertake a systematic literature review of recent research on PMOs, noting how knowledge management practices underpin much of the core function and role of the PMO, despite differences in their configuration according to different contexts.

One way projects can become more complex while pursuing an innovative agenda is when they are run under a consortium, for instance involving collaboration between industrial firms and universities. Baptista, Santos, Páscoa, and Sändig (2016) highlight the importance of projects that span different sectors, such as between industry and universities. University-industry collaboration has become a vibrant domain for innovation; universities benefit by accessing private sector knowledge and capabilities in commercialization, and industry benefits through access to state-of-the-art scientific endeavor (Williams and Allard, 2018). Baptista, Santos, Páscoa, and Sändig (2016) point out that project management methodologies need to be appropriate for the complexity of projects and that, when projects are collaborative between universities and industry, particular features of the project management framework need to be adopted. These include a new way of mapping the phases of a project to allow for preliminary and upfront work to identify and manage risks, monitoring the project process through collected data, and greater flexibility. The main phases presented by Baptista, Santos, Páscoa, and Sändig (2016) in their specific case are *deliberation* (including searching for and negotiating with partners, setting project strategy, and financing), *candidature* (a wide range of tasks including idea generation and clarification, contributions to society, developing the work program, and guides for project units, development of proposal), *execution* (from submission of proposal, negotiating with funding sources, scientific coordination, proof of concept), and *finalization* (from practice case presentation and prototype construction to legal aspects, report submission, and defining future steps). The interesting point about Baptista, Santos, Páscoa, and Sändig's (2016) approach is how it allows for different options to be defined and considered in each phase of the project, and for enough preparation to be carried out in advance, such that future phases are not held up.

Buganza and Verganti's (2006) work on life-cycle flexibility argues that managing for innovation in fast-moving and turbulent environments requires more than just being flexible during the project development timeline. They argue that what also is needed is for the end-product or service (i.e., the innovation itself) to have flexible characteristics and capabilities. After all, we should never expect the environmental context to stop being dynamic, competitive, and disruptive after product launch! Buganza and Verganti (2006) refer to this as life-cycle flexibility (LCF) and this is comprised of three aspects: frequency of adaptation, rapidity of adaptation, and quality of adaptation. Adaptations should be expected pre-launch as well as post-launch. Importantly, each of these three dimensions can be measured (meaning that it is possible to assess the performance of competitors) and managed through combinations of five practices: (1) back-end technological competence management, (2) sharing front-end technological competence with partners, (3) utilizing open technologies, (4) low formalization of procedures, and (5) high formalization of organization. Not all of the practices impact the three dimensions all of the time. For example, use of open technologies has a positive impact on rapidity of adaptation but not necessarily on the frequency or quality of adaptation. Project managers need to be cognizant of this contingency approach to understanding life-cycle flexibility and how these organizational practices matter in a given project in terms of frequency, rapidity, and quality of adaptation.

# Consultancy and innovation in a disruptive context

The consultancy industry is a dynamic, knowledge-intensive environment (Creplet, Dupouet, Kern, Mehmanpazir and Munier, 2001; Wood, 2002a). When consultants innovate, either for themselves or for their clients, the consultants are contributing to this dynamism. Indeed, the consultancy industry is in a constant state of flux and needs to continually change in order to keep up with client organizations that are evolving all the time (Poulfelt, Olson, Bhambri and Greiner, 2017).

A question arises on how to manage innovative projects in such an environment; by definition client relationships and client situations change all the time, and they can change rather suddenly and abruptly. Collyer, Warren, Hemsley, and Stevens (2010) carry out exploratory research on the question of how to plan in such environments through inductive interviews with 31 project managers. They identify a number of strategies (or approaches) to optimize planning in dynamic and changing environments: *make static*, where the project actually attempts to resist change – only reported in 2 out of the 31 respondents; *emergent planning*, where the detail of each phase of an overall plan is only done at the time, and an acceptance is made that plans should not be perfect – supported widely by respondents; *staged releases*, where an emphasis is made to reduce project delivery scope in order to obtain real-world feedback before deciding whether to broaden scope; *competing experiments*, where alternative approaches can be tried out and tested, allowing the project manager to eventually choose the one which has the best chances of achieving goals; and *alternate controls*, where a choice is made between input controls (controlling the resources made available to a project) and output controls (the goals of the project).

A slightly different perspective is offered by Wright, Sturdy, and Wylie (2012), who show that consultants can lead innovation projects not necessarily through disruption and dynamism, but through standardized approaches. While this idea might be counter-intuitive for some, and at odds with what the authors refer to as the "post-/anti-bureaucratic discourse of revolutionary change" (Wright, Sturdy and Wylie, 2012: 653), it becomes clear that consultants are often acting as 'standardizers' within their client organizations. They are setters of management fashion across clients, often using codified systems to implement change. Through 61 interviews in seven case organizations, the authors uncover how the process of consultancy when geared towards innovation does not necessarily mean that rules have to be broken. Two standardizing aspects are uncovered: *standardizing agendas*, where an overall strategy of change – including internal cultural change – is in force, and *standardizing methods*, entailing well-documented and tried and tested ways of performing consultancy tasks. One note about Wright, Sturdy, and Wylie's (2012) study: it was limited to internal consultants. Nevertheless, it does show that there does not necessarily have to be a conflict between innovation and standardization within the consultancy industry.

Bessant and Davies (2007) note that while service companies such as consultants do not have formal R&D labs, much of their service innovation mirrors that taking place in manufacturing sectors. It is "creative work undertaken on a systematic basis" (Bessant and Davies, 2007: 65, citing the OECD Frascati Manual). The process of innovation in services involves a search aspect, an experimentation and prototyping aspect, and a scaling up and preparation for launch aspect (Bessant and Davies, 2007: 65). The different forms that innovation can take, i.e., product, process, position, and paradigm, can all be present in services industries as well as manufacturing. Bessant and Davies (2007) draw on Christensen's (1997) view of disruptive innovation which highlights the need to know when to listen to client needs in order to provide a somewhat tried and tested solution for short-term goals vs. when to essentially ignore client needs in order to push for a fundamental paradigm shift and break-through technology that may unsettle clients initially. They argue that this principle applies in services industries as much as it does in manufacturing and the decision on whether to promote existing solutions or develop new ones hinges on four factors: embedding disruptive projects within clients, pursuing small opportunities in a disruptive way, planning to fail early and inexpensively, and finding new markets that value the disruptive innovation, rather than compete with existing offerings.

Nah, Lau, and Kuang (2001) research the process of implementation of enterprise resource planning (ERP) systems in large organizations. Consultants are often used to assess how such systems can be utilized by clients, and this involves a deep understanding of client needs as well as the customizable capabilities of such systems. Their review leads to a number of critical successful factors that fit into the four-phase model put forward by Markus and Tanis (2000). These four phases are a *chartering* – defining the business case and solution constraints; the *project phase* – getting both users and the system up and running; a *shakedown phase* – stabilizing and eliminating bugs; and an *'onward and upward' phase* involving maintenance and user support. Important to note here is that consultants can be involved in any or all phases. Nah, Lau, and Kuang (2001) argue that it is in the shakedown phase that business disruption can be keenly felt. There may be the most bugs in the live system during this phase and there may be a reduction in productivity.

Winsborough and Chamorro-Premuzic (2013) put a spotlight on how the field of consulting psychologists is changing: becoming more commoditized while the gap between science and practice is widening. Psychological consulting requires an application of knowledge from the field of psychology to client organizations (ranging from individuals through to teams) and typically in support of the HR function and dealing with behavioral issues and problems within organizations. The methodologies used by consultancy firms – particularly the large ones – have become more open and transparent over time, hence the expression: 'commoditization'. Examples include 360 reviews, employee engagement surveys, and personality assessments. They note how "New vendors offer incremental improvements or small changes, but the underlying science seems not to have shifted a great deal" (Winsborough and Chamorro-Premuzic, 2013: 321). They conclude by encouraging consulting psychologists to reconnect with academia to promote a two-way flow of knowledge, linking problems and solutions between client organizations and academia, pushing the boundaries of the field in order to solve significant problems, working in collaborative networks, and having an orientation towards new technology and data processing capability.

Werth, Greff, and Scheer (2016) (in German) examine digital consulting and remote consulting based over the Internet as disruptive innovations. They point out that disruptive innovation with respect to the way consultancy services are offered represents an evolving story. Their own innovative suggestion is for consultancies to use an eConsulting store in projects: a "platform for integrated sales and fulfillment of consulting services" (Werth, Greff, and Scheer, 2016: 56). The eConsulting store is a piece of software: it is technology; it is not a 'place' that customers physically visit. By using this software, clients can effectively purchase consultancy services. The sales process involves the user of the software requesting services that are placed in an online shopping basket. Against this the pricing is applied. The fulfillment process is a separate process and involves the client opening a consulting dashboard and assigning resources to be used in meetings with the client to fulfil the service to the client. The eConsulting store concept is another example of how a deliberately constructed and formalized approach can be used to disrupt traditional approaches to consulting. In Christensen's (1997) terms, it is a kind of straightforward technology that has the potential to be used initially on a very small scale (the lower end of the market), and then slowly but surely to move 'upmarket' and displacing other, more established approaches.

Brescia, McCarthy, McDonald, Potts and Rivais (2014) describe how the process of disruption has already gained traction in the legal services profession. The authors cite Christensen, Wang, and Van Bever's (2013) article that points out that professions such as consultancy and legal services had traditionally been characterized by an opacity and an agility that made them "immune to disruption" (Brescia, McCarthy, McDonald, Potts and Rivais, 2014: 563). One of the developments that changed this was the setting up of in-house legal counsel by large corporations (Brescia, McCarthy, McDonald, Potts, and Rivais [2014] give the example of General Electric). Something similar might be said of the consultancy industry, where many large firms themselves have in-house consultancy units, such as the *iCon* case (Chen, Tran and Williams, 2018) reproduced in this book. Other competitors come along, using new technology to streamline processes and reduce costs. Brescia, McCarthy,

McDonald, Potts, and Rivais (2014) also make an important point that disruptive approaches in legal services took place before the dawn of the Internet. Examples include how to use trusts in order to avoid the costs and complexity of probate. Again, similar examples may be found in the consultancy industry where firms developed proprietary approaches to address client needs in ways that moved from smaller scale (down-market) to eventually displace approaches at the higher end.

## Practice insight

The following practice insight was kindly provided by Switzerland-based consultant Kamales Lardi.

### The shift to modular consulting

Several key factors have caused lifecycle disruption in management consulting over the last decade. Firstly, there has been an accelerated rate of technology development resulting in transformative breakthrough technologies such as artificial intelligence, robotics, and blockchain. These are fundamentally changing the way companies (including consultancy firms) do business. Secondly, there has been a rapid adoption of new technologies and online platforms by clients resulting in higher client expectations in terms of superior customer service, quick response time, and 'instant gratification'. Thirdly, there has been a democratization of knowledge. Technology platforms enable instant, anytime anywhere access to information, making it possible to leverage knowledge and experience of the crowd. Also, top management consultants take up industry positions, taking their experience of frameworks, tools, and methodologies with them. Fourthly, technology enables new ways of working, e.g., mobile workforces, virtual teams, and flatter organization structures. And this has been increasing in the consultancy industry. Fifthly, changing attitudes in the workforce have resulted in a focus on work-life balance and a shift towards entrepreneurship and freelance working models. Lastly, there is a transformed competitive landscape, and increase in the number of agile, smaller firms offering specialized consultancy services.

These factors combine to result in the disruption or unbundling of the management consulting life-cycle. Since starting my company in 2012, I have seen a shift in the market as client companies are disrupted, resulting in subsequent disruption in the management consulting industry. With platforms such as LinkedIn and mobile apps offered by industry events, access to top decision makers is easier and accessible to all. In the past, this was a competitive advantage of top leadership in management consulting, who closely guarded access to client relationships.

Access to big data and analytics capabilities (a combination of data from various sources, structured and unstructured, social data) offers the possibility to pinpoint challenges for a specific industry or company, or even predictive analysis for strategic decision making. Client companies have also adopted these capabilities internally, reducing the need for using consultancies and putting pressure on the consultancies to change appropriately.

As a transformative move, I introduced a new business model for my company when I launched in 2012 – modular consulting. What does this mean in practice?

Working with a community of proven experts from various specialized areas, I plug them into projects as and when required by clients. This 'plug and play' approach to consulting enables me to create experienced teams that are able to quickly deliver client projects. The lean operations of my company allow me to offer clients cost-effective projects, even for very specialized work. Also, our model enables working with virtual/remote teams, giving clients access to experts from across the globe. The organization structure is flat: all team members are responsible for their own work product and fully in control of delivering high quality. This approach also allows the company to rapidly innovate and transform according to market changes, offering new services based on market shifts. For example, this year we moved into offering blockchain business model assessment within a few weeks, as client demand for this area rapidly grew. Based on my experience over the last few years, client companies are not only happy with this transformation, they have quickly adapted to the new model of working.

In the traditional approach, a partner does the sales pitch for a large project for a client organization. If they win the deal, they may never see the top people again. Analysts and consultants then come in, being placed on the client site. While it still works in many situations, clients have become increasingly wary of this model. Now, with modular consulting, experts come in with me and deliver directly to the client on a one-to-one basis for the specific part of the project. We recently delivered a project on organizational change to move towards digital delivery for a client. I brought in one person who had 15 years relevant experience – they came in and delivered on that one piece. We have access to these people from various walks of life and we can leverage this flexibility. From their point of view, they don't need to be in one long-term engagement with clients.

I see now how larger organizations are interested in moving towards this model. We see this in blockchain clients. One of the challenges in the market is addressing the question of "what's the future of work?" for larger companies. They are more worried about human capital atrophy – consultants leaving to do their own thing. This includes women leaving the workplace. Larger consultancies find it hard to switch and re-position themselves quickly. It is still a very traditional work environment with project and team structures.

## Case reflections on the theme of disruption

In the case of McKinsey and the Globalization of Consultancy (Jones and Lefort, 2005), a number of (now well-known) disruptive forces are highlighted that pre-date the Internet era by decades! These include Marvin Bower's various initiatives such as bringing in new recruits directly from business school (1953), the intro-duction of an 'up or out' policy (1954), and the company's first international office (1959). These disruptions changed the way McKinsey & Company operated, but also became commonplace across the consultancy industry. And they were orga-nizationally oriented, changing the way the consultancy firm operated in order to maintain competitiveness and continue to give clients what they wanted. They were not based on the massive computing power and the potential of the Internet that we have today. They were moves that became taken for granted in the decades that followed. It may be hard to imagine that, at one point in time, they displaced previously accepted ways of working. What these types of disruptions meant for the management of consultancy projects is open for discussion. But at the very least they meant that clients would (suddenly) find themselves interfacing with relatively young consultants, fresh from business school. This may not have been something they were used to. And these young consultants, if they did not perform, may not be employed by the consultancy firm for very long!

The case of Global Consulting Services (GCS) Consulting (Batra and Puri, 2015) describes a more recent situation surrounding an Indian IT consultancy firm offering both business consulting and technology consulting. The managing direc-tor positioned his boutique consultancy firm as an advisor with a strong belief that IT should not be seen merely as a support function, and that it goes hand in hand with business strategy. The GCS approach in projects involved a kick-off meeting with teams from both client and consultant side coming together. Given the com-plexity of projects, this created trust and synergy and enabled client expectations to be managed. By 2014, non-linear models were increasingly used for projects in India's IT space. New technologies were emerging in the areas of social media, mobile computing, data analytics, and cloud computing. These provided opportu-nities for consultants and GCS itself had shown its stature and thought leadership by publishing its own white papers on topics such as business analytics. Clearly any future investment and growth in GCS would need to account for these trends and develop a mindset in the company that would be flexible to client needs and the ability to design projects for clients in ways that were suitable given the nature of the emerging technology and its use in the client's strategy.

In a separate case on Transforming the Business Service Portfolio at Global Consultancy (Su and Pirani, 2014) (Global Consultancy is a disguised name), the company was at a decision point in terms of how to improve its efficiency across its operations in Canada. It was considering strategic sourcing options for four of its internal, back-office functions: marketing, HR, finance, and IT. These internal, back-office departments are essential in large consultancy firms. However, they themselves need to be efficient, and strategic sourcing was considered an option to transform each of them. The puzzle is that strategic sourcing can be achieved in various ways: delivering the services in-house or through third parties on the one hand, and on the other hand, delivering the service in the home country vs. in another 'offshore' location. These internal services act as vital supports to the client-facing side of any large consultancy firm, but nevertheless, are not themselves immune from being disrupted through a strategic transformation involving multiple possible organizational solutions. While such a strategic change at the 'back-office' side of a consultancy business ideally should not affect the client-facing side, there is always a chance that, during the implementation of the transformation, the processes that client-facing consultants are using in their execution of projects with clients, will be impacted. For instance, it is likely to take considerable time and effort to ensure that a transformation of back-office services towards an offshore outsourcing model has achieved the desired efficiency goals while not interrupting client-facing work. There are always likely to be teething problems.

## Implications

The foregoing literature review and case examples clearly illustrate the importance of life-cycle disruption to innovation in management consultancy. Disrupting life-cycles means a new way of working for both the consultant and the client. It implies a questioning and a revising of the traditional ways of executing projects with clients as well as a willingness to continually review the way projects are managed in order to create innovative outcomes. Firstly, we see from the project management literature that important paradigmatic issues have been raised in recent years: is it best to assume a hard paradigm or a soft paradigm? What are the contingencies under which one or the other (or a combination of them) are adopted? The literature shows there has been a massive shift at the paradigm level. We would not even be talking about the nuances of a soft paradigm for project management if the world of project management was happy with traditional, linear and predictable approaches. The literature also tells us that there is a lot to be gained by adopting a contingency approach to managing projects in consultancy. Consultancy firms need to listen to the needs of clients and the imperatives of individual projects in terms of innovation before deciding which type of stance to adopt. It does not necessarily have to be about radical disruption in each and every client project. Indeed, as some have argued, innovation can come about by adopting standardization. Moreover, what is important is to determine the desired level of innovativeness both before and during a project; this is an ongoing process requiring a mentality that is open to adapting the organizational system (including the specific project management practices and tools) for the project accordingly. Consultants must always be ready to disrupt their tried and tested ways of doing things and to be aware of the degree to which they are required to generate innovation for themselves or for their client.

On top of this contingency logic relating to the overall approach at the level of individual projects, another theme that comes up is the role of technology, including, but not limited to, how the Internet is used. We see this theme in the cases highlighted, as well as in academic articles such as the presenting of the results of prototype 'tools' (the eConsulting store), insights into why it is necessary to build flexibility into end-products and the role of consultants in helping clients implement ERP systems. We see the theme of technology also in the practitioner insight provided by Kamales Lardi, in particular how Internet-based applications have allowed access to key decision makers in client organizations, as well as to other consultants who might be brought in to work on projects on a modular basis. While technology underpins practically everything that happens in a virtualized context (discussed in more detail in the previous chapter), it is also an important theme when we discuss the issue of disruption.

In addition, something that is not at the level of individual projects and also not necessarily linked to specific technology platforms is the overall disruptive forces within the consultancy industry. Some organizations' actions have a bearing on how projects with clients across the industry are executed. The case of McKinsey & Company highlights this. Marvin Bower led new initiatives and ways of working within the industry that others then followed. And all this happened before the advent of the modern era of technology. So the lesson with this point is that consultancy firms are able to provide disruption to themselves, to their own way of working, and such disruptions may end up diffusing across other firms in the industry. Other forms of disruption here may include the calls for consultants to work more with the field of science, i.e., at research-led universities and ways in which consultants can be recruited and selected based on their ability to cope with uncertainty in projects with clients.

Overall, these three themes (contingent project management, use of technology for disruption, disruptive forces in the organizational system) have implications for consultancy firms in terms of their ability to be creative and original, and how well they are able to create new knowledge as a basis for innovating for themselves and their clients. Contingent project management that caters for a soft – as well as a hard – paradigm, and that is selected and adjusted on a situation-by-situation basis, means the consultant does not fall into a trap of being locked in to one predetermined way of doing things. With a mindset and ability to adjust the project system to cope with new learning and unforeseen events during a project, the consultant is able to absorb new tacit knowledge, identify new opportunities, and work with others on ways of addressing new opportunities. The use of technology for disruption, while innovative in its own right, has the potential to 'breed' further innovation during the life-cycle of projects. Users of the technology – whether on the supply or demand side – will inevitably, through their use of it, spot deficiencies in the technology and this will lead to incremental adaptations to the technology itself. But the technology will also allow knowledge of new opportunities to be shared, perhaps more quickly than ever before, and for new ideas for solutions to these opportunities to be discussed and disseminated. Disruptive forces in the broader organizational system of the consultancy will have a direct impact on how consultants operate. The strategic sourcing of back-office operations, for instance, and the inevitable shakedown period that will ensue following such a change, will create new problems that need solutions, and therefore a strategic imperative on the part of the consultancy firm to be creative and generate new ways of providing services to the market.

## Summary and learning points

In this chapter on Pole 4: disruption in the consultancy life-cycle, we have seen the following:

- How disruption in the life-cycle can be seen as part of a broader paradigm shift in the field of project management, namely a shift from the traditional hard paradigm to a newer soft paradigm that emphasizes human action and interaction, social complexity and the continual restructuring of problems.
- How the traditional hard paradigm does not need to be dispensed with in consultancy assignments, rather, consultants should work with clients in order to understand the fundamental nature of the problem in context in order to design and use the most appropriate project management approach.
- A disrupted life-cycle is essentially about a non-traditional way of working with clients; while this might be seen as an innovation in itself, the 'new' way of working can also yield new products and services, i.e., innovations.
- The project management body of literature has been reflecting and re-evaluating itself for over 20 years as it tries to keep up with the changing nature of project management practice – e.g., the reviews by Koskela and Howell (2002), Söderlund (2011) and Svejvig and Andersen (2015).
- There is a need to be aware of how innovative a project will be before and during its life-cycle in order to assess the most appropriate tools and practices –

this requires learning in the local context and an ability to continually review what is expected of a project in innovative terms.

■ That technology plays an important role in how disruption takes effect – new applications that allow consultants and clients to network with each other in new ways, and web-based solutions for managing the engagement process are examples.

■ That changes in the broader organizational system in which projects are set up and executed are also an important part of the disruption equation in consultancy – these changes can be seen as innovations themselves, but, like new technology adoption, they also can breed an innovative culture within the consultancy firm and this will get carried through into individual projects.

## Note

1  Darling and Whitty (2016) point out a number of synonyms are used for PMOs, including project office, project management office, program management office, project or program management center of excellence, project portfolio office, and project performance office!

## Suggested additional cases for analyzing life-cycle disruption and innovation in consulting

Batra, S. and Puri, S., 2015. 'GCS consulting: Should corporate or personal interests come first?' *Ivey Publishing* (product number: 9B15M042).

Jones, G.G. and Lefort, A., 2005. 'McKinsey and the globalization of consultancy', *Harvard Business School* (product number: 9-806-035).

Su, N. and Pirani, N., 2014. 'Transforming the business service portfolio at Global Consultancy', *Ivey Publishing* (product number: 9B14E001).

# 6

# Pole 5: reflective ability in consultancy

## It's all about taking stock

This chapter will examine innovation in consultancy firms from the perspective of reflective ability within consultancy firms. The working definition of reflective ability that we will use is this: the *ability of consultants to stop and reflect on what they have learned and how they have been doing things with a view to innovating, either for themselves, or for their client.* David Maister (2003) emphasizes this theme in his book on *Managing the Professional Service Firm*, at a key point in the book when he talks about augmenting the knowledge of the firm:

> In a variety of contexts, I have asked members of professional service firms to write down what they have learned from their activities over the past year that has made them better at what they do-to identify something they learned about serving clients, managing projects, or approaching certain matters in a new way.
>
> (160)

This reflective ability is, I argue, similar to virtual organization and disruptive life-cycles in that it is a form of organizational capital relating to a practice that supports how the firm functions at a fundamental level (Acs and Fitzroy, 1989; Prescott and Visscher, 1980). It happens in teams as well as at an individual level (Engeström, 1999) and is seen as a value-added knowledge exchange practice in business services (Amara, Landry and Doloreux, 2009). But reflective ability is different in one important respect: it goes to the heart of one of the most important aspects of consultancy, namely the need, indeed the pressure, for consultants to be highly utilized (O'Mahoney, 2011). Maister (2003) continues:

> In many cases, this has proven a difficult exercise. The professionals seem to have been too busy rushing from project to project to stop and reflect on their

experiences. They say that they *feel* they have learned something, but they cannot either identify or communicate what it is.

(160)

If our consultants are all fully utilized on client projects, we may think we have a very successful consultancy firm: a popular one, one that is good at selling projects to clients. But a firm that has 100 per cent fully utilized consultants will leave little time for those consultants to *collectively* stop and reflect on what they are doing and how they are doing things with clients. They will not have given themselves the time and space to reflect as a group (Edmondson, Bohmer and Pisano, 2001; Engeström, 1999). A tension arises when consultants do not find the time (because of utilization rate pressures) to 'take time out' within their employers (rather than their clients) to reflect, share knowledge of new opportunities and solutions, and work towards new creative activities in a *non-utilized* (*i.e., non-billable*) manner (O'Mahoney, 2013; Taminiau, Smit and De Lange, 2009). However, to be innovative in the consultancy firm, some level of collective reflection is important. Think about it: human capital gives us the ability to advise, social capital gives us the ability to relate, virtualization gives us the ability to work from anywhere, and disruptive life-cycles gives us the ability to confront the way we do things with clients. At some point we need to stop and reflect on how this is all working out!

Mirroring the structure in previous chapters, we will examine the academic literature on reflective ability – this often subsumed into a broader narrative on team learning (Senge, 1990). We will also review real-world examples in the form of published cases and insights from practice before synthesizing our main implications.

Figure 6.1 provides a schematic for Pole 5. As we go through the discussion on this Pole, please try and imagine a consultancy firm that has a maximum value for reflective ability, and at least for now, ignore the other Poles.

## Exploring reflective ability

We see from the literature on reflective ability that the concept is very familiar in fields as diverse as architecture and the arts (Schön, 1987), education (Braun Jr and Crumpler, 2004; Cheng and Chau, 2013; Ross, 1989), and health care practice (Hays and Gay, 2011), as well as within the project management profession (Winter, Smith, Morris and Cicmil, 2006). The essence of reflective ability is the capability for professionals to perform reflection-in-action (Schön, 1987). Cheng and Chau (2013), for instance, examine the practice of students generating ePortfolios in order to promote their reflection and learning. Student-generated ePortfolios are created and updated over the duration of a course and contain different types of media to allow students to keep track of their own learning. Importantly, they also contain a

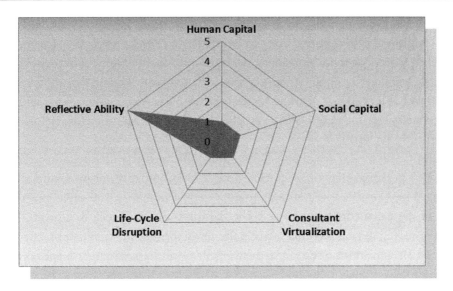

**Figure 6.1** Pole 5: A Focus on Reflective Ability

reflective writing component in which students review collected artifacts in their ePortfolios. Cheng and Chau (2013) find that students with the most aggressive set of goals (comprising mastery goals to develop competence as well as performance goals) have the highest level of reflective ability.

Braun Jr and Crumpler (2004) study autobiographical writing in pre-service teachers' social studies methods courses as a way of reflecting on, and learning from, their practice. They describe reflective teachers as having "developed the capacity to think about their teaching behaviours and the contexts in which they occur . . . they can look back on past events; make judgments about them; and, they can alter their teaching practices and beliefs based on the needs of their students" (Braun Jr and Crumpler, 2004: 60). If we replace the word 'teacher' in this definition with the words 'management consultant', the word 'teaching' with 'consulting', and the word 'students' with 'clients' we arrive at a definition of reflective ability in consultancy. It entails consultants looking back on events, making judgments about them, and altering behaviors accordingly. Braun Jr and Crumpler (2004) find that student teachers are able to develop skills in reflective ability before actually going into the world of practice: it allows them to understand how their identities came about; their own social development.

Hays and Gay (2011) also underline the importance of understanding, fostering and measuring reflective practice. While their focus is on learning in medical professionals, the principle that reflection forms the basis of keeping up to date and relevant over a long career holds for consultants as well. They point out how reflective practice has been well-established in nurse education, where it has often been formalized. In medical schools, student doctors are often taught 'how to reflect' from an early point in their studies. However, Hays and Gay (2011) are somewhat critical of how the literature treats the construct of reflective practice: for instance, whether it is a single, stable construct; whether it is measurable; or whether it should be assessed on a verbal basis rather than on a written basis. The final point is relevant to reflective ability in consultancy firms. It is more likely that consultants will share their experiences with each other verbally than through the use of social memoirs and written biographical pieces.

Mann, Gordon, and MacLeod (2009) also look into the literature on reflective practice in health professionals, noting how it is a foundation of professional competence. They conduct a literature review of research into reflective practice in health professional education. One of the key questions they seek to answer in their literature review relates to what enables the development of reflective practice. This would be an important question to answer in a consultancy firm as it speaks to the organizational environment and managerial intervention that might be required in order to encourage consultants to reflect as a basis for learning and innovation. Through their literature review, Mann, Gordon, and MacLeod (2009) find a number of factors: "a supportive environment, both intellectually and emotionally; an authentic context; accommodation for individual differences in learning style; mentoring; group discussion; support; and, free expression of opinions" (Mann, Gordon and MacLeod, 2009: 608). Clearly a supportive and open environment is needed in which individuals feel comfortable to reflect on their experiences with others.

In a study of third-year undergraduate medical students, Grant, Kinnersley, Metcalf, Pill and Houston (2006) find that those that volunteered to take part in a reflective learning exercise (by keeping written learning journals over two terms and attending regular group meetings to discuss their entries in the journals) were better able to identify their learning goals, i.e., what they needed to learn. There were no differences in exam performance between those that took part in this reflective practice and those that did not. However, it is interesting that those that participated in reflective practice were better able to identify what they needed to learn. They were able to acknowledge that their understanding was incomplete and identify gaps in knowledge and what they needed to learn to make their knowledge base more complete. The process of reflection also allowed individuals to become aware of their own learning style.

Ross's (1989) work on developing a reflective approach in teacher education makes some useful points about how reflection allows students to identify practices linked with teacher effectiveness. Firstly, reflection allows the "components of competent practice" (Ross, 1989: 29) to be identified and articulated. This is a first step in developing a reflective approach. In a consultancy setting, a consultant that is able to articulate such components of competence with his or her peer group will be providing a base layer for reflective ability. Ross (1989) goes further, however, arguing that students are able to perform reflection at a higher level than they demonstrate. This is also interesting if we translate it into a consultancy context. Consultants may be encouraged to be reflective, and may, to a limited extent engage in this practice. However, line managers should be sensitive to the possibility that they may be capable of more reflection than they are actually showing.

These insights from the literature on professions such as teaching and health care are useful because reflective ability has been a core element of education and career-long learning in these professions for decades. In the wider management literature, and especially the literature on learning, the construct of reflective ability does take a central position (e.g., Engeström, 1999; Gibson and Vermeulen, 2003). In learning theory, learning is seen as a process in which individuals or groups reflect upon the consequences of their actions, and based on this reflection are able to modify their behaviors accordingly (Dewey, 1922; Edmondson, 1999; Engeström, 1999). We see this principle applied in a broad range of professional services settings, including in project management (Winter, Smith, Morris and Cicmil, 2006) and business services offshoring (Williams and Kumar, 2014).

What role does reflective ability play in determining performance outcomes of teams? In Edmondson, Bohmer, and Pisano's (2001) study of team learning in hospitals that were implementing a new technology for cardiac surgery, differences were found between teams that implemented the new technology successfully and those that did not. Implementation of the new technology is seen as a learning process with four steps: *enrollment* (which motivated the team), *preparation* (involving practice sessions), *early trials* of the technology, and finally a *reflective phase*. This reflection involved reviewing data and results and planning future trials. It was a collective process involving the whole team. As noted by Edmondson, Bohmer, and Pisano (2001: 705), the team reflection involved formal and informal conversations, in the latter case: "grabbing whatever time was available rather than scheduling formal meetings". Team-level reflection happens in a public space. It involves groups of individuals reflecting on their work, not just one individual reflecting on his or her work. The team is using the reflecting time to ask questions such as: "What are we learning? What can we do better? What should we change?" (Edmondson, Bohmer and Pisano, 2001: 705). The model that emerges emphasizes the importance of taking time out (i.e., away from a regular or main task) to complete this step. The team's ability to reflect is an important determinant of successful outcomes.

In Edmondson's (1999) study of psychological safety, learning and performance in manufacturing teams, the operationalization of team learning behavior included the item: "In this team, someone always makes sure that we stop to reflect on the team's work process" (383). This goes to the heart of the issue in this chapter. When a consultant 'stops' work on a client project, even temporarily, he or she is not being utilized and may not even be billable. And the idea that 'we stop' (with the emphasis on the 'we') in a consultancy setting implies multiple consultants, working on different client projects in different locations, all downing tools and finding time to communicate with each other – face-to-face or virtually – in order to ask all-important questions of themselves concerning what has worked well, what has worked less well, and what might they want to do differently in the future. In Edmondson's (1999) study, the psychological safety in the team (that is, a belief that it is safe to take personal risks in the team) has a positive impact on team learning behavior, and this in turn drives team performance (satisfying client needs). So for a group of consultants in a consultancy firm, perhaps working on different client accounts, all to engage in team learning effectively, they need to feel 'safe' that there will be no personal risk to them. In other words, the consultancy firm would need to endorse and encourage such team learning and reflection, and see long-term value in it, even if there is a short-term loss of billable hours.

Gibson and Vermeulen (2003) argue that team learning behavior is optimal when all of three necessary steps are present: experimentation, reflective communication, and codification. During *experimentation*, exploration takes place: new ideas are generated and explored and team members are engaged in a searching activity. During *reflective communication*, the team is able to reach a common understanding, a clear agreement on what any new information gleaned through experimentation actually means. During *codification*, tacit knowledge becomes explicit; the new knowledge is made concrete in terms of the writing down of any new discrete steps to use in the future. Their study concentrates on the role of subgroup strength, which is the "degree of overlap across multiple demographic characteristics among a subset of members in a team that is not shared with other members of the team" (Gibson and Vermeulen, 2003: 203). When a team has subgroups that are strong, there are discrete units within the overall team where viewpoints will be common and easily shared. This centers on the argument that a group with more than one person with the same or similar demographic characteristics will share the same or similar viewpoints. Gibson and Vermeulen (2003) find that moderately strong subgroups within a team (as opposed to very weak or very strong ones) encourage learning behavior. Subgroup strength also moderates the effects of aspects of the organizational environment (such as degree of empowerment to the team) and team learning. Overall, their study highlights the importance of team composition, and the demographic characteristics of subgroups of individuals in the team, to how learning unfolds.

Bunderson and Sutcliffe's (2003) study warns against too high a level of team learning orientation. They argue – and show empirically – that a short-term emphasis on team learning can be detrimental to team performance; there will be decreasing returns as team learning increases. The reasons include the issue that team learning takes time and can take the team away from tasks focused on core performance. There will be costs associated with too much experimentation (the first phase of team learning according to Gibson and Vermeulen [2003]) – too many new ideas will be generated and the team might not be able to fully evaluate them and be able to choose the right ones for further development. There will be "more variation than can be effectively assimilated (i.e., selected and retained)" (Bunderson and Sutcliffe, 2003: 554). This finding has implications when applied to a consultancy environment. Too much time taken away from client projects will negatively impact revenues (by reducing utilization) and may create too much variation when consultants get together to try to find new ways of working and new offerings. Bunderson and Sutcliffe's (2003) results, if applied to a consultancy setting, suggest that consultancy teams need to find the right balance between too low and too high a level of reflection and not try to attempt team learning in a rush.

Zellmer-Bruhn and Gibson (2006) show that learning in teams that operate within multinational corporations (MNCs) will be influenced by what they refer to as the macro organizational context. More specifically, they look at the extent to which the MNC pursues a globally integrated strategy and the extent to which it pursues a locally responsive strategy. According to the logic of the integration-responsiveness paradigm (Williams, Colovic and Zhu, 2017), these are separate organizing variables. It is possible to have high global integration and high local responsiveness (this is referred to as a transnational strategy – Bartlett and Ghoshal, 2002). In Zellmer-Bruhn and Gibson's (2006) study, global integration in the MNC has a negative impact on team learning, while local-responsiveness has a positive impact on team learning. Given that many consultancy firms are international and will find it necessary to make strategic decisions relating to whether to assume a globally integrated posture and a locally responsiveness posture (they will have common processes and systems to allow them to service global clients, but they will have to be sensitive to local host country contexts), this finding creates a paradox! If the firm wants to encourage team learning as a basis for innovating, it will need to find ways of reducing or overcoming the negative effect of global integration, while promoting or encouraging the positive effect of local responsiveness.

## Reflective ability and innovation

Learning and innovation are closely linked in the literature (Brown and Duguid, 1991; Engeström, 1999; March, 1991; McKee, 1992). Furthermore, a number of studies have examined the links between reflective ability and innovation. Yu and Sangiorgi (2018), for instance, argue that the process by which heterogeneous knowledge and skills are internalized is central to the ongoing capability development needed to generate new service innovations. Many of these studies draw on the construct of reflective ability through a broader conceptualization of organizational or team learning (Senge, 1990). However, this does not change our interpretation for the purposes of this chapter. As shown in the literature in the previous section, reflective ability (in teams as well as in bigger organizational units – Engeström, 1999) is at the core of all organizational learning (Buckler, 1996; Huber, 1999). So how does this then impact innovation in organizations?

Stata (1989) argues that organizational learning is the essential ingredient for achieving management innovation, not just product or technology innovation. Management innovation relates to how an organization is managed: the knowledge, tools and methods that managers use to organize activities. Without an ability to reflect and learn from past success and failure, managers will never be able to come up with new ways to organize. The ways in which an organization memorizes past events are important; there are certain institutional mechanisms that retain organizational knowledge, not just knowledge retained at an individual level. This knowledge is shared across the key members of the organization. Because shared knowledge is important in organizational learning, the encouragement and facilitation of internal communications becomes important. Failure to allow effective internal communications through teamwork and openness will undermine the learning organization and prohibit effective management innovation.

Hirst, Van Knippenberg, and Zhou (2009) examine employee creativity from the perspective of learning, exploring how the interaction between learning at an individual level and at a team level influences the creativity of the individual. Given that creativity is centerstage in the process of innovation, it is important to understand the influence of different levels of learning on creativity. Studying 25 R&D teams in a large pharmaceutical company, the authors find a number of interesting interaction effects between individual and team learning on creativity. Arguably the most interesting from our perspective is the finding that individual learning orientation has a positive impact on employee creativity, but this is moderated by learning behavior within the team. At higher levels of team learning behavior, the positive relationship between individual learning orientation and employee creativity is amplified, although the relationship is non-linear and it becomes attenuated at higher levels of learning orientation. The result emphasizes, in the authors' words, how "we must consider not just the individual but rather the individual in his/her context" (Hirst, Van Knippenberg and Zhou, 2009: 291), this context relating to the extent of learning behavior in the team in which the individual works. It also highlights a potential boundary condition on creativity at higher levels of individual learning, something that managers will need to pay attention to if they want to promote creativity.

Teams are typically based around specific projects. They may span organizational departments and even national borders. Teams can make mistakes in much the same way that individuals can, and if they are not able to learn from their mistakes, performance will not only be impacted at the level of the team; it will also affect the wider organization. Barker and Neailey (1999) cite Kransdorff's (1996) work on post-project analysis in identifying reasons for ineffective team learning, these being "a disinclination of managers to be reflective, the uncertain nature of accurate memory recall and a tendency for those involved in the process to be defensive" (Barker and Neailey, 1999: 61). Barker and Neailey (1999) point out that if innovation is a motivation for team learning, members of a team need to respond accordingly. Their study of a project to develop a new automotive vehicle highlighted how post-project reviews can facilitate team learning and innovation. Of particular interest to the theme of reflection is they find that individual learners in teams need managerial support: "detailed reflection over a long period of time is a difficult process" (Barker and Neailey, 1999: 67). Learning logs provide the structure to do this and set the foundation on which team learning then happens.

Lynn, Skov, and Abel (1999) study 95 new product development teams to understand the factors that facilitate learning in teams. They examine a number of team-level practices that have the potential to influence team learning: recording information, filing information, reviewing information, goal clarity, goal stability, vision support, and having a new product development (NPD) process. These team-level practices are assumed to have a positive influence on information acquisition and implementation. Interestingly, the team practice of reviewing has a strong overlap with the construct of reflection and reflective ability discussed in this chapter. The four questionnaire items used by Lynn, Skov, and Abel (1999) to capture reviewing include having weekly team meetings during the project with all department heads, team members systematically reviewing action items from meetings, team members systematically reviewing prototype test reports, and team members systematically reviewing customer reaction reports. In this study, the ability to reflect at a team level is seen as a practice that is antecedent to team learning. Results show that reviewing is the only one of the team practices that leads to information acquisition, again underscoring the importance of reflective ability in teams.

Drach-Zahavy, and Somech (2001) also see team reflection as a central component of the learning function, in particular the "overt reflection" on objectives, strategies, and processes and how this is geared towards initiating change in the organization (Drach-Zahavy and Somech, 2001: 112). Their study on elementary and secondary school educational teams in Israel uses a questionnaire survey. One of their questionnaire items for team learning reinforces the point concerning reflective ability in team learning: "My teammates are prepared to reflect on the way we act" (Drach-Zahavy and Somech, 2001: 116). Importantly, the study finds team learning to be the sole predictor of team innovation; exchanging information, motivating and negotiating are all insignificant.

Huber (1999) reviews literature on the relationship between team learning and innovation, arguing that new knowledge for innovation is often created in project teams within organizations. These teams also need to assimilate pre-existing knowledge from the wider organization and integrate this with newly created knowledge in order to be successful in their innovative activities. This process is underpinned by a number of factors, including what Huber (1999: 74) refers to as "meta-management of project team members". This essentially relates to how HR practices can be used in a very deliberate manner to stretch team members; identifying and assigning them to projects, and finding new projects for them to work on where they will gain new knowledge. Another factor is the enhancing of learning "in and by teams" (Huber, 1999: 74). This has a strong reflective aspect, including institutionalized practices of "subjecting [evolving knowledge] to examination, critique, and revision" (Huber, 1999: 74). A third area relates to the transfer of team learning: having a culture of – and practices for – transferring knowledge from a focal team to need-to-know units around the organization.

Ahmed (1998) reviews literature on innovation from an organizational culture perspective, identifying a wide range of factors to do with what stimulates innovation in an organization and how prevailing norms within the organization impact creativity and change. Of interest to Pole 5 is the observation made by Ahmed (1998) that internal debates (within and across teams) within the organization should be part of the cultural norms that facilitate innovation. Debates allow minority views to be expressed and employees should not feel hindered to enter into debates. In Ahmed's (1998: 37) words, debates as part of the norm of the organization should have the following attributes: "expect and accept conflict; accept criticism; don't be too sensitive". This opens up the possibility that tolerating team-level reflection will inevitably lead to some kind of internal conflict – there will be different viewpoints on what constitutes an innovative opportunity, how to evaluate it, and whether or not to pursue it (Williams and Lee, 2009).

Buckler (1996) presents a learning process model for innovation. He sees reflection as "probably the most important part of the learning process" and where "deep learning takes place" (Buckler, 1996: 34). Flatter structures, a tolerance for experimentation, and participative team leadership are all elements of the learning system that Buckler (1996) sees as supportive of effective learning. However, perhaps the most prominent theme in Buckler's (1996) essay is the importance of reflecting on prior actions; some may have led to successful outcomes, others may have failed. Omitting the reflection stage of the learning process is catastrophic and organizations will not be able to formulate and implement change initiatives effectively.

Verdonschot (2006) takes this one step further and identifies specific methods for supporting reflective ability in innovation. Her work is based on a literature review. She identifies five methods (what she calls 'elements') that enable the tracing of learning processes within innovation: *focusing in daily practice, paying attention to personal stories and emotions, reflection needing to be appreciative and not focusing only on things that went wrong, needing to take into account the social context of learning*, and *understanding the starting point for reflection* (past, present, and even future!). Her suggestion that reflection might go beyond a singular view of the past (and of what is currently happening in the present) but also taking an "imaginary stand of learning in and from the future" (Verdonschot, 2006: 683) stands out as an interesting point. Here there are no experiences to reflect on. However, she argues that a future can be constructed by imagining different scenarios of what might happen, and breaking the "dominant way of thinking in the past" (Verdonschot, 2006: 675).

Jack and Anderson (1999) examine reflective ability from the perspective of entrepreneurs and entrepreneurship education. Given the increase in education on the topic of entrepreneurship, a question arises as to how such education can satisfy the demands from multiple stakeholders within an enterprise economy. Stakeholders include the students learning about entrepreneurship, as well as the government promoting it, and the firms themselves. Jack and Anderson (1999) point out that some have even criticized entrepreneurship education: as an 'art form', is it really something that can be taught? Others point out that there is a scientific aspect to entrepreneurship that can be taught in the classroom. Nevertheless, entrepreneurial acts are often difficult – if not impossible – to predict with any certainty. Following an extensive literature review, Jack and Anderson (1999) conclude that educators of entrepreneurship can play a vital role in enabling students to reflect on the entrepreneurial landscape, i.e., to become *reflective practitioners*. They note: "the outcome of entrepreneurial education should be the creation of reflective practitioners fit for an entrepreneurial career" (Jack and Anderson, 1999: 122). This reflective ability allows entrepreneurs to constantly update their knowledge about the process of entrepreneurship – of identifying opportunities, knowing how to evaluate them, and then deciding whether to attempt to exploit them (Shane and Venkataraman, 2000; Venkataraman, 1997). Reflective ability in entrepreneurs is also a skill that is transferable to larger corporate environments in which corporate venturing takes place.

Schweitzer, Rau, Gassmann, and van den Hende (2015) explore how a technological reflective ability in individuals can impact the generation of social innovations, i.e., innovations that have a benefit for society. They define technological reflectiveness as "a tendency to think about the societal impact of an innovation" (Schweitzer, Rau, Gassmann and van den Hende, 2015: 847). They generate and test a seven-item scale in their study. The scale consists of items for the individual: (1) thinking about how a new technology can provide for society, (2) being interested in studying the impact of technical products on society, (3) relating new products to the reduction of social problems, (4) enjoying thinking about how new technical products can help society, (5) reflecting on the consequences of a new product for society, (6) enjoying thinking about how future technology can benefit society, and (7) thinking about how technical products can impact the self-determination of individuals and social groups. They use the scale in a number of studies including a study of users of a health monitoring system in a lab setting. This finds technological reflectiveness to be positively and significantly correlated with product involvement and general creativity. After controlling for these factors, technological reflectiveness is found to be positively and significantly associated with the number of improvement suggestions as well as the elaboration of improvement suggestions. Individuals who have a technological reflectiveness are able to contribute to the new product development process. While the study focuses on social innovation, the core principle can apply to other types of innovation projects. Interestingly, in Schweitzer, Rau, Gassmann, and van den Hende's (2015) scale, we see the concept of the individual 'enjoying' the activity of reflecting. This will have implications for the organizational system surrounding individuals in innovation projects and how they are motivated and incentivized to contribute. Reflecting can be fun!

## Innovation in consultancy through reflective ability

The previous sections introduced the concept of reflective ability in individuals and teams, and showed how a literature has emerged examining its links with innovation in organizations. We now examine some key literature that has looked at this question in the context of professional services and consulting organizations. Researchers have argued that consultancy firms can be seen as knowledge systems; they allow different types of knowledge, some based on theory and some based on practice, to be continually comingled and integrated (Werr and Stjernberg, 2003). Consultancy firms, through their embeddedness with their clients are able to learn from their clients – particularly new clients and those in new settings (Taminiau, Smit and De Lange, 2009). But they also need to reflect and take stock. One key question is how much time out from client projects is needed to allow an appropriate amount of reflection between colleagues to take place (Taminiau, Smit and De Lange, 2009). While this may be debated depending on individual circumstances, one thing is clear from the literature: a reflective ability at the heart of the knowledge system within management consultancy firms is a primary determinant of innovation among those firms.

Anand, Gardner, and Morris (2007) explore the way in which new practice areas emerge and become established in professional services firms. This is a classic example of innovation in these types of organizations; new practice areas embody specific and distinct knowledge and expertise to be used on assignments with clients.

A new practice area can be seen as an emerging knowledge-based structure. Larger management consultancy firms are typically structured and organized around such distinct practice areas. Through in-depth case studies of the emergence of four practice areas, followed by a validation exercise in 25 further emerging practices, Anand, Gardner, and Morris (2007) are able to identify three types of pathway to practice emergence. The first is based on *expertise*, where a consultant is driving the formation of a new center of expertise that is new to the firm. The second pathway, which the authors refer to as a *turf-based* pathway, involves a consultant in the company using an existing relationship with a client to drive new ideas. These ideas, if successful, can then be deployed in assignments with other clients, and the practice is born. The final pathway, a *support-based* pathway, is more of a top-down approach with senior managers in the consultancy firm identifying a new market need that a consultant picks up on and tries to develop a new practice area out of. Important in all of these pathways is individual agency; the role of a particular 'champion' or lead individual to push for the formation of the new practice. When such innovative forces are aligned with the over-arching organizational goals and interests, we see a form of innovation in management consultancy firms that can have huge implications not only for the firm and its clients, but also for other consultancy firms that seek to mimic the new practice in their own organization. Again, what is critical in this process of internal organizational innovation in consultancy firms is the ability of key individual consultants to reflect on knowledge in three broad areas: existing areas of expertise, initiatives and ideas emanating from existing clients, and knowledge being passed down from senior managers. At the heart of practice emergence and innovation in management consultancy firms is a multi-level reflective ability.

O'Mahoney and Sturdy (2016) use the case of McKinsey & Company to show how different forms of power influence the diffusion of management ideas in and across organizations. While this is not the focus of the current chapter, their study is relevant in that it shows how large 'omnipresent' consultancy firms have a role to play in influencing which new ideas become diffused across organizations and how this process happens. The big consultancy firms are not the only sources of power that determine this diffusion process, and the article also points to formal institutions such as governments, courts, and professional accrediting bodies. Special interest bodies and client organizations also wield considerable power as new management ideas take hold. Nevertheless, consultancy firms are seen as knowledge creating entities that are able continually to reflect on what they are doing as they seek to identify, pursue, and make a profit from 'the next big idea'. Recruited consultants are mentored by partners and given continuous feedback. They engage in 'thought leadership' and publish articles and white papers on new ideas in order to demonstrate their relevance and influence. And their knowledge management systems and cultures form a model on which executives from client organizations may base their own ideas for change. Using the McKinsey & Company case as an example, O'Mahoney and Sturdy (2016) highlight how a reflective ability at the core of the consultancy firm's knowledge system will allow it to build power and exert its influence in the diffusion of new management ideas.

Plattfaut, Niehaves, and Becker (2012) use the case of an IT consultancy firm in Germany to expose weakness in how the traditional dynamic capabilities view (Teece, Pisano and Shuen, 1997) explains service innovation. They propose a new class of capabilities, namely, systemic capabilities, that relate to how operational capabilities and assets are utilized. Systemic capabilities are "based on the organizational culture of open doors and minds, low hierarchies, basic rules, [and] small teams" (Plattfaut, Niehaves and Becker, 2012: 9). In essence, they are event-independent capabilities that are not intended for any one specific change event. In Plattfaut, Niehaves, and Becker's (2012) case, regular team meetings were used to share knowledge and engage in team reflection, and a Wiki was used to store and share knowledge arising on an event-independent basis. Accordingly, reflective ability amongst consultants is event independent. When consultants meet and interact in order to reflect on what has worked and what has not worked, and share ideas on where potential new opportunities for innovation may lie, they will not be focused on one specific client or one specific project. Reflective ability for innovation, if it is to take place in a consultancy firm, is part of the organizational culture of that firm. It will be part of the established norms and rituals and ways of doing things that will encourage the coalescing of knowledge and experience from multiple projects and clients.

Crevani, Palm, and Schilling (2011) review academic research on innovation in service firms and point out that there have been some important gaps between what academics have researched and what actually happens in practice. One major theme identified as a gap by Crevani, Palm, and Schilling (2011) is the fact that much innovation in services takes place in and through everyday operations. It is less common in services to have a separate R&D function or R&D department as it is in manufacturing. So innovation in services is *less* formalized and will come about as a consequence of feedback received on a day-to-day basis in generating and delivering the service offering (O'Mahoney, 2011). However, that does not mean no formalization is necessary. And the reflective ability of team meetings comes up again as a means to share knowledge of opportunities for new innovations. One of the practitioner interviewees in Crevani, Palm, and Schilling's (2011) article says the following:

In order to make use of ideas we have regular and structured meetings with the co-workers, both in larger and in smaller groups. We have had a number of meetings spanning over professional boundaries in which we have worked on trying to develop new ideas. The problem has been that different professional groups work with very different things and it is hard to get everybody motivated. We are trying to change this by now working divided more by function. (CEO of a training company).

(184)

This highlights both the reality of (1) business services firms explicitly engaging in reflection in order to stimulate innovation, and (2) the difficulties they may face in bringing people together to share knowledge who might otherwise be assigned directly to clients.

Taminiau, Smit, and De Lange (2009) examine knowledge sharing in management consultancy firms in the Netherlands and the impact this has on innovation. They argue that management consultants are under pressure to be billable, i.e., utilized on assignments for their clients, and subsequently have little time for innovation. In O'Mahoney's (2011) study of management innovation in the UK consultancy industry, a lack of time driven by high utilization rates was seen as a major impediment to innovation. Literature reviewed indicates that innovation will arise in management consultancy as a consequence of knowledge gained through relationships with clients, but this can be augmented with other knowledge from within the consultancy firm. Formal mechanisms such as explicitly articulated methods and cases (Werr and Stjernberg, 2003) may play a role. But so may informal mechanisms such as "lunches, drinks and dinners" (Taminiau, Smit and De Lange, 2009: 45), i.e., accumulated tacit knowledge and experience from practice (Werr and Stjernberg, 2003). Taminiau, Smit, and De Lange (2009) argue that direct sharing of knowledge between consultants will lead to innovative outcomes through both formal and informal routes. They describe the formal route as leading to collective learning because knowledge is institutionalized. In the informal route, creative ideas come about because of its "accessibility and free character" (Taminiau, Smit and De Lange, 2009: 47). Based on their interviews with 29 consultants in the Netherlands, mostly from large and well-established firms, they see the route to innovation through knowledge sharing being an interlinkage of informal and formal routes: direct knowledge sharing between consultants leads to knowledge creation through informal mechanisms, this is then formalized to allow collective learning to take place. In many ways, this finding mirrors that of Plattfaut, Niehaves, and Becker (2012) who identify both informal and formal elements within the event-independent capabilities for learning and innovation in business services. And they also underscore the importance of reflection between consultants (not just interactions between consultants and clients) to provide impetus into the creativity and innovation process in consultancy firms.

Den Hertog (2000) draws on Nonaka and Takeuchi's (1995) socialization-externalization-codification-internalization (SECI) model of knowledge creation to discuss how knowledge exchange underpins innovation in knowledge intensive business services (KIBS). Importantly, the 'externalization' step in Nonaka and Takeuchi's (1995) model involves a "dialogue and collective reflection" (den Hertog, 2000: 14) among members of a KIBS team. Once again, this puts a focus on interaction between individuals and the importance of knowledge sharing on a collective basis. Den Hertog (2000) identifies three ways in which a KIBS provider can stimulate innovation: (1) as a *facilitator*: helping a client firm innovate but not being the source of the innovation per se; (2) as a *carrier*: helping transfer innovations from one sector of the economy to another; and (3) as a *source* itself: generating innovations for use amongst client firms. In all of these roles, the KIBS provider facilitates knowledge transfer. Through a SECI knowledge creation process, KIBS providers enable their own consultants as well as client employees to talk about and share their collective experiences as a basis for facilitating, carrying, and generating new innovations.

Canato and Giangreco (2011) review literature to examine the role of management consultants in innovation, and identify four different types of roles: (1) as an *information source*, the consultancy firm can use its experience and position in networks of organizations and institutions to provide specific and relevant information to clients; (2) as a *standard setter*, the consultancy firm diffuses the same solution across multiple client organizations; (3) as a *knowledge broker*, the consultancy firm helps clients to develop their own innovations by linking the client with multiple external knowledge sources; and (4) as a *knowledge integrator*, the consultancy firm helps clients integrate solutions using its own specific expertise. Underlying all of these roles, the consultant is helping and supporting the client to learn. While the way this happens may be different across the roles, the importance of this support function for client learning during innovation is underscored. In terms of the consultant's own ability to reflect and come up with new innovations, what is clear is that the consultant will not be able to maintain its support function to clients' learning if it itself is not able to reflect on what has worked and what has not worked in the past. As Canato and Giangreco (2011: 236) point out: "to remain competitive and nurture their reputation, standard setters must regularly update solutions in their portfolio". And in knowledge brokering and knowledge integrating roles, the consultancy firm is leveraging its *previous* experience; clearly the reflective ability of the consultancy firm plays a central role in how it is able to leverage previous experience and how it is able to regularly update its own solutions.

Martinez, Ferreira, and Can (2016) also examine this knowledge sharing and learning facilitation within consultant-client relationships. Consultants act to challenge clients and through this process of being challenged by an independent 'outsider' the client is able to learn. Consultants need to do this in a clear way. Their messages of communication must be clear and unambiguous and, in this way, can also boost the motivation of clients to learn for themselves. While these points echo those of Canato and Giangreco (2011) and den Hertog (2000) with respect to the role of consultancy firms in enabling the learning for clients, Martinez, Ferreira, and Can (2016) also point out that the credibility of the source (i.e., the credibility of the consultancy firm as an expertise provider) will matter to the effectiveness of knowledge transfer and learning. Clients will not gain any new learning from a consultant unless the consultant is able to learn for him or herself. Again, this goes to the heart of our emphasis in this chapter. In order to maintain credibility and to be seen as a source of the latest knowledge and expertise, the consultancy firm will need to be able to reflect on its own knowledge stocks regularly and update them accordingly. Martinez, Ferreira, and Can (2016) highlight the sharing of context in a consultant-client relationship, in particular, the establishing of intimacy and shared norms in the relationship. Building such intimacy over time will be helped when the consultancy firm has shown it is able to reflect on what it knows in order to stay relevant. A failure to do this may appear as self-oriented and perhaps arrogant on the part of the consultant, undermining trust in the consultant-client relationship (Maister, Green and Galford, 2000).

Von Platen (2015) argues that communication consultants need to be able to operate in multiple contexts in order to translate and interpret meanings across contexts. They operate across various organizational boundaries, allowing management practices to be "decontextualized, materialized and recontextualized" (Von Platen, 2015: 154). This is more of an art than a science, and clients should be wary of communication consultants offering 'cut and paste' solutions. The kinds of knowledge that an effective communication consultant needs includes factual knowledge of the topic being translated, knowledge of the cultural contexts, how a concept has been practiced in other organizations, awareness of the history and norms of the organizations concerned, linguistic skills, and knowledge of how to be creative! This is clearly a tall order and one which underscores the need for consultants to provide sense to clients in complex and ambiguous situations, rather than being a "neutral transmitter" of information (Von Platen, 2015: 154). This sense-giving function requires the consultant to actively re-interpret knowledge on an ongoing basis, again underscoring the importance of reflecting on what is known and how knowledge needs to be continually upgraded.

Sturdy (2011) takes a critical view of the impact of consultants on management and highlights how innovation and organizational change do not necessarily come about because of consultants. In Sturdy's (2011: 527) words, there are "alternatives to consultancy as a means of innovation, change management and legitimation". He also points out how the boundaries surrounding consultancy have become blurred. Some organizations (such as the *iCon* case in this book) (Chen, Tran and Williams, 2018) have internal consultancy units. In other situations, management is influenced by sources which have nothing to do with consultants. Client organizations may be inspired to innovate, for example, because of what they have learnt through working with various operational partners around the world. Management ideas do not necessarily have to come from consultancy firms! This perspective is very interesting not least because it raises questions about how consultancy firms draw in knowledge in order to be reflective. To some extent, we have assumed thus far that the reflective ability of the consultancy firm entails taking time away from clients and to encourage groups of consultants to discuss their experiences with a view to generating new innovative ideas for their firm. However, Sturdy's (2011) critique puts a spotlight on the fact that this reflective process may need to extend beyond the consultancy firm, beyond the array of client firms, and into a myriad of other sources that may provide impetus for new ideas.

## Practice insight

The following insight is adapted from an interview with an experienced senior partner in a top global consultancy firm and is reproduced here confidentially.

### Informal knowledge sharing in a practice of a global management consultancy firm

Control in professional services firms is almost a contradiction in terms because it is quite hard to control professionals. The only way you can grow the business successfully is to 'uncontrol' those professionals, to give them freedom and let them do what they think is the best thing to do – to give them freedom and stimulate them to develop themselves.

In terms of control you need to bring people together every now and then and give them the feeling that they belong to the same group. That can be in many different forms, that's what many of us do. It can be from an expertise theme – we have tips and tricks meetings where every consultant can show what he or she has learned, and convince others that it's good, and to standardize it and put it on a server so others can use it. Let's call it the 'substance' part.

There is also the 'play' part – which I like the most. We have a beer and talk about cars, or do some sports in order to get a group feeling. Next week we have a half day where everybody has prepared short-term attack plans because the market is very difficult at the moment for us. I asked my team to prepare certain sub-plans for the very short term. People will present, we'll discuss, and afterwards we'll go to the beach, kiting, surfing, other things, and we have a barbecue with drinks and go home. It's always a very stimulating event. It gives a form of control because you get the group together. Now that I think about it, it's possible to control consultants, but it's very, very soft – all soft controls.

## Case reflections on the theme of reflective ability

In the case of Deloitte Consulting GTA: The Deloitte Dads Initiative (Konrad and Shuh, 2013), a manager in the corporate strategy group at Deloitte in Toronto had started an initiative called 'Deloitte Dads', which would be a new group within the organization that would hold one event per quarter to promote the cause of working fathers within the firm. While there already was a similar forum for working mothers, the manager recognized the need for a formal way of providing some paternal support. He had clearly reflected on the situation. He had gained access to data that indicated up to 60 per cent of working men experienced a work/life balance conflict. He had also found out that the HR department did not have up-to-date information on the number of fathers in the organization. By pitching his idea to the senior management team in Toronto, the manager activated the reflective ability of the organization at a senior level. He made others think about the core issue and how his initiative would benefit the organization. He made sure the initiative was aligned to the firm's core values. The questioning by the members of the senior team and the informal discussions that inevitably would have happened outside the actual pitch meeting constitute an important reflective ability on the part of Deloitte. The initiative was given the go-ahead and the group was launched in the Greater Toronto Area (GTA), reaching around 130 members. The combined reflective ability of one proactive individual working with an experienced top management team led directly to an organizational innovation that ended up getting reported on the cover of *Bloomberg Businessweek* magazine. Perhaps a more subtle point about this case but nevertheless an important one is as follows. By implementing the Deloitte Dads initiative and giving the fathers of the company an opportunity to take time away from clients together (albeit with their children), they actually have an opportunity to build and cement relationships with colleagues and have informal discussions with each other. In other words, the initiative itself provides a zone for reflective practice to actually take place. Perhaps the fun activity with their children also would spark some creativity and innovation that could spill back over into the corporate side of life!

In the case of Innovation at the Boston Consulting Group (BCG) (Eccles, Narayandas and Rossano, 2013), a new CEO had a strong belief that the success of the company – in an environment of intensifying market competition – would be dependent on the company's ability to innovate. It needed to show clients that it was still able to innovate for them, creating new products and services for them as it had in the past. This view was shared by other senior leaders in the company. Innovation always had been part of the company's heritage and it needed to continue. One way the company supported innovation was to give the consultants time to reflect on and be exposed to innovation. The culture of innovation at BCG also emphasized decentralized idea generation during projects with clients, but then seeking ways to take the best ideas into a wider domain, normally driven by a champion. Among other communication channels, practice area meetings were used to discuss emerging ideas and case teams would take them forward. The company also had a 'Tier One' project format in which exploratory research was done to pursue new ideas. These mechanisms illustrate the essence of reflective practice in management consulting.

The case of Ergonomica Consulting (Williams, 2017) was discussed earlier in the context of our first Pole, namely, human capital. There are, however, some useful links to the theme of reflective ability in this story as well. In the main case itself it seems the company has not had much time to reflect! As a small and fast-growing consultancy firm it was keen to have its professional staff fully utilized at all times. And when the company was disrupted by the effects of the financial crisis, some long-standing clients were lost. Ergonomica's response was to cut the headcount by eliminating "a large portion of a program management and quality assurance office that had only been set up in 2006" (Williams, 2017: 4). It is a worthy point of discussion about whether this inadvertently led to the situation facing the consultant some years later as she grappled with an error in her spreadsheets that would undermine the company's relationship within one of its key clients. In the subsequent events, we note that Ergonomica indeed ended up losing the client. But the consultant was not sacked. Instead, she was invited to work on revising the guidelines and processes for quality assurance in the company. This was a clear example of a consultancy firm reflecting on the situation, learning from it, and innovating in terms of instilling a new mentality for quality as well as implementing new and concrete processes across the organization. On the flip-side, perhaps the lack of reflective ability in the early years – and especially during a time of crisis during the financial crash – can be seen as going hand-in-hand with a rather narrow-minded focus on utilization and growth. This came at the expense of allowing time for the consultants and partners to reflect and take stock of what they were doing, how they were working and how they might improve their quality assurance processes.

## Implications

Looking at these case examples and literature we see very strong links between reflective ability and innovation. Indeed, innovation is one of the greatest benefits of reflective ability and we see these links playing out in the consulting context as much as they do in other service contexts such as health care practice and education. Coming up with new ideas and progressing them towards implementation or commercialization is not possible without knowledge of what has happened in the past. There needs to be due consideration for the diverse experiences of different people. This is not possible without an opportunity to take time away from current projects and assignments which are always, in effect, about executing against a previously agreed brief to deliver service in the moment. What this literature tells us is that the past matters, different people's experiences of the past matter, and the ability of the consultancy firm to harness these experiences in order to create something new is a principal determinant of lasting innovative performance.

Unfortunately, management consultancy firms do not typically have formal networks of R&D labs as their engines of innovation in the same way that high-technology equipment manufacturing, telecoms, or pharmaceutical companies do. They do not have bench scientists peering down microscopes. Their inspiration for innovation comes largely through engagement, mostly with clients on real-world problems facing their clients, and by reflecting – with others – on the knowledge gained through these relationships and engagements. This reflection shapes new ideas. Nevertheless, the literature and case data suggest that an innovative consultancy can, and indeed should, have a number of organizational features that would assist it in its ability to be reflective.

Firstly, there is a *leadership* aspect. Leaders provide legitimacy for behavior within the firm. They set the management control systems and incentivize staff to behave in certain ways. If leaders are hell-bent on utilization (a case in hand being the Ergonomica case) and do not allow the time and freedom for decentralized professional staff to reflect (a case in hand being the BCG case) then they will dampen the potential of their organizations to create long-term value. Their obsession with the short term may eventually backfire, especially as intense competition in the industry erodes market share. Secondly, there is a *cultural* aspect. Much of the literature emphasizes aspects of the learning environment in which reflection is enabled and can take place. People contributing to a reflective process need to feel that what they are doing is the norm; that it is acceptable to be away from billable projects, even for short while. They should feel encouraged to challenge established ways of working in the firm and encouraged to listen to the past experiences of colleagues and other outside experts as they form their own contribution to the creative process of innovation. Thirdly, there is a *structural* aspect, and here we see a divergence away from the modus operandi in non-business services and R&D–intensive firms. I refer not to structure in a control or hierarchical sense, but to structure in a temporal sense. When is the best time to bring consultants together to have a practice-focused reflective meeting? How long should the meeting take such that all participants can have an opportunity to share their experiences and comment on those of others? How often should such a get-together take place? These are effectively all temporal questions, rather than questions about formal position within the organizational hierarchy. In the UK, for example, it is not uncommon for a General Practitioner (GP) medical practice to close for half a day every month for training purposes. If this is mirrored in a large practice area in a leading consultancy firm, perhaps clients would begin to ask about where their highly paid consultants have all disappeared to! But the point is clear: without leaders incentivizing professionals to engage in reflection and allocating this time accordingly, the potential of the consultancy firm to innovate will be dampened. Fourthly, there is the *knowledge management* aspect. The literature and cases such as BCG highlight how knowledge management systems can be used to capture and share knowledge about past experiences with clients, new opportunities and ways to target and harness those newly identified opportunities. In large consultancy firms and those with global operations and hundreds of clients, this is a formidable challenge. Sophisticated systems have been developed to manage and share knowledge globally, as in the cases on knowledge management at McKinsey & Company (Bartlett, 1996) and Tata Consultancy Services (Sharma and Koh, 2008). These can be seen as event-independent capabilities in Plattfaut, Niehaves, and Becker's (2012) terms, allowing an institutionalization of knowledge for innovation within the organization's memory (Stata, 1989).

While the discussion shows how these imperatives (leadership, culture, temporal structure, and knowledge management) will need to be tackled for reflective ability to be used as a foundation of an innovative consultancy, the literature and cases also alert us to pitfalls in these areas. Leaders may be easily and understandably seduced into going against the grain and downplaying utilization in favor of reflective activity. But if they do this to an excess, and particularly in times of operational stress (e.g., the Ergonomica case during the financial crash period) they may undermine narrow margins and this might even threaten survival. In other words, there may be periods of time where the environmental conditions indicate that reflective initiatives actually need to be de-emphasized, at least temporarily. In terms of culture, a potential pitfall could be if reflection is over-emphasized to the extent that consultants on engagements with clients are side-tracked from the main task at hand because they are constantly setting up and attending knowledge sharing and lessons learnt meetings. This could be an annoyance to clients who expect the consultant to deliver on a tightly defined brief. In terms of temporal structuring, having review sessions that are too long, too frequent, and bringing in consultants (on Skype or video conferencing) from too many different time zones could also be dangerous. It will be more difficult to coordinate and make sense of diverse knowledge and experiences and will take people away from the situations in which they actually obtain the experience that is needed to be shared! And in terms of knowledge management, and in particular the 'hard' IT side of knowledge management systems for capturing and sharing the outcomes of reflective sessions, there will be a cost of setting up and maintaining these systems. Many IT set-up projects overrun, both in terms of time and cost. It will be important for IT development and support staff – as part of the operational infrastructure of the consultancy firm – to work closely with the consultants in order to really understand the requirements for knowledge management and build solutions that support the relationship between reflective ability and innovation. So a key implication here is that care will be needed in all of these areas for a consultancy firm to balance pressures for utilization and pressures for reflective non-utilized time in a strategic way.

## Summary and learning points

In this chapter on Pole 5: reflective ability, we have seen the following:

- That it is possible to draw from the literature on reflective ability and reflective practice in skilled workers such as teachers, architects, and health professionals and apply these concepts to the world of management consultants.
- How reflective ability is a seminal construct in learning and how this applies at individual, group, and organizational levels.
- That it is at the team level in consultancy firms that reflective practice will be especially useful, giving a responsibility to those defining and controlling team membership to select the most appropriate individuals to participate.
- That leading global consultancy firms use explicit mechanisms to encourage reflection and they use this to promote the exploration and development of new ideas.
- How reflective ability also can be seen as part of the organizational culture of the management consultancy firm; it can become engrained in the norms and rituals of organizational members.
- How leaders in management consultancy firms need to consider the temporal dimension to reflective practice and pay careful attention to the point in time that reflection takes place, the amount of time consultants spent reflecting, and the frequency in which they engage in reflective practice.
- How reflective ability cannot only provide a basis for innovating for clients or developing new products and services for future clients, but that it can also be used to instill organizational changes for the consultancy firm.
- That knowledge management systems can be used to codify the output from reflective sessions, capturing a record of individuals' and teams' experiences on key issues and questions.

# Suggested additional cases for analyzing reflective ability and innovation in consulting

Bartlett, C., 1996. 'McKinsey & Company: Managing knowledge and learning', *Harvard Business School* (product number: 9-396-357).

Eccles, R.G., Narayandas, D. and Rossano, P., 2013. 'Innovation at the Boston Consulting Group', *Harvard Business School* (product number: 9-313-137).

Konrad, A. and Shuh, A., 2013. 'Deloitte Consulting GTA: The Deloitte Dads initiative', *Ivey Publishing* (product number: 9B13C046).

Sharma, R.S. and Koh, S., 2008. 'Managing intellectual capital at Tata Consultancy Services', *The Asia Business Case Centre* (product number: ABCC-2008-001).

Williams, C., 2017. 'Ergonomica Consulting and Solltram Hotels: An ethical dilemma', *Ivey Publishing* (product number: 9B17M153).

# 7 Connecting the Poles to form the innovative consultancy

## So far so good

This chapter will bring the discussions of the previous five chapters together to shed some light on how the Poles can be inter-linked and connected in order to achieve innovative outcomes in management consultancy firms. The core argument is that, in order to achieve positive innovation outcomes for clients as well as for the consultancy firm itself, attention must be paid to how human capital, social capital, and organizational capital interact. In other words, consultancy firms need to 'connect the Poles' in the most appropriate way in order to maximize their chances of producing useful and valuable innovation.

We start with a series of dyadic analysis between various combinations of the Poles. We find that the literature provides some interesting insights about these dyads. We explore five examples of such two-way interactions. These are as follows: (1) human capital interacting with social capital, (2) human capital interacting with reflective ability, (3) social capital interacting with consultant virtualization, (4) disruptive life-cycles interacting with reflective ability, and (5) disruptive life-cycles interacting with consultant virtualization. We then move on to some more complex constellations, i.e., between human, social, *and* organizational capital. We look at two examples of such three-way interactions: (6) human capital and social capital together interacting with consultant virtualization, and (7) human capital and social capital together interacting with reflective ability. These selected interactions are clearly not exhaustive. But we do not have space here to follow up on each and every combination. However, they do represent some of the important combinations of the various forms of capital to be deployed for innovation in consultancy and for which literature and case insights exist. Moreover, they should get you thinking about how you can analyze, lead, and manage consultancy firms for innovation in an holistic way. Firstly, we have the important interactions between human and social capital. Secondly, we have the possibility that this interaction itself can be moderated by a third set of variables related to organizational capital. Thirdly, we have the potential for the lower-level forms of organizational capital to interact with each other.

## Human capital and social capital

The interaction between human capital and social capital is a commonly found one in the literature. It is interesting for us because it talks squarely to the basis for competing in the industry, namely that (1) our firm has well-trained and highly experienced consultants, who are (2) socially embedded in long-term relationships with clients and others. The implications of this are manifold. For example, the skills and experience of the consultants will allow knowledge coming through the relationships with clients to be effectively absorbed; this will form the bedrock for new innovation. Also, social capital has an important function in enhancing the value of human resources; without social capital with clients, our human capital may end up being under-utilized and 'collecting dust'.

Figure 7.1 depicts a firm that is high in both human and social capital simultaneously.

Studies have shown positive correlations between human capital and social capital, suggesting they influence and reinforce each other. In Florin, Lubatkin, and Schulze's (2003) study of new ventures, human resources and social resources were found to

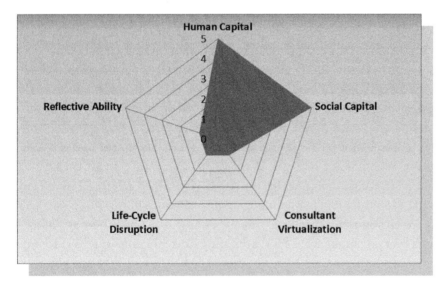

**Figure 7.1** Two-Way Interaction #1: Human and Social Capital

be strongly positively correlated. In Williams and Lee's (2016) study of subsidiaries of Korean MNEs in Europe, human capital and socialization were positively correlated. In Nielsen and Nielsen's (2009) study of international strategic alliances, levels of know-how were found to be positively related to levels of trust between alliance partners. These are just some examples of the correlation between these two forms of capital. Let's now dig a little deeper, as there are some nuances in the literature.

Davidsson and Honig (2003) showed that while human capital amongst Swedish entrepreneurs explains their decision to becoming an entrepreneur, it does not necessarily explain their ultimate success at being entrepreneurs. Social capital – particularly weaker ties as indicated through bridging social capital – has a bigger role to play here, especially in terms of the likelihood of achieving the first sales and giving the entrepreneur a greater chance of success at exploiting the opportunity.

Goyal and Akhilesh (2007) conduct a literature review in the fields of social capital, innovativeness, emotional intelligence, and team performance and conclude that social capital is a key determinant of innovativeness at the team level. They highlight the interplay between social capital, cognitive intelligence (related to intellectual ability and intelligence), and emotional intelligence (non-intellectual abilities including the ability to monitor the feelings of others as well as oneself) as the main factors that will predict team innovativeness. This insight is interesting because it highlights the value of social capital in conjunction with – what are ultimately – the abilities of people.

In Florin, Lubatkin, and Schulze's (2003) study, the researchers interacted human resources with social resources and found social resources elevated the relation between human resources and financial capital of a venture at the time of an IPO (a positive relationship), as well as the relation between human resources and eventual return on sales (a negative relationship). In other words, social capital acts to heighten the effect of human capital on outcomes. As Florin, Lubatkin and Schulze (2003: 376) say: "an individual's achievement is conditioned by the social context".

According to Wu, Chang, and Chen's (2008) study of Taiwanese firms, human capital is an important part of a firm's intellectual capital. While the study finds a positive and significant effect on innovation in its own right, the study also shows how intellectual capital mediates the effect of social capital on innovation. In the authors' words: "social capital seems to be a catalyst for the influence of intellectual capital on innovation" (Wu, Chang and Chen, 2008: 267). In Bontis and Fitz-enz's (2002) survey of 75 executives, a causal map of human capital is developed showing investment in training to lead to human capital, which in turn has a positive impact on relational capital and human capital effectiveness. Bozeman, Dietz, and Gaughan (2001) make an important distinction between individualist human capital and social human capital in the field of science and technology. Individualist human capital can be assessed through formal education and training, consistent with the theory of human capital. Social human capital recognizes that trained individuals work in groups and the productivity of groups and networks of trained individuals can be assessed in terms of their collective ability to produce new knowledge and new applications of knowledge.

These associations are also conspicuous in our case data and practice insights. Consider how the specialist trained consultants at iCon (experts in the energy sector) have strong social ties with various internal clients within innogy (previously the RWE Group). Consider how Qiang Li uses both his ability in turning various types of businesses around alongside his investment in physical space for maintaining good quality relationships. Consider also how a consequence of Jeroen Brugman's training in process mining was the development of new social networks as he set up and delivered a project with his client.

## Human capital and reflective ability

The interaction between human capital and reflective ability is also an important one to dwell on. It has a strong theoretical overlap because of the importance of knowledge in the industry. In this scenario we would have a consultancy firm that has highly trained and skilled consultants who are able to meet – in groups – on an internal basis and away from client engagements in order to reflect on their experiences with clients. Individuals share their knowledge with others whilst listening and learning themselves. This reflection process will then boost each individual's level of knowledge, improving their ability to perform for clients in the future. Being trained will mean an enhanced knowledge base which helps in the recognition and absorption of new knowledge from others during the reflection process. This will then boost innovative potential amongst the consultants.

Figure 7.2 depicts a firm that is high in terms of human capital and at the same time puts a strong emphasis on reflective ability.

Schön's (1987) seminal work strikes at the heart of the interaction between reflective ability and human capital. Schön (1987) emphasizes how it is necessary to find a balance between reflection and acquisition of knowledge and skills needed to do a job. As Schön (1987) noted, reflection allows problems to be framed. When conducted collectively, it also allows information about how skills are applied and how these are brought into the reflective conversation. In other words, collective reflection allows human capital to be stimulated. Similarly, McKee (1992) discusses organizational learning skills and how they may be used for different types of innovation in the organization (incremental, discontinuous, institutionalization). This puts an emphasis on learning as a skill. In other words, part of our human capital in consultancy is the ability of our consultants to learn, including their ability to self-organize into reflective groups. Consultants can, in essence, continue to learn

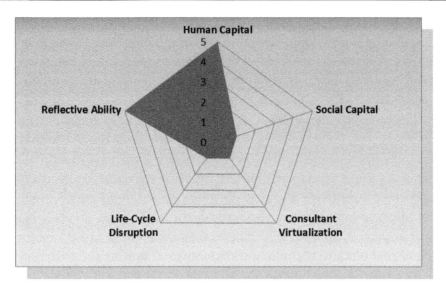

**Figure 7.2** Two-Way Interaction #2: Human Capital and Reflective Ability

how to learn, this happening traditionally through client engagement and through in-house training. But this also can happen through collaborative reflective ability within the consultancy firm.

Chen and Huang (2009) examine the link between strategic human resource practices, knowledge management capacity and innovation performance. In a sample of 146 firms, they find knowledge management capacity mediates the relationship between strategic HRM and innovation. HRM practices including staffing, training, participation, performance appraisal, and compensation are all practices that develop and maintain human capital in the firm. Knowledge management capacity includes knowledge acquisition, sharing, and application. The sharing aspect closely resembles reflective ability in our sense and includes the sharing of knowledge between colleagues and between supervisors and subordinates. In the authors' own words, their "findings highlight the critical roles of human resource management and knowledge management in the process of innovation" (Chen and Huang, 2009: 112). Similarly, De Winne and Sels (2010) examine the interplay between knowledge-related HRM practices, human capital and innovation. Within their set of HRM practices they include practices designed for knowledge retention, including participation mechanisms that underpin knowledge creation and transfer within the firm. The more of these practices that are present the greater the innovative output. Also, when human capital levels are high, the more pronounced the positive effect of these knowledge-related HR practices. These two studies clearly demonstrate an interaction (the first being based on mediating effects, the second based on moderating effects) between human capital and the learning environment of the firm.

In the Deloitte Dads case, we see a highly trained Deloitte consultant instigating an initiative to support working fathers in the organization. The person in question was able to conduct some basic research and create a persuasive argument to convince senior managers of the benefits of the initiative. He used his abilities to create an environment for reflection between colleagues. In the subsequent events of the Ergonomica case, once the problem in the focal consultant's calculations are made open to others, we see a reflective process taking place inside the organization. This was even more important given the loss of the client contract as a result of the issue. But the subsequent reflection and quality assurance work that involved a number of people in the company led to new operating procedures designed to prevent a repeat of this type of problem happening again. In the BCG case (Eccles, Narayandas and Rossano, 2013), we see the role of a champion used to help facilitate the diffusion of an innovative idea into a wider domain, following the reflection phase. Such a role enshrines the human capital needed to persuade and 'sell' the idea to others. In different ways, such real-world examples show powerful chemistry between human capital and reflective ability.

## Social capital and consultant virtualization

When we talk about social capital and consultant virtualization in the same breath, we may be concerned about contradicting ourselves. It is a combination that may appear as a paradox to some. How can consultants build social capital with clients when the consultants themselves are virtually organized and not working in physical proximity with the clients? It might seem that the basic elements of social capital that are useful for innovation, such as the building of trustworthy relationships and the flow of tacit knowledge that can be useful during exploration and creativity, will be entirely absent when the consultants do not actually share the same physical space with their client base. The interaction of these two Poles explores this in more depth.

Figure 7.3 depicts a consultancy firm high on social capital with clients while also operating in a virtually organized way.

A number of research studies have shown ways of resolving the apparent paradox of being virtually organized while building social capital. Afsarmanesh and Camarinha-Matos (2005) put forward the concept of a breeding environment for virtual organizations. These are defined as

> an association of organizations and their related supporting institutions, adhering to a base long term cooperation agreement, and adoption of common operating principles and infrastructures, with the main goal of increasing both their chances and their preparedness towards collaboration in potential Virtual Organizations.
>
> (36)

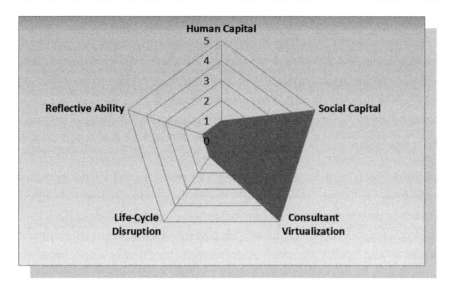

**Figure 7.3** Two-Way Interaction #3: Social Capital and Consultant Virtualization

Such a breeding environment means like-minded organizations enter into this partic-ular form of collaboration, that they are prepared for it and that a base level of trust is established from the outset. They may share the same IT infrastructure and different members may assume different roles over time. Importantly, an explicit recognition is made of the role of an 'opportunity broker' – an explicit function that identifies oppor-tunities around which new virtual organizations form. The broker is responsible for selecting members from the breeding environment in order to pursue the opportunity.

Jarle Gressgård (2011) emphasizes the need for a shared understanding in IT-enabled virtual environments where more than one organization collaborates on innovation projects without actually being in close proximity. Is this shared understanding achievable? If so, how? Afsarmanesh and Camarinha–Matos (2005) argue that it is, and that the breeding environment for like-minded organizations is needed as a starting point. Jarle Gressgård (2011) stresses the need for mutual under-standing between members of the virtual organization. Such mutual understanding is particularly useful to the question of how to access and manage the knowledge required for the innovation process as well as the establishment of a shared social context. One challenge for virtual organizations when it comes to socialization is that non-verbal cues are not easily communicated. These can be used to establish trust and psychological comfort when sharing information between team members (Gibson and Gibbs, 2006). Non-verbal cues are important in the early phases of innovation projects (Jarle Gressgård, 2011). However, Jarle Gressgård (2011) also points out that culturally diverse teams (such as those often found in international virtual environments) can form sub-groups when physically co-located and this can be detrimental to innovation performance. One conclusion is that an appropriate mix of face-to-face interactions and virtual interactions are used in order to build the social context needed to allow knowledge access and knowledge exploitation in the innovation process. Dispersed members have their own social networks *outside* of the virtual organization and these are also important as they provide tacit knowledge to support innovation *within* the virtual network.

Kirkman, Rosen, Gibson, Tesluk, and McPherson (2002) use in-depth data from the Sabre, Inc. case, an innovative technology company that developed solutions for the global travel industry, to identify challenges facing virtual teams when it comes to innovation. These authors find some key responses made by the organization to deal with those challenges, and especially the challenges arising because of a lack of face-to-face meeting opportunities. For instance, building trust can be achieved by enforcing rapid responses by teammates, by having established norms around how to communicate, and having the team leaders enforcing timeliness and consistency in communications. Isolation and detachment can be problematic for the social health of the virtual team. However, a managerial response to this can include the following: (1) selecting members based on their preference for working virtually, (2) preparing members on the issue of detachment, (3) team leaders maintaining continuous contact with remote members, and (4) having opportunities from time to time for face-to-face meetings (Kirkman, Rosen, Gibson, Tesluk and McPherson, 2002).

In sum, the interaction between social capital and consultant virtualization does not necessarily have to be a negative one when it comes to innovation. The important point in the literature is the need to harness the diversity of the virtually organized form for creativity and innovation, while at the same time having effective team leadership and management to address the pitfalls associated with limited opportunities to socialize.

In the Hongxin case we see a business model that has largely been centered around face-to-face meetings in dedicated socialization spaces in Xiamen, China. This is now being challenged to become extended across the whole of China by making use of the Internet. The early years of the Hongxin incubator had Qiang Li as the central node in the social networks; this allowed the incubator to flourish. Through his relationships with local companies that joined the incubator, he was able to advise them and oversee his advice being put into practice. The next stage in the organization's evolution (which would involve collecting information about more remote clients over the Internet and there being a certain 'distance' emerging between client and consultant) is made possible by the fact that remote clients are willing to engage in this model. To a large extent, the credibility and prior success of the Hongxin incubator allays fears or concerns that more remote clients may have. Again, we have another external factor (this time, the stage of development and credibility of the consultant in social networks) helping to overcome the potential pitfalls of building social capital through virtualization. It could be argued that it is the organization's pre-existing social capital that allowed Hongxin to 'go virtual'.

## Disruptive life-cycles and reflective ability

Let's now consider interaction amongst the organizational capital Poles. Having reflective ability while at the same time being open to disrupting the way work is carried out with clients is an intriguing combination. On the one hand, disrupting life-cycles might be seen as risky, and reflective ability allows multiple consultants to share their experiences of where they have been disruptive, whether the approach worked and why. Having a reflective ability might encourage life-cycle disruption because it allows for an awareness of how to approach disruption, and in particular how to 'sell' the idea of disrupted life-cycles to clients. Examples and cases from previous attempts at disrupting life-cycles can be shared through reflective meetings and consultants will be able to consider (and re-consider) the use of disruption over traditional approaches through reflective discussion with others who have used similar approaches in the past.

Figure 7.4 depicts a firm that puts a strong emphasis on disrupting the life-cycles of its projects with clients while at the same time being serious in terms of reflective ability.

As noted in Chapter 5, Westerman, McFarlan, and Iansiti (2006) show how contingencies in innovation projects change over time. Along with these changes, organizations need to be able to adapt the way they manage and control innovation activity. More decentralization is likely to be needed during exploration, and more centralization during exploitation. They also note how a provision should be made for learning mechanisms in innovation projects. Reflective ability is at the heart of this. It will

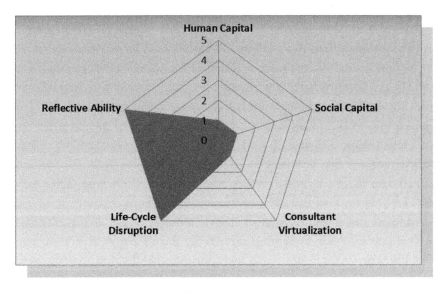

**Figure 7.4** Two-Way Interaction #4: Life-Cycle Disruption and Reflective Ability

allow project managers to decide when to change the organizational system around an innovation project, and, indeed, how to change it. Other consultants' knowledge, perhaps gained on assignment with other clients and in practice areas, will be useful and will act as a reference point when making these on-going decisions.

O'Leary and Williams (2008) describe how Centres of Excellence (CoEs) can be used to intervene directly in innovation projects as problems arise. Knowledge, expertise, and ways to solve problems are embodied in the CoE and its main function is to transfer best practice when required. Importantly, O'Leary and Williams (2008) describe this best practice transfer as a social process, not one that easily can be codified. The intervention of a CoE into a project will disrupt the way the project is carried out. It also allows all parties to stop and reflect on what has happened, and what should happen next. In the same line of thinking, Julian (2008) describes how project leaders in Project Management Offices (PMOs) have a key responsibility to make sure lessons are learned and shared across projects. As he notes: "By far the most common activity associated with learning from projects is the practice of reflecting on project experiences after a project is complete" (Julian, 2008: 44). Indeed, he notes Mezirow's (1991) definition of three types of reflection: *content* (reflecting on how ideas are applied), *process* (reflecting on procedures and assumptions in previous projects), and *premise* (uncovering the fundamental assumptions behind the project).

While this might assume lessons get learned from one project to the next in a sequential order, reflective practice can also allow lessons to be learned across live projects, thus providing impetus to disrupting some projects that take these lessons on board while they are in full swing. This could happen in content, process or premise reflection, although given our emphasis on life-cycle disruption as a way of changing the way we carry out projects with clients, we might expect cross-project process reflection to be highly salient. Lévárdy and Browning (2009) in their discussion on the Complex Adaptive Systems (CAS) view of project management argue that the organizational system surrounding product development needs to change over time. They also emphasize the role that learning plays in this. Indeed, in one of their 'motivations' (akin to propositions), they state: "Adaptability in PD [product development] projects is facilitated by advance knowledge of the potential activities and their relationships (planning) and their rules for combination (work policy), because this enables the activities to be quickly and effectively re-evaluated and reorganized over the course of a project" (Lévárdy and Browning, 2009: 605). The emphasis for us here is on the advance knowledge that is needed to reduce uncertainty related to any altered way of managing a project. This, as the authors claim, happens through systematic learning and making this a part of project management.

In this literature we see life-cycle disruption and reflective ability going hand in hand. It is not at all wise to attempt a dramatic change to the project approach without engaging in reflection first, and being supportive of ongoing reflection as any newly changed project process unfolds. We also see these themes interacting in the cases. In the Ergonomica case, for instance, a period of reflection following the loss of the main client account – which itself occurred as a result of errors within one consultant's spreadsheet – resulted in new ways of working in the company. And the shift to modular consultancy, as described by Kamales Lardi in her Practice Insight in Chapter 5, only happened after reflecting on what clients were saying they needed.

## Virtual organization and disruptive life-cycles

Having your consultants organized on a virtual basis and expecting them to disrupt life-cycles of projects with clients . . . is this even possible? In the same way that we needed to dig deeper when considering social capital with clients and consultant virtualization, we should be diligent and do the same here. We found that while social capital and consultant virtualization did not – on the surface – make sense, there are conditions under which it can be a useful combination of forms of capital for driving innovation in consultancy. With virtual organization and disruptive life-cycles we are effectively considering the situation in which consultants are not co-located with each other or with clients, that they are connected by advanced IT systems and the Internet, and they are open to challenging the way projects are run with clients, both before commencing the projects and during them.

Figure 7.5 depicts a firm that puts a strong emphasis on disrupting the life-cycles of its projects with clients while at the same time organizing on a virtual basis.

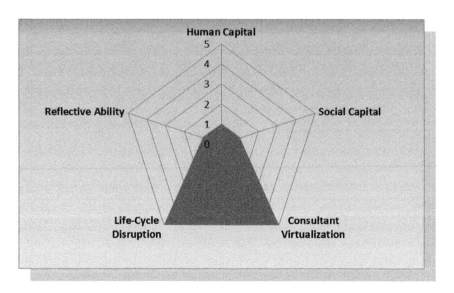

**Figure 7.5** Two-Way Interaction #5: Life-Cycle Disruption in a Virtually Organized Consultancy

As discussed in Chapter 4, one way for consultants to innovate is to organize in virtual way. This is indeed seen by some as an innovative organizational form. Nissen and Seifert (2015) point out that the decision to adopt a virtual form for a specific client need is part of the life-cycle of the sales-consulting-cycle of consultancy firms. Using insights from leading experts in the field, they derive a decision process to assist firms in making the decision on whether to adopt an organizational form based on virtualization. Importantly, this stresses the need for a business case that accounts for the benefits (savings) and the downsides (costs) of a virtual approach. Both the client and the consultant need to have input into the assessment of the benefits and risks of a virtual approach, as well as in the assessment of its overall upside. What this effectively means is that the option to use a virtual organization form for a given project with a given client is potentially a disruptive option, especially if it has not been used with the client previously. However, risks can be mitigated by having a structured approach to assessing its value, and this being driven by input from both the client and consultant side.

Bergiel, Bergiel, and Balsmeier (2008) note how virtual teams allow firms to recruit talented individuals who might not want to re-locate or travel. Such talented individuals may have the experience to know when to challenge an established way of working on a project. They will have a reference point with which to justify a change of approach for a project. Bergiel, Bergiel, and Balsmeier (2008) also note how such teams can be more creative due to their heterogeneity. This makes them more likely to come up with new ways of working for a specific project. Furst, Reeves, Rosen, and Blackburn (2004) tracked six cases of virtual teams over time, identifying the managerial interventions that kept them on course through Tuckman's (1965) phases of forming, storming, norming, and performing. In line with others that stress the potential pitfalls of virtual organization (Bergiel, Bergiel and Balsmeier, 2008; Gibson and Gibbs, 2006; Kirkman, Rosen, Gibson, Tesluk and McPherson, 2002), they find variance in terms of performance outcomes. The more successful cases had managerial interventions throughout the team's lifecycle. These included coaching from experienced team members in the formation phase, face-to-face team-building sessions in the storming phase, assigning a team coach skilled at managing virtually in the norming phase, and having a sponsor to support the team in the performing phase. For the full list of interventions, please see Table 3 in Furst, Reeves, Rosen, and Blackburn's (2004) article. What is important to note here is how these managerial interventions disrupt the way the virtual team is working over time. The team leadership needs to account for the fact that different interventions will be required and this will be dependent on the phase in the life-cycle at which the team is at.

Similarly, in Strader, Lin and Shaw's (1998) life-cycle model of virtual organization (identification-formation-operation-termination) we have an explicit focus on the birth, life, and death of the virtual team, and the fact that different information processing requirements are needed in each phase. The virtual team can expect itself to only last a certain amount of time. The key characteristic of virtuality means its life expectancy and very existence is brought into question at the outset! It is going to be constantly disrupted in terms of the types of decisions it needs to make, the information it needs to gain access to in order to make those decisions, and the external partners with which it connects in order to operate. As a result, we may expect the life-cycle of the underlying project on which the team is working also to be disrupted.

The Hongxin case shows how ambitious Qiang Li was to expand the incubator's presence across China using a virtual model. The implications of this for Hongxin itself? It would need to find a new way of interfacing with clients in locations a long way from Xiamen, where Hongxin originated. It would need to find new ways of collecting and processing information about clients, as well as building relationships with them. And the implications for clients? They would start to see Hongxin differently, in some instances interfacing with the incubator on a virtual basis. As projects progressed, and in particular if Hongxin eventually made a large-scale investment in a new client in a far-flung location, we might expect there to be an increase in socialized contact with the client and a blending of virtual communication with face-to-face interaction. So the company would disrupt the way it works with clients by allowing a multitude of ways of interacting. The chosen mechanism at any point in time depends on the importance of the client, and the phase of the project in terms of investment and restructuring. Likewise, the practice insight provided by Claire Agutter in Chapter 4 (Pole 3) on Scopism's model for eConsultancy sees virtualization and disruption working together. The consultants are spread out all over the world. They offer training and advice in defined areas to clients online, and their inclusion into Scopism was done after the vetting of their skills and profiles. Clients would be disrupted because they would no longer have an (expensive) consultant walking around their offices or factories. The client would have to organize itself in order to be in attendance at certain times in webinar or video conference facilities in order to receive the consultancy online from one of Scopism's eConsultants. This is likely to entail a change of mindset on the client's side, especially clients not used to this approach. Clients could also use a blend of traditional consultancy as well as one of Scopism's eConsultants, again putting an onus on the client to change the way he or she views, selects, and retains consultants for key projects.

## Virtual organization and human and social capital

Let's now look at important three-way interactions on our Innovation Radar. When we consider high human capital with high social capital with high consultant virtualization at the same time, we have a situation where our highly trained and experienced consultants are deeply embedded with clients, but are not physically co-located with them. Companies such as PricewaterhouseCoopers have used virtual organization for many years, for instance to "bring employees around the globe 'together' for a week or two to prepare work for a particular client" (Bell and Kozlowski, 2002: 15). Much of the previous discussion on the two-way interactions between human and social capital on the one hand, and social capital and virtualization on the other, will apply. But when we combine these constructs together, we find some interesting twists and turns in both theory and practice.

One question we may ask relates to the role that social capital has in influencing human capital (discussed earlier, see for example Bontis and Fitz-enz [2002], Florin, Lubatkin and Schulze [2003], Williams and Lee [2016], and Wu, Chang, and Chen [2008]). If the individuals are socially related only through virtual platforms, can we expect any mutual influence between social capital and human capital to apply? Will such individuals still be able to develop themselves from a human capital perspective as effectively as they would do through close physical relationships? The consultancy industry has not shied away from these issues.

Figure 7.6 schematizes a firm whose high levels of human capital are virtually organized, while at the same time having high levels of social capital with clients and others.

Bell and Kozlowski (2002) note how virtual team members are chosen because of their skills and abilities to operate effectively in a virtual form. This suggests certain types and levels of human capital are a pre-requisite to make a virtual team for a client operate effectively. But they also suggest that the maintenance and

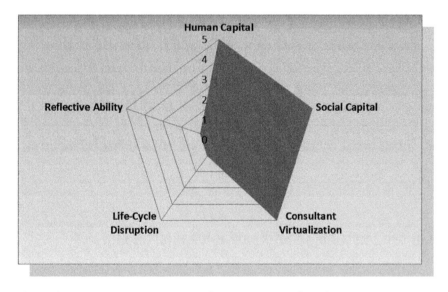

**Figure 7.6** Three-Way Interaction #1: Virtually Organized Human and Social Capital

development of skills within the team should be distributed to the team itself. Virtual teams are self-managing and should take responsibility for their own human capital development. Echoing the work of others (Bergiel, Bergiel and Balsmeier, 2008; Jünemann and Lloyd, 2003), Bell and Kozlowski (2002) shine a light on the leadership imperatives in virtual teams. Leaders should monitor how the social interactions develop over time, intervening where necessary. And they should also monitor how the human capital is utilized and developed over time, again intervening where necessary. So one answer to the question of how to combine human capital, social capital, and consultant virtualization in order to innovate in consultancy is to have strong leadership within the team. This will act to provide clear direction. It will also act to monitor and intervene where appropriate as the different forms of capital interact. So there can be a mutual influence between social and human capital in the virtual form, and the key role is for leaders to be cognizant of this link and to intervene to nurture it where necessary.

Literature also exists on the beneficial outcomes of virtual organization for human and social capital. Building on their work on virtual breeding environments, Camarinha-Matos, Afsarmanesh, Galeano, and Molina (2009) argue that a key area of motivation for organizations when considering virtual organization relates to organizational reasons, on top of market-related reasons. This is interesting because it talks to organizational benefits from pursuing virtual organization. Camarinha-Matos, Afsarmanesh, Galeano, and Molina (2009) note how a virtual breeding environment can help an organization develop its core competences and engage in learning and training. These motivations are clearly related to human capital. They also note how virtual organization can be used to build new collaborations (e.g., for concurrent engineering or scientific experiments), working with other organizations with a shared common goal, building trust and generating social contributions. These motivations are clearly related to social capital. Applying this view to the consultancy industry we would see both consultants' levels of skills and expertise as well as their social connectivity being enhanced as a direct consequence of their virtual involvement.

Martins, Gilson, and Maynard (2004) review the literature on virtual teams, decomposing the field into three main components: team inputs, team processes, and team outputs. A fourth component referred to as moderators of virtual team performance contains a set of contingency variables (including support and coaching, leadership structure, and organizational culture) that determine how characteristics of the virtual team will impact outcomes. An important aspect of Martins, Gilson, and Maynard's (2004) review is that it shows how outcomes of virtual teams have been researched not just in terms of performance. Human and social capital are conspicuous as aspects of inputs and processes to help make virtual teams effective. However, another category of outcome relates to affective outcomes including member satisfaction and also levels frustration. Member satisfaction matters; without it, members will be less willing to share knowledge and engage constructively in virtually mediated social networks. Martins, Gilson and Maynard (2004) show also how outcomes relate to behavioral outcomes. These include team creativity and learning. Again, we see a connection between a well-functioning virtual team and improved levels of human capital in terms of the ability to be creative and to learn through participating in a virtual environment.

The example of Scopism outlined in Chapter 4 (Pole 3) brings into focus a clear example of how a central coordinator and knowledge broker (namely Scopism) aims to use the human capital of highly geographically dispersed consultants to provide solutions for clients. The ability of Scopism to develop social capital with clients in advance of setting up a project where the human capital of the dispersed independent consultants can be tapped into by the client is critical. From each eConsultant's points of view, they may not have been alerted to the client opportunity – or even been aware of the existence of the client, given that the client can very well be located in a completely different country – without the social capital of Scopism in developing and nurturing client relationships prior to any sale. Once the projects have been delivered, clearly each eConsultant's level of social capital has increased. In this sense, we can see human capital as a key input to the client engagement, facilitated by the social capital provided by Scopism, but then the social capital between the eConsultants and the clients being enhanced as a consequence of the work. The eConsultants are able to innovate as a consequence of what they learn through feedback from the client engagement. Scopism facilitates innovativeness in their eConsultant network by using their social capital to connect eConsultants with clients.

## Reflective ability and human and social capital

Another example of a three-way interaction on our Innovation Radar is between human capital, social capital, and reflective ability. When we consider high human capital with high social capital with high reflective ability simultaneously, we have a situation where our highly trained and experienced consultants are deeply embedded with clients, but are putting a big emphasis on stopping to reflect on what they are learning as they are going along. From a client's point of view, the consultants are highly capable people. And they are engaged at a personal level within the client organization, possibly having a permanent desk there, and having familiar, friendly, and cooperative relationships with members from the client organization. So does it become a contradiction when these consultants frequently take time away from the client in order to all gather together (amongst themselves) to share experiences (with themselves)? The client may question the frequent reflecting: seeing the consultant 'disappear' for periods of time, perhaps wondering whether they (the client) are being used as a way for the consultant to gain and share knowledge about their (the client's) industry and organizational challenges with other 'unknown' consultants in the consultant's firm. In other words, there could be a perception of high self-orientation that undermines any long-standing trust in the client-consultant relationship (Maister, Green and Galford, 2000).

Figure 7.7 schematizes a firm whose high levels of human capital enjoy high social capital with clients but are also able to find the time and space to reflect on their experiences.

Again, the literature and case data provide some insights here. Malhotra, Smets, and Morris (2016) note how 'leverage' (the ratio of associates to partners) in a professional services firm affects innovation capacity. Associates who report to a single partner typically do so because they have knowledge and expertise (human capital) in a defined area. The partner has social capital with clients that can be used to identify and prioritize problem areas that need new solutions. And within the partner's direct reports we expect a sharing of explicit and experiential knowledge (akin to a reflective ability). Malhotra, Smets, and Morris (2016) argue that high leverage teams are good for solving routine problems while low leverage teams are better for novel, highly complex problems. In particular, the latter allows for reflective ability to take hold in a meaningful way. Swart and Kinnie (2003) highlight ways in which barriers to knowledge sharing in knowledge-intensive firms can be overcome, putting a spotlight on the role that HRM plays in this. HRM policies and practices

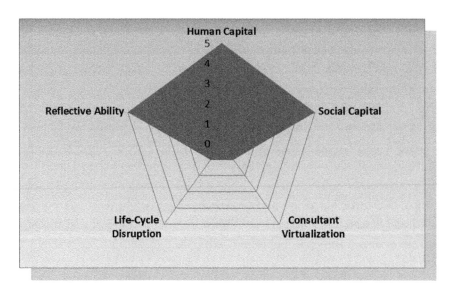

**Figure 7.7** Three-Way Interaction #2: Human and Social Capital under High Reflection

can be used to facilitate social capital within the firm. These practices include some based on the nurturing of human capital and some based on encouraging social interaction and bonding between employees in the firm. Practices useful for integrating knowledge include recruitment and selection (with a focus on prospective employees that would 'fit' with the organization), employee development (with an emphasis on learning by doing and learning across fluid boundaries), and participation (strong cultural controls to achieve social consensus). These are reinforced by a fairly homogeneous culture, social support for knowledge, and commitment to sharing knowledge. What this suggests is that the consultancy firm, through its HRM practices, is able to make reflective practice effective and efficient. It does not necessarily have to be the case that the client notices – at least not enough to make an issue out of it – the extent to which any given consultant engages in reflective practice within his or her own firm.

Mosey and Wright (2007) examine different types of academic entrepreneurs and how they form different types of social capital through their entrepreneurial activity. Those that are nascent rely on more experienced academic colleagues, and they seek to learn specifically in terms of how to recognize opportunities. More habitual entrepreneurs focus on academic colleagues, equity funders, and professional managers in their social networks, with an emphasis on learning about new technologies. Mosey and Wright's (2007) study is relevant to the question of how human capital, social capital, and reflective ability can interact in the pursuit of new innovative ideas. The level and type of human capital will determine how a network structure will form as well as the type of learning that needs to take place. Translating this to the case of a consultant embedded within a client and seeking to have time to practice reflection with his or her own colleagues could lead us to think that the draw (or the motivation) for the consultant to 'down tools' and become temporarily non-billable will be determined by (1) the consultant's own skills and experience and (2) the skills and experience possessed by other consultants that will take part in the same reflection process.

Nielsen and Nielsen (2009) examine determinants of innovation between alliance partners, showing how tacitness of knowledge has a positive impact on innovation while having a negative impact on learning. In our context, consultants' human capital will embody a high level of tacit knowledge, and it is this tacit knowledge that we would expect to be shared during reflective practice, especially when this reflection takes place in a physically co-located (i.e., meeting or workshop) setting. Nielsen and Nielsen's (2009) finding might suggest that this is a good thing as far as innovating is concerned, while we might not necessarily expect levels of learning (i.e., human capital) to increase as a result. Bringing together and sharing tacit knowledge between consultants will help them be creative and innovative. Now, what happens when we bring in social capital (with clients) into the equation? According to Nielsen and Nielsen (2009), there will be a positive interaction between knowledge tacitness and trust such that any positive relationship between knowledge tacitness and innovation will be stronger where there is a higher level of trust. Tacit knowledge – stored across the human capital of the firm – requires a verbal and social process in order to be effectively accessed (from clients and between consultants) and utilized (by consultants in a reflective practice session). While Nielsen and Nielsen's (2009) study is not about the consultancy industry per se, the central finding and theoretical assertion point us to a strong interaction between human capital, social capital, and reflective ability as a social process that will be supportive of innovation in the firm.

In the Ergonomica case we see a situation of high levels of social capital between the consultancy firm and the client. The head of Ergonomica has built a long-standing relationship with the head of the main client. As the case notes, he had become a 'trusted advisor' to the client on how to keep energy costs under control and had earned a regular and steady fee from the client over a number of years. One of the consultants was trying to build a solid relationship with the same client. Her human capital in the form of knowledge and experience in HF fluorescent lighting was an important factor. She was only one of two consultants in the company who knew how to handle and analyze complex hotel energy data. Unfortunately for her, at a critical moment in the sales process she discovered an error in her main spreadsheet. This affected the projected payback period for the client, and once corrected increased it from two years to four. Owning up to the issue could cost her reputation, her prospects for promotion, and potentially the whole account. The subsequent events in the case reveal how she informed her boss of the issue and how he reacted to the news. He brought in another consultant, the only other person in the company with the skills to analyze the type of data in question. He confirmed the error but also argued it was one that anyone could have made. The head of the consultancy firm tried to salvage the client's interest by meeting with them the next day with a revised proposal containing the new payback period. The client was not impressed and the account was eventually lost. However, he insisted on a reflective exercise and asked both the two consultants to conduct an internal audit of Ergonomica's quality assurance and control processes. The idea was that the consultancy firm could learn by its mistake. It was not the sole responsibility of one consultant. It was an opportunity for collective learning. The outcome was a revised set of quality assurance guidelines and processes and the main consultant in the case was eventually rewarded with a promotion on the back of this. A combination of social capital, human capital, and reflective ability brought about a new organizational innovation that would strengthen the company's competitive position in the long term.

## Case reflections and connecting the Poles

Let us now reflect on the four cases in this book and see if we can discern differences between them in terms of how they 'connect the Poles'. We can do this by plotting an interpretation of the position of each case on the Innovation Radar. You may also like to do this for consultancy firms or other cases you are familiar with. For each plot it is important to ask the question: how does this particular shape impact potential or actual innovation for the firm? My interpretation of the four cases is summarized in Figure 7.8. Unsurprisingly, we detect high levels of human capital and social capital across all cases – these are omnipresent features of this industry. However, we do see some subtle differences and dynamics in the three organizational capital variables.

Firstly, in the *Deloitte Dads* case, we see a very high level of human capital in the Toronto-based consultants of the firm. The firm has been ranked as a top employer and clients of the management consultancy practice are from a wide range of industries. Consultants would spend a large amount of time away from home on project assignments with clients. There was therefore also a high level of social capital. This feature of the case is also indicative of a low emphasis on consultant virtualization. In many ways, the 'traditional' model of onsite representation being pursued in the case is at the completely opposite end of the virtualization spectrum that we see at Scopism or in the Pay Zone case (Munro and Huff, 2008). Furthermore, we do not see a great deal of emphasis on life-cycle disruption in the case. Perhaps, as a traditional consultancy firm with long-standing established clients across a range

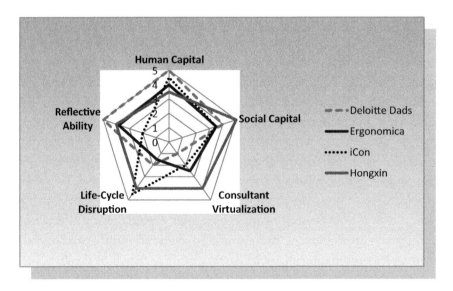

**Figure 7.8** Comparison of the Four Cases Using the Innovation Radar

of practice areas, Deloitte is not one of those companies that necessarily needs to push for continual disruption. That said, outside of this particular case, we are aware of Deloitte's work in new digital transformation practices. Where I think the *Deloitte Dads* case really stands out is in terms of reflective ability. The company has already put in place a number of diversity initiatives. It has a history of taking stock and reflecting on what it needed to do to appeal to broader community segments, including minority groups and new Canadians. The new Dads initiative then comes on the back of that heritage; there are organizational systems that kick in to allow consultants' voices to be heard. Consultants are free to be proactive and research the background to a new opportunity before presenting it to senior management in order to secure an approval to progress to an implementation phase. This phase then involved cementing the initiative and building a strong network to support working fathers within the firm. Key to the incremental innovation in this case is the combination of human capital and reflective ability that allows the firm to link new initiatives with its overall strategy (encapsulated in its scorecard criteria) as well as the needs of its employees.

Secondly, in the *Ergonomica* case, we again see high levels of human capital and social capital. The firm's head has a long-term relationship with the client and this speaks to enduring social capital. The consultant's skills and expertise in energy-saving projects speaks to human capital. We see only modest evidence of consultant virtualization. In fact, one of the reasons that the consultant is under time pressure and working on the proposal late and at night – including sending important emails to the client in the early hours – is because she has been spending a great deal of her time 'on the road' trying to sell new projects to prospective clients. This has been a face-to-face effort during the day and a virtual effort at night. The pilot program to implement energy-efficient lighting in a few of the client's hotels is also an implementation part of the project that cannot be done on a virtual basis. As a consultant overseeing the implementation, she needs to visit the various premises and see for herself how the implementation is progressing. So virtualization is moderate in this case. Life-cycle disruption does not really feature. The types of projects the consultancy firm is trying to sell and deliver are not ones that are amenable to agile or non-traditional methods. A great deal of effort will need to be spent calculating, preparing, and planning for the implementation of energy-saving upgrades to the client's asset base. Reflective ability is a little higher. Indeed, as noted already, the main role that reflective ability plays really comes in during the subsequent events. It was only *after* the revelation that the consultant had made a critical mistake in her calculations. During the main case storyline, we could be critical of the consultancy firm for not investing enough in reflective practice. Since the financial crisis, the strategic emphasis had been on sales and utilization. So, on balance, I would argue the reflective ability in this case is mixed. Key to the organizational innovation that occurred in this case is the combination of human capital, social capital, and reflective ability. Virtualization and life-cycle disruption do not matter for the type of innovation in this situation.

Thirdly, in the *iCon* case, I would argue that the firm is high in human and social capital: they are experts in the energy sector, they have a passion for the energy sector, and they are deeply embedded with their 'internal' client. I would also argue iCon is high in terms of life-cycle disruption. It is not married to one way of working with clients, and to some extent this is a legacy from its early days in information systems projects, some of which required a traditional waterfall model, and some of which required an agile, rapid application development approach. However, there is not a lot of information in the case on reflective ability and its approach to virtualization is not a strong feature of the case (note its direct investment into countries where it hopes to embed with clients). The type of innovation we see at iCon is strategic. It is attempting to re-position towards external clients, to remove its dependency on the internal client. And it is hoping to win contracts in new sectors. Clearly, human capital and social capital are important for this. And so is the ability to run projects in different ways and to be able to challenge potentially new clients on how to run projects. Virtualization could be a hindrance for this strategy, however. Trying to penetrate and win new clients in new sectors with a message that the consultants work mostly on a virtual basis might come across as a reason not to take on the consultant. There would be little by way of previous relational experience and trust with new clients. So this makes sense. The lack of evidence on reflective ability should encourage us to dig deeper into whether iCon is able to pool its considerable expertise and learn in order to innovate in the existing client base.

Finally, for the *Hongxin* case, we see a relatively high level of human capital as embodied in the key individual in the case, Qiang Li. Li has an MBA from Xiamen University and a PhD from Wuhan University of Technology. In the early and formative years of the Hongxin Incubator he was personally involved in guiding nascent entrepreneurs to a successful outcome with their businesses, as well as providing guidance in restructuring and turnaround scenarios for larger and more established clients that were facing difficulties. Li's personal human capital was of tremendous importance during those years. That said, he did not have experience in the newer industries, such as the Internet industries. The social capital Pole, however, is a considerable feature of this case. His emphasis on building personal and enduring relationships with clients, government representatives, and a wide range of stakeholders puts him in a central and influential position in his network. He is able to secure land at preferential rates, providing an incentive for clients to work with Hongxin. Indeed, the whole 'Cloud Entrepreneurship' concept has relational capital and *guanxi* at its core. In terms of life-cycle disruption, we also see a new emphasis on changing the way prospective clients engage with Hongxin. The case finishes at the point in time when Qiang Li is pushing for an expansion of his incubation and consultancy services across the whole of China. The way to realize this was to use the Internet. What this would mean in practice is that new clients would not necessarily need to meet face-to-face and there would be a new way of interacting with clients, particularly during data collection. In a country where personal ties and face-to-face meetings really matter, the new proposition is a strong disruptive force. It is also disruptive for Hongxin. They had no experience of this type of business model. Linked closely to this is the fact that consultant virtualization would also be high with the new proposal. We must, however, be careful in our assessment here. The current 'Cloud Entrepreneurship' model does not feature high on virtualization. It is the proposed new approach that would entail – somewhat suddenly – a higher level of virtualization. And in terms of reflective ability, we also see an environment in the premises in Xiamen (Exhibit 3 of this case study gives an example of one of the meeting rooms) that encourages meeting and reflective practice. Employees of Hongxin can meet together to discuss what has worked well and what has not worked so well. They can also meet with representatives from member firms in order to reflect on practice and discuss new innovative ideas. Recall that many of these firms would have had an equity stake taken in them by Hongxin, integrating the boundaries between them. Key to the strategic and radical innovation in this case is the combination of a wide range of Poles; they all seem to play their part.

## Finding the right fit and managing the right fit

What emerges from this discussion is the idea that there is an ideal fit between the different Poles and the type of innovation to be pursued by the consultancy firm. Firstly, it seems that for different types of innovation in consultancy, both human capital and social capital must be present. The skills and experience of our professional workforce matter, as does knowledge and trustworthy relationships with clients that help guide where the firm wants to head next. Then we see that, for relatively small incremental changes, such as the Deloitte Dads initiative, only one of the organizational capital Poles matters – that of reflective ability. That, in combination with human capital, is a potent mixture for driving and implementing internal organizational innovation on an incremental basis. If we move along the spectrum to Ergonomica, we also see an internal organizational innovation occurring; that of the review, design, and setting up of new quality assurance and control systems. Again, reflective ability in combination with human and social capital plays a role here. But so too does a modest amount of virtualization; recall how the consultant works remotely in the evenings, partly because she is 'forced' to be on the road in her sales efforts for clients during the day. So we see a second of the organizational capital Poles creeping into the picture as the innovation increases in its degree of impact for the consultancy firm. For more radical changes, let's consider the *iCon* case first. Here the company is seeking to penetrate new markets for the first time, to grow out of its internal consultancy past, and to take on new clients in new sectors and geographies. We see a big emphasis here on life-cycle disruption, as well as some virtualization. It is unclear whether – and how – reflective ability plays a role. Nevertheless, as the scale of the change increases, so does the number and intensity of the Poles that are relevant. And finally, arguably the most radical change program that is being proposed in the four cases is that of Hongxin, i.e., taking Qiang Li's Xiamen-based 'Cloud Entrepreneurship' across the whole of China in a short space of time and to do this using Internet technology, technology which the organization has not used in this way before. This proposal has the biggest impact on both the consultancy firm and the client base out of our four cases. And it is here we see all of the organizational capital Poles at play.

In sum, what seems to be occurring here is the notion that a high amount of human capital and social capital will always be required to innovate in consultancy, regardless of the type of innovation being pursued. We see these two forms of capital playing key roles in the incremental innovation and the more radical innovation cases. However, as the degree of radicalness increases, and by association the scale and scope of the innovative activity, the more the organizational capital Poles will be required. Furthermore, as radicalness increases, the higher the number of organizational capital Poles that are required.

We might consider this observation to be aligned with the contingency approach in organization theory. This sees the organization as an open system that is influenced by its environment (Burns and Stalker, 1961; Lawrence and Lorsch, 1967; Thompson, 1967). It asserts that the situational factors in which the firm finds itself will determine the appropriate organizational structure and managerial approach. If an optimal form is adopted and is appropriate given the environmental situation, then superior performance will follow. However, in our analysis, the consultancy firms in the cases described have put themselves in a particular situational context by embarking on a certain form of innovation. In each case, this was a deliberate strategic choice. Similarly, levels of human, social, and organizational capital are all variables that are influenced by the firm itself; they are a consequence of the historical choices made by the firm and are shaped in the future by new decisions that the firm can make. So we see an alignment between and amongst the choices made by the firm, and, while context matters, it is a much more complex context than that described in traditional contingency theory (Burns and Stalker, 1961; Lawrence and Lorsch, 1967; Thompson, 1967). So traditional contingency theory is less appropriate here as a way of explaining innovative outcomes. Instead, what we see is an internal coherence and integrity between the choices managers make for the organizational system and the goals they are trying to achieve in terms of innovation. In essence, the ways in which managers 'connect the Poles' need to be consistent with the innovative goals they have.

While this 'finding of the right fit' is an important insight, managers and leaders of consultancy firms will also be interested in the imperatives of *managing* a combination of Poles as a particular form of innovation is pursued. Clearly, the demands put on an organization such as Hongxin as a consequence of what Hongxin wants to achieve, will be greater than those imposed on Deloitte Dads as a consequence of what Deloitte wants to achieve in that case. The latter is an incremental innovation that builds on a pre-existing cultural norm for diversity initiatives and internal procedures for airing and reviewing important suggestions for change. The former is a radical innovation that aims to take the organization into new geographical areas across a country as vast and diverse as China, while requiring the organization to gain new technological knowledge and capability, as well as finding new ways of relating with clients. This is a tall order. In the latter case, pre-existing reflective ability is the key organizational enabler that links the firm's human and social capital with the purpose of the change. In the former case, it is a combination of organizational enablers that would inter-relate with human and social capital in order to achieve the change.

Managing the issue of 'connecting the Poles' therefore requires leaders of the consultancy firm to have absolute clarity about the nature of the innovation they want to pursue. Elevating to higher levels on all Poles at the same time could challenge the workforce of the firm. Highly trained employees who are embedded in relationships with clients will be asked to work more on a virtual basis, look for new ways to disrupt client projects, and engage in reflective practice *all at the same time*! This will be challenging for many people, especially when they have been entrenched in a certain way of working over a long time period. And it won't be appropriate in many situations.

Choosing the right Pole from the organizational capital group is a key consideration, especially for innovations that are less radical. Perhaps a relatively incremental innovation is put forward as the future direction of the firm. Which of the Poles should be emphasized? Clearly, leaders need to think carefully about which Poles to prioritize and change first. A clear thinking and articulation of the rationale should be made. Leaders then need to monitor outcomes in terms of employee adoption of the desired change for that Pole. If no material effect on the desired level of innovation occurs, perhaps the wrong Pole has been emphasized. Reviews and internal discussion should be used to gain opinions and input across the employee base to isolate any fault in the cause-effect logic. Leaders then are free to slide the levers on the other Poles. But caution might be needed to avoid creating the impression that leaders are acting randomly (i.e., they that don't know what they are doing!), and are simply treating the organization as an experiment. Perhaps a certain degree of experimentation is not a bad thing, as long as leaders do not elevate all five Poles to extremely high levels abruptly and at the same time. Such a move might be fun, but it would be fraught with risk and costly if the consultants that are being managed under such a regime end up becoming confused. Existing client contracts could suffer as staff try to adjust. Any radical innovation that is being sought might not materialize because staff are diverted to maintain the status quo with existing client accounts.

Despite these words of caution, the key implication of this chapter remains: it is possible to form the innovative consultancy by adjusting levels of human capital, social capital, and consultancy-specific organizational capital, and aligning these with the nature and purpose of the innovation that is required by the firm.

## Summary and learning points

In this chapter on connecting the Poles, we have seen the following:

■ How it is possible to analyze innovation in consultancy by combining any two of the Poles on our Innovation Radar – we find academic literature and case examples that shed light on how any two Poles will interact.
■ How, arguably, the biggest area of interaction found in the literature, as well as practice, is between human capital and social capital.
■ That the presence of both human capital and social capital is high in all of our case examples.
■ How we can then add any one of the organizational capital Poles into a three-way interaction with human capital and social capital to create an interesting view of innovation in consultancy.
■ That a situation in which all five Poles are elevated to high levels in a consultancy firm would present a managerial challenge to the firm and would need to be monitored and controlled carefully and appropriately.
■ How our four main cases – which each have a different type of innovative outcome ranging from incremental to radical – can be seen through different Innovation Radar profiles; the main implication of this is that every consultancy firm has a unique profile, and that these profiles are likely to change over time as managers elevate or reduce the emphasis on each Pole.
■ How a consultancy firm's overall profile on the five-Pole Innovation Radar is likely to determine the type of innovation that it would be best suited to pursuing.

# Implications of the innovative consultancy

This chapter will discuss implications of the perspective on innovation in management consultancy explored in this book. These implications are in three areas. Firstly, in terms of *ethics*, we need to ask what the innovative consultancy means in an industry that has often been highly criticized in terms of its ethical standards. Secondly, in terms of the *academic research agenda*, we need to push academics to do work that is practically relevant as well as theoretically stimulating. How can academic research and postgraduate research projects (e.g., DBA and PhD) utilize the perspective presented in this book in future work? Thirdly, what does our perspective on the innovative consultancy mean for individuals' *careers* . . . for your career? In other words, how can students and early career consultants benefit from the ideas of the book? What about senior and experienced consultants acting in a strategic and/or stewardship capacity in their firms?

## Ethics and the innovative consultancy

O'Mahoney and Markham (2013) devote a whole chapter to the topic of ethics in consultancy, and rightly so. Hodges (2017) does the same, highlighting its 'dark side'. Consultancy is an industry that has attracted a lot of attention from an ethical standpoint – much of it in the form of criticism and bad publicity. O'Mahoney and Markham (2013: 327–331) summarize the charges very neatly for us. The first charge is that *consulting advice is not value for money and it does not work*. This speaks for itself. There are sceptics out there who point to evidence indicating the money that clients spend on consultants does not get returned in terms of cost savings or other benefits. However, O'Mahoney and Markham (2013) point out how many consultancy interventions are difficult to measure and that there are also countless examples of successful projects. The second charge is that *consulting solutions are fads or 'boiler-plated' templates.* Such solutions seem popular at the time; everyone seems to be adopting them. But they soon disappear. As O'Mahoney and Markham (2013) note, the negative side of this charge is that these fads do not work. This is linked to the first charge with respect to the connection between high client spending and advice or solutions that are ineffective. The authors also point out that, while the label on a fad may go out of fashion, the underlying logic and principle may still endure. The third charge asserts that *consultants cannot be trusted.* This, clearly, is a serious charge. Critics point to the fact that some consultants want to string out contracts to gain higher fees for themselves, make problems seem worse than they are, and embed themselves so deeply inside a client organization that they become indispensable. Here the authors note how it is never in a consultant's interest to create a lack of trust with a client; too much repeat business is at stake. Finally, there is a charge that *consultants prey on the insecurities of client managers.* Client managers can be insecure, suffering from high anxiety levels because of the rapid changes in the environment around them. Consultants are able to exploit their vulnerability in this respect. However, O'Mahoney and Markham (2013) make a very important point in that managers themselves are often highly educated and able people. They have attained their senior positions because of their skills and experience; they do not need to feel insecure.

Nevertheless, these charges go to the heart of the question of ethics in consultancy. And every time a news story breaks concerning unethical behavior of consultants or poor client performance as a consequence of poor advice, this only adds fuel to the fire. In the *Ergonomica* case, we encounter a situation in which the ethical dilemma falls squarely on the shoulders of one consultant within the company. In this case it is not as if the company at large is deliberately acting in an unethical way. But a situation has arisen that makes it plausible that a consultant could knowingly lie about the basis for his or her sales pitch. An error in the analysis, if not disclosed, would mean that he or she would be misleading the client. On closer scrutiny we see that the strategy of the consultancy firm in which the consultant was employed has contributed towards this situation. No one is suggesting the consultancy firm has deliberately acted unethically. And no one is suggesting that the consultant has behaved unethically in the run-up to the point in time that she discovers the error. But, put in this type of situation, many people would be tempted to not disclose the error, brushing it under the carpet in order to secure a short-term gain for themselves. It is noteworthy that, in the *Ergonomica* case, the company was ultimately willing to change the way it operated as a consequence of the consultant's disclosure of the error. They were able to reflect and improve their internal quality control systems to avoid a repeat of the situation in the future. This was a long-term view that accepted the short-term loss of the immediate client project.

When we consider this type of situation – that unfortunately can occur all too often in consultancy – as well as the charges outlined by O'Mahoney and Markham

(2013: 327–331), we should ask the question about what the innovative consultancy really means. How can innovative efforts be orchestrated and harnessed to limit the effect of these charges and these types of situations in consultancy? One way of addressing this is to think of innovative responses as either proactive or reactive.

In a proactive sense, being innovative through the different forms of capital discussed in this book can allow a consultancy firm to identify, predict, and defend against ethical dilemmas before they occur. For the *Ergonomica* case, if the management team had the foresight and it was possible to predict the onset of the situation in which the consultant found herself, then it could identify and prepare suitable organizational responses. Such responses would reduce the chances of the situation arising in the first place. Some upfront reflective ability would clearly help here. This could be used to identify bottlenecks and risks associated with the sales process, and share knowledge internally on the difficulties of assessing the accuracy of econometric models based on complex hotel energy data. The reflective ability could be combined with human capital to assess how the rotation of expert staff could be used to help in proactive quality control and proactive audit of the analysis.

In a reactive sense, the different forms of capital discussed in this book can be harnessed in order to respond to ethical dilemmas once they have come to light. This is the actual storyline of the *Ergonomica* case. While it would have been more beneficial to have been proactive to innovate before the situation arose – and hindsight can be a great thing – the reality was that it was the reaction that led to the organizational innovation. Oftentimes it will be necessary to react to unethical situations quickly. Lingering over the issues and delaying an effective response could be damaging to a consultancy firm's reputation and undermine trust with the wider client base. To this end, consultant virtualization may play a key role. One of the benefits of consultant virtualization is the ability to set up temporary constellations of experts at short notice in order to work on urgent problems. The diverse nature of members of a dispersed virtual team could add to the creativity needed to deal with an urgent issue in the event that it unexpectedly arose.

In terms of the charges against consultancy highlighted by O'Mahoney and Markham (2013), innovation can play an important role in dampening or eliminating their effects. For the charge that *consulting advice is not value for money and it does not work*, consultancy firms can point to their innovative efforts to argue that they are continually looking for ways to make their offerings cost-effective and impactful for clients. They can point to their reflective ability as one mechanism that elevates their overall innovativeness while not being billed to clients. They can point to the creativity in their virtual networks that helps produce new offerings in the longer term while keeping costs low (as noted in the Scopism example in this book). And they can point to how they are able to disrupt the life-cycle of projects with clients in order to provide benefits for clients. Overall, they may also be able to point out that innovation comes with risks – bringing novelty into the client organization cannot always be assumed to work first time. The decision on whether – and how – to bring novelty into the client organization is one that arises through joint discussion, awareness and negotiation between the client and the consultant, and therefore the client will need to shoulder some of the blame if results are not as expected.

Similarly, with the second charge that *consulting solutions are fads or 'boiler-plated' templates*, consultancy firms will be able to argue that their innovative competence means that their solutions are quite the opposite of being fads or template-driven. They will be able to show prospective clients – as well as other bystanders and critics – how they combine human, social, and organizational capital in order to generate new approaches for themselves (i.e., far from being template-driven). They will also be able to show how they encourage and push for their clients to adopt an innovative mindset and agenda where appropriate – again, far from being followers of fashion. Their social capital with clients can be used to encourage clients to write testimonials on the innovative nature of the solutions provided in previous projects. And their human capital – perhaps articulated in the form of consultants' biographies and CVs containing prior engagements and impact, publications, social initiatives, TED talks, etc. – as evidence of how they emphasize internal human capital as a way of continually innovating. The underlying message here would be that such highly talented and experienced consultants would not want to work on fads or boiler-plated solutions – this would stand in stark contrast to their 'DNA'!

When we consider the third charge that *consultants cannot be trusted*, we also can provide some rebuttals based on the core idea in this book. Trust relates to the expectation that another party will not exploit a vulnerability (Nikolova, Möllering and Reihlen, 2015). It is a "psychological state comprising the intention to accept vulnerability based on positive expectations of the intentions of behaviour of another" (Nikolova, Möllering and Reihlen, 2015: 233). As Maister, Green, and Galford (2000) and others have argued at length, without trust we will have no client-consultant relationship. However, when a consultancy overtly demonstrates its ability to harness human capital, social capital, and organizational capital in pursuit of innovative outcomes for itself or for clients, it is putting itself in a vulnerable position. Firstly, by sharing information on its innovative work, it is giving sensitive information away on what it thinks its priorities are and why it is willing to take risks and bear the potential costs of failure of those projects. Secondly, by sharing information on how it is combining human capital, social capital, and organizational capital in pursuit of innovation, it is also putting itself in a vulnerable position. It is sharing its secrets; potentially sensitive information on how it seeks to build competitive advantage in the long term. In many respects, a consultancy firm that is not able to indicate to clients and critics what it considers to be areas for investment vis-à-vis innovation, and provide at least some clues about how it thinks it can achieve innovative outcomes, is a firm that cannot be trusted. By involving clients on innovation projects through its social capital, it will also reduce skepticism.

Finally, we have the charge that *consultants prey on the insecurities of client managers*. Again, the notion of the innovative consultancy can provide some counterpoint to this charge. One of the areas in which managers may feel insecure is in terms of how they should devote scarce or slack resources to innovation. It is difficult to think of a greater area of insecurity for managers. Of course disruptions and uncertainties abound for all managers in all organizations. But when it comes to the what, how, where, when, and why of innovating, most managers will suffer from insecurity. Does any manager want to be the one that was responsible for a high profile innovative investment that ended in humiliating disaster? While the charge is that consultants are only there to prey on these insecurities while not necessarily providing a helping hand in times of insecurity, the thrust of the innovative consultancy argument is that 'we're in this together'. No consultancy firm wants to be the one that was responsible for a high profile innovative client investment that ended in disaster either! The innovative consultancy firm is able to share the insecurity. It is able to empathize with the client. It is able to share risks with the client. And it is able to mobilize and change its constellation of capitals (human, social, organizational) in order to align with the particular insecurities of the client in order to make the client feel more secure during an innovation process.

## Research and the innovative consultancy

Academic research, both by established scholars and early career or post-graduate students, usually involves testing new – or re-testing – theoretical ideas (in a positivist paradigm) or developing new theory entirely (in a phenomenological paradigm). Sometimes academic projects involve a mix of both.

There are some new theoretical possibilities and combinations highlighted in this book that could be tested in a positivist approach. Firstly, the idea that different *interactions between human capital, social capital, and organizational capital* will have a bearing on innovation in management consultancy has been a central thrust of our story, mainly in the previous chapter. New hypotheses could be developed and tested to show which interactions matter and also how they matter (e.g., for the consultancy firm's own innovations, or for that of their clients). Data can be collected using large-scale surveys of consultants in different locations and segments of the industry. The key thrust here is on the interactions as moderating or mediating effects between the different forms of capital.

Secondly, a broader stance could be taken on the variables of interest (the independent variables) and *a structural equation model could be developed* involving multiple direct and indirect effects between the variables. Again, data for this could be gained through questionnaire surveys and tests could be carried out using structural equation modeling tools.

Thirdly, more nuanced and *fine-grained analysis of the sub-components of each form of capital* discussed in this book could be included, as well as new forms of organizational capital not included. For example, a particular focus on consultant virtualization and social capital could be made in a given study, with a spotlight on the number and distribution of the consultants in the virtual team, as well as their proclivity and experience. In this way, the forms of capital could be broken down and literature used to develop new hypotheses and conduct tests on moderating, mediating, curvilinear, or path model effects.

The ideas in this book can also create some interesting possibilities for phenomenological work that aims to develop theory. Firstly, *longitudinal case-based work* that tracks the progress of innovative projects over time would be particularly useful. This kind of approach could be used to chart the unfolding nature of an innovation project from idea generation and conception all the way through to commercialization and impact. Data could be collected on how the different forms of capital matter at different moments in time and stages during the innovation process. A dynamic theory of innovation in services could emerge from this. Also, new forms of capital, particularly different types of organizational capital specific to how consultants are managed and controlled, could be uncovered in an inductive, explorative way. The key point here is that the mapping of the organizational system that surrounds the innovative effort can be achieved and discussed vis-à-vis extant literature and theory. Along these lines, more teaching cases can also be developed. Many of the teaching cases on management consultancy firms are anonymized. Perhaps more efforts can be made for the industry to open up to case researchers and case writers. Business and management students the world over are hungry to learn about innovation and this industry. While an anonymized case is better than no case at all, it would be great to have more transparent stories. That said, we must recognize the difficulties, particularly of cases that depict individual behaviors and interactions with – and interests of – clients.

Secondly, *action research* (Kemmis and McTaggart, 2005) could be conducted in a phenomenological way. In action research, the researcher is involved as a change agent in the action process, dealing with a client problem or issue of practical concern to people (Rapoport, 1970). The individual therefore has a dual role as a consultant and as a researcher. This could be interesting for active consultants who are engaged with clients while also conducting academic research work, for instance those studying for a PhD or DBA on a part-time basis. In this instance, the consultant would adopt the role of an 'action researcher' whose goal it is to help a client. For projects based with an external client that aim to promote innovation within the client, assuming attention is paid to obtaining permissions to use insights gained for academic work, the researcher is able to provide the academic world with insight into micro-dynamics and outcomes given specific interventions. Similarly, for innovative projects within a consultancy firm, the 'action researcher' will be able to describe the nature of the interventions made, why they were necessary, and what the outcomes were.

Thirdly, there are possibilities to use *alternative participative approaches* for generating new theory on innovation in consultancy. Given the range of different forms of capital discussed in this book, and the numerous sub-dimensions and variables within each category, it could be argued that it will be inappropriate to take a positivist stance. It could be argued that the combinations are endless and the situation is too complex. One way of developing new theory in situations of high complexity, data poor situations and soft knowledge is to use Fuzzy Cognitive Mapping (FCM) (Özesmi and Özesmi, 2004). Fuzzy cognitive maps help researchers make sense of organizational phenomena by modeling variables, the links between variables, and the direction of interaction (Harary, Norman and Cartwright, 1965). They even allow feedback loops from the dependent variable (innovation) to the independent variables, and relationships between the independent variables. The strengths of the relationships between variables can be captured as part of the process (Özesmi and Özesmi, 2004). This modeling can be done in a number of ways, including through direct interaction between the consultant and the researcher (i.e., participation). Given that management consultants are generally highly educated and experienced, they should be able to understand what is required from them in the process of producing the map, including the identification of variables and why it is important to graph the links between variables and attribute strengths to them. They should also be interested in seeing feedback from the researcher in terms of an aggregated (social) cognitive map (Özesmi and Özesmi, 2004). Condensed forms of these maps account for sub-graph groupings of variables and can be produced in a form that consultants – as participants to the research process – will be able to understand and make sense of. The FCM approach could be useful therefore to encourage open debate and dialogue between researcher and consultant on the complex topic of innovation.

In both of the scenarios described (i.e., the positivist approach and the phenomenological approach), the emphasis was on collecting data from consultancy firms. However, the perspective of clients should not be ignored. The client view should also be taken into consideration by the researcher where possible. Triangulation of data can then be carried out between data from the consultant side and data collected from the client. For innovative projects in client organizations where there has been significant consultant involvement, clients will be well placed to answer questions relating to the nature and impact of the innovation itself. They will also be able to provide their perceptions on the consultancy firm's human capital as well as how social capital played out in the relationship. One pitfall of relying only on data from clients is that clients may not have an in-depth understanding of the intricacies of the organizational system within the consultancy firm. The opaque quality of professional services firms is a challenge. Clients are not always able to assess the quality of experts' output or understand where and how that expertise originated (Von Nordenflycht, 2010). In our case, they may not be able to say with any certainty how consultant virtualization or reflective ability played a role on an innovative project. Data on these will be more forthcoming from the consultancy firm side. That said, if life-cycle disruption took place during the innovative project, and the consultant was a force behind this, then the client's perception of this could be useful.

In addition to these general considerations, we may also like to think about specific research stemming from the discussion in this book that can be addressed in future work. Firstly, the main focus of this book has been on the forms of capital that can help to create the innovative consultancy. These are effectively the determinants of the innovative consultancy. We have not directly talked to the question of the consequences of the innovative consultancy. What we do know is that this is an industrial sector where innovation is needed. And we know innovation is rife within this sector. But the short-term and long-term consequences of being innovative in this sector warrant further research. A consultancy firm that is always trying to be on the edge of novelty and creating new ways of working and new offerings for clients might perform at a lower level financially compared to one that tends to prefer tried and tested ways of adding value to clients. The consequences of the innovative consultancy are not only for financial performance but also for performance in terms of corporate social responsibility, capability development, and learning (i.e., non-financial indicators of performance). These may also be considered in future work. Also, the contingencies under which an innovative stance in management consultancy influences performance outcomes for the consultancy firm and for clients is a topic worth exploring in greater depth. Secondly, we might want to think more about the different forms of innovation in management consultancy, and how different forms of capital influence different types of innovation in different settings. Management consultancy firms may innovate in terms of their service offerings, but some may also branch out into developing tangible product offerings, including IT systems and books and publications. Some innovations are internally oriented and based on changing the way the firm is organized. Others are externally oriented and focused on what is actually delivered to clients. Some may occur in traditional consultancy firms, others in internal consultancy units, or as a result of engaging with non-traditional types of consultants. Comparing across these different types of – and settings for – innovation in management consultancy can lead to new insights and implications for theory and practice. Thirdly, there are other forms of capital that we did not (and could not for space reasons) consider in this book that can have a role to play in determining innovation in management consultancy. For instance, what role does financial capital play? Innovation does not come for free. Someone somewhere will need to foot the bill for the human capital, social capital, and organizational capital (including the cost of reflective practice) needed to be innovative in this sector. While consultant virtualization might be cheaper than having co-located staff, there might also be difficulties and costs attached that need to be considered. The role of financial capital in enabling the different forms of capital to be applied in different ways at different times can be investigated. And what about natural capital (Costanza, d'Arge, de Groot, Farber, Grasso, Hannon, Limburg, Naeem, O'Neill, Paruelo, Raskin, Sutton and van den Belt, 1997)? In a world where climate change, environmental degradation, and natural ecosystems are important concerns for organizations, one might ask some probing questions about the role of innovative consultants in providing solutions that have a positive impact on the natural world.

## Careers and the innovative consultancy

From a career perspective, the professional services sector at large was traditionally characterized by the 'up-or-out' paradigm pioneered by McKinsey & Company (Jones and Lefort, 2005). In the up-or-out model, more junior professionals compete for promotion in a 'tournament'. The main evaluation criterion was utilization (billable hours), although other factors also play a role depending on the management style in a given firm. Overall, the up-or-out model dictated that, should an associate not fulfil the criteria for promotion, then he or she would be encouraged to leave the firm to find a new employer.

One main criticism of the up-or-out model is that the intensity of internal tournament competition puts pressure on young consultants. It affects their work-life balance by encouraging them to spend all the hours in the day (and sometimes night) working on selling and delivering to clients. However, attitudes to work-life balance have changed over the years (Malhotra, Smets and Morris, 2016), particularly amongst Generation Y (the Millennials). Questions have been raised about whether performance at work comes at the expense of work-life balance, or whether it can be achieved while enjoying a work-life balance (Bloom, Kretschmer and Van Reenan, 2009). Citing numerous studies from the management literature, Bloom, Kretschmer, and Van Reenan (2009) note that work-life balance policies have been found to have a positive effect on workplace performance. However, they argue that these findings in the literature suffer from an omitted variable bias and that it is management quality (a measure of 'good' management) that correlates highly both with work-life balance in a firm and performance. Work-life balance would mean that the employer is sympathetic to flexible working, working from home, family-friendly policies, and the like. But we need to think more carefully about the drivers of work-life balance in the managerial approach used by the firm and how this may actually account for the firm's performance.

What this debate in the literature highlights is that the nature of work in management consultancy has changed, as has the nature of the organizations themselves. The up-or-out model may persist in many consultancy firms, but there will be others that do not use it or use it less extensively, offering alternative ways of giving people career fulfilment while allowing them to contribute to the goals of the organization. The levels of diversity in management consultancy firms have also undergone change. Tomenendal and Boyoglu (2014) note large gender imbalances at the higher levels of management consultancy firms. Indeed, in certain European countries, the share of female partners in firms like McKinsey & Company, BCG, and Bain & Co. was less than 10 per cent (Tomenendal and Boyoglu, 2014). However, for companies like Accenture, the ratio was higher: Accenture reported 36 per cent of its independent board members to be women. It also reported 29 per cent of its executive level managers and 45 per cent of its new hires in 2017 to be female (Accenture, 2017). The *Deloitte Dads* case (Konrad and Shuh, 2013) also illustrates how management consultancy firms listen to both genders of parents and how they allow work-life balance initiatives to be conceived and implemented.

In terms of the links between work-life balance, diversity and 'good' management practice on the one hand, and innovation on the other hand, Malhotra, Smets, and Morris (2016) find that there is a positive link. The introduction of a career path model that differs from the up-or-out approach will mean that the transition between exploration and exploitation (and back again) during the innovation process will be more seamless and efficient. They point to a negative side of the up-or-out model in terms of sharing knowledge, prioritizing work, and bundling knowledge under partner-led practices. Having alternative roles that are under the partner level but which nevertheless give employees a sense of career progression and fulfilment are good for innovation: they allow ambidextrous capabilities of exploitation and exploration to coalesce. In one sense this echoes Bloom, Kretschmer, and Van Reenan's (2009) finding that it is 'good' management that is responsible for both work-life balance policy and outcomes. The installation of an alternative career path system may be seen as an organizational innovation in its own right. The mentality and willingness of the leadership team to do this will also rub off in terms of other types of innovative outcomes.

This backdrop is important as we consider careers in the innovative consultancy, hopefully, your career as an innovative consultant. If an individual wants to enter the management consultancy industry or move within the industry, and is looking to work for an innovative consultancy, it will be necessary to look at the fundamental make-up of the organization in terms of its diversity policies, its work-life balance policies and how it promotes people. These will be indicators of the mindset of those who run the firm – the management quality in Bloom, Kretschmer, and Van Reenan's (2009) terms – that will determine not only the proclivity of the firm towards innovating, but also whether the firm intends to incentivize innovation and provide a creative and diverse environment for working in that does not hinder innovation.

Furthermore, the various forms of capital we have discussed in this book also have a bearing on how careers will progress. New recruits and those contemplating new positions can look at the various forms of capital that are in use and evident in the firm or unit that they are targeting. Levels of human capital will say something about whether the individual will 'fit' in the target firm or unit. A relatively lower level of human capital may make the individual seem like a big fish in a small pond. A relatively higher level of human capital will imply a stretch in terms of knowledge and skills. This stretch can be an incentive to move; it offers an opportunity to gain new knowledge and develop new skills, hopefully ones that will be useful in future innovation projects. The extent to which the new firm or unit has deep, embedded social relationships with clients will also be a good question to ask, as will the question of how those ties influence innovative outcomes. Moving into a new firm or unit that has strong ties with long-standing clients may be a good thing if the individual wants to work in those client accounts. On the other hand, perhaps the individual is interested in spearheading new project work with new clients. The point is the pre-existing social capital of the target firm or unit is something that should be understood; it can have a bearing on whether the individual will stand to gain by working in that firm or unit. And the different aspects of organizational capital will also have a role to play. We have discussed how these can lead to innovative outcomes for consultancy firms and clients. Examining the type and forms of organizational capital at play in a prospective future employer or different unit within an existing firm will help an individual understand how the organization works and how it may use organizational capital in order to promote innovation. Again, should the individual value an innovative environment and actively seek an innovative environment to work in, these factors will be important to understand.

We should also think about the size and structure of the consultancy firm or unit which we are targeting for a career move. Individuals need to find the right fit in any career move. Larger and older firms like Deloitte are likely to have established systems and processes for handling innovation projects and innovative initiatives. Smaller, boutique consultancies – which have been growing in number and often have a unique and fresh image – may still be in a growth phase and what may be lacking in terms of formal systems and processes might be made up for in terms of culture and social control.

We also see different forms of management consultancy in the modern era. Internal consultancy units like the *iCon* case in this book may be in transition and seeking to absorb or adopt some of the standard industry-wide ways of working as they grow away from their main internal client. They may, however, be tightly embedded with their internal client and wish to stay in that structure. These imperatives and strategic intentions will be important to understand so that any career move does not end in disappointment. Similarly, other types of organizations such as the Hongxin entrepreneur incubator in Xiamen may offer great benefits in terms of work-life balance and fulfil all the career needs of someone wishing to be engaged in turnarounds and implementation of strategic and operational advice in client firms. But organizations like this are not one of the 'traditional' Western consultancy firms. Perhaps the substance and content of the role is more important to a career-progressing individual than having a famous global name on the CV.

Another important point is that large consultancy firms are mostly divided up into discrete practice areas (Anand, Gardner and Morris, 2007; Christensen, Wang and Van Bever, 2013). Such practice areas are centers for knowledge and identity. Individuals will need to consider the specific practice area they are targeting and why. Management control systems can differ across practices. So it is not only a question of how a particular firm runs things, it is also a question of what happens in the given practice.

We made the point in the opening section of this book that not all innovators are consultants, and not all consultants are innovators. For someone entering the consultancy industry for the first time, it will be worth reflecting on the types of innovation projects they have worked on in the past and to identify transferable skills and knowledge that can be applied – and valued – in the new consultancy setting. Consultancy firms should not need to be reminded of why innovation matters in their sector. But at a minimum, a gentle nudge during the application and interview process could be useful. For people who have been in consultancy in the past and are looking to make a shift within the same industry, a self-reflection along the lines of experience and capabilities in innovation projects is worthwhile. Not all consultants are innovators. It may be the case that prior skillsets and experience gained on projects have been highly standardized and routinized. An emphasis – through no fault of the consultant – might have been on exploitation rather than exploration. For an entry into a highly innovative consultancy firm or unit, it will be useful to reflect on this as a potential weak spot and to find ways of addressing it during the application and interview process. One way is to identify how exploitative forms of innovation took place within standardized and routinized projects. After all, scholars have noted how innovation can come about in this form (Wright,

Sturdy and Wylie, 2012). Another way is to identify the experience gained in the various forms of capital and show how these will be transferable to more explorative innovation environments with any new employer or unit within the existing firm. Ultimately, the various forms of capital discussed in this book are more than ways in which consultancy firms as a whole may innovative; they are also domains in which individuals can grow and develop in order to make an innovative impact in their career journey in the future.

# 9 Concluding remarks

## A capital problem . . .

At the outset of this book we asked a simple question: *What makes some consultancy firms more innovative than others?* We noted that the management consultancy sector – as well as the broader professional services industry of which it is a part – *is* innovative. It is a hugely influential sector that is in demand the world over. It does, from time to time, come up with grand innovations in its own space that shape the way the industry operates for decades to come. And it comes up with smaller and incremental innovations all the time too. Many are not visible to outsiders, and they may not be patented. But they are there in no small volume with clients all over the world feeling their effect. Innovations in this large and complex industry are broad and diverse. They can be categorized in multiple ways: innovating for clients vs. innovating for the consultancy firm, innovating in the product or service offering sense vs. innovating in the process sense, and explorative innovation vs. exploitative innovation.

The question does not really find a clear answer in extant literature. Many of the textbooks on management consultancy do not cover the topic of innovation in any depth. Much of the academic literature on innovation does not talk specifically about the unique situation of management consultancy. However, there are some notable examples where consultancy firms have been used to study innovation and these studies are very interesting and insightful. But – by and large – they are too few and far between in my opinion. And there is no single, over-arching theory that explains innovativeness or innovation in an industry containing firms that are led, managed, operated, and (sometimes) owned by management consultants!

We see blurriness in field of management consultancy too. It is an industry that is not formally regulated (in the same way law or accounting are). Who has the right to offer managerial advice that has the potential to be innovative and where does this advice come from? The *iCon* case illustrates that, for one large energy company in Germany, an important source is an Internal Consultancy Unit. The *Hongxin* case shows that, for small-scale entrepreneurs and large-scale industrial firms needing turnaround in China, an important source is an entrepreneurial incubator. The practice insight into the HIV/AIDS awareness campaign in Nigeria (Chapter 3) shows that an advisor from a bank can be involved to help formulate and execute the new idea. So it is not just about the bigger and older traditional firms in the developed world.

Perhaps these features of blurriness, diversity, and complexity provide a clue as to why not enough scholarly attention has been paid to innovation in management consultancy. Maybe it is a fundamental, organized human function that cannot be delineated in a traditional industrial classification sense. Maybe it has been so opaque, aloof, distant, and special that many academics are put off. Hard data may be easier to obtain in other settings.

## . . . needs a capital solution

Our approach for understanding what makes some consultancy firms more innovative than others has been to use a capital approach, depicted visually by the Poles of an Innovation Radar. There are rich and substantial literatures on human capital, social capital, and organizational capital, and these provide useful theories as we seek to explain variance in innovation in consultancy. These literatures also contain instances of empirical fieldwork conducted in professional services and consultancy settings that guide our thinking. The human and social capital logics may be self-evident to many. It's all about our people. It's all about our relationships with clients . . . and others. But what we see when we delve into these literatures are many nuances and strands of thinking that encourage us to stop and think more carefully. We then continue with the organizational capital angle. There are various organizing principles and decisions to be made about how we do things in the consultancy sector that influence innovation. It's all about working from anywhere. It's all about how we execute client projects. It's all about taking stock. We then consider the possibility of interaction between the various forms of capital and here we find more evidence in the literature for how combinations of capital can determine innovativeness in management consultancy.

Finally, we have the stories as told through the cases. These all have elements of human capital *and* social capital *and* organizational capital. The four main cases can be laid out in a spectrum of least innovative (*Deloitte Dads*) to most innovative (*Hongxin*). While they are all innovative stories at a base level, they are innovative in different ways and with different degrees of impact for the firms involved. What we see when we line up the different forms of capital for these cases is that human and social capital is prevalent in all of them. However, the intensity and the constellation of different types of organizational capital vary across the cases.

Consultancy firms can and do manage these forms of capital. They have managerial control over them. They are able to influence the intensity of these capitals and how they interact. If managers of consultancy firms can only be aware of how the interactions between these forms of capital will impact innovative outcomes, then they will be able to use them at the right times and for the right reasons. With any luck, some of the innovative outcomes that emerge will then form a new basis for staying ahead of the pack in the fascinating and intriguing world of management consultancy.

# APPENDIX: CASES OF INNOVATIVE CONSULTANCIES

1 Deloitte Dads
2 Ergonomica
3 iCon (innogy Consulting)
4 Hongxin Cloud Entrepreneurship

**Ivey** | Publishing

9B13C046

## DELOITTE CONSULTING GTA: THE DELOITTE DADS INITIATIVE

*Amy Shuh wrote this case under the supervision of Professor Alison Konrad solely to provide material for class discussion. The authors do not intend to illustrate either effective or ineffective handling of a managerial situation. The authors may have disguised certain names and other identifying information to protect confidentiality.*

It was the first week of June 2013, and 29-year-old Andrew Hamer, recently promoted manager in the corporate strategy consulting group of Deloitte (Canada) LLP (Deloitte), was admiring the headline on that week's cover of *Bloomberg Businessweek* magazine: "Lean Out, Working Dads Want Family Time, Too." ("Lean Out" is a reference to Facebook Chief Operating Officer Sheryl Sandberg's 2012 feminist manifesto *Lean In*.) Hamer himself was central to the cover story, with the group he founded, Deloitte Dads, the main topic of discussion. He wondered whether this positive press coverage would help further the goals and strategy of his initiative and how he could maintain the momentum for Deloitte Dads, which had approximately 130 members across the company's management consulting practice in the Greater Toronto Area (GTA). Hamer knew his time was restricted, the common paradox for parents juggling priorities. He wanted to maintain his high level of performance at the firm, work on the Deloitte Dads program and still balance life as a father of two young children. What was he going to do?

## DELOITTE (CANADA) LLP

Deloitte employs over 8,000 people in 56 locations across Canada. It is a legally separate and independent member firm of the Deloitte Touche Tohmatsu Limited global network of member firms, one of the largest of the Big Four[1] firms in terms of number of employees and total revenues. Deloitte's service arm included practices in assurance and audit, consultancy, enterprise risk, tax and financial advising. The management consulting practice was further divided into three groups: human capital, strategy and operations and technology. Deloitte's consulting practice included clients in industries ranging from government, financial services, consumer products, health care, media and communications and energy and resources. The firm had consistently been ranked as a top employer.

Life at work in any management consulting firm was widely regarded as a rigorous career choice for business school graduates. Firms invested a great deal of time acquiring and securing project contracts of varying lengths from clients. Often a consultant at the staff level would be required to work at the client site, resulting in a large amount of time spent travelling and on the road. A typical week for a travelling consultant would consist of flying to a client site late Sunday evening or Monday morning, working on site until Thursday and returning to home office to work on Friday. Key skill requirements for those working in the management consulting industry included proficiency at working in teams, analytical competency, aptitude in "thinking outside of the box" and the ability to multi-task differing priorities. Additionally, 70- to 80-hour workweeks were a norm within the industry as clients expected consultants to fulfill their expectations within tight work deadlines.

### Deloitte's diversity initiatives

In 2013, Deloitte's diversity initiatives included developing women in business, supporting new Canadians and encouraging the development of "People Networks" to give employees the opportunity to connect with others on similar issues and values. With a core focus on integrating diversity in the workplace, Deloitte's Chief Diversity Officer Jane Allen led the firm-sanctioned initiatives. In 2012, 38 per cent of new partners were women or visible minorities, and 23 per cent of the leaders were women. Additionally, as a part of their performance review, employees were asked to incorporate "giving back" to the community in some way as an important facet within their career development goals.[2]

### Andrew Hamer

Andrew Hamer, an Ivey Business School Honours Business Administration (HBA) graduate in 2006, began working at Deloitte in the GTA consulting office as a consultant in 2010 after four years at a boutique consulting firm in Toronto. He was promoted to senior consultant in 2011 and to manager in 2013. At Deloitte, Hamer worked with global banks and global wealth managers in areas including distribution strategy, growth strategy, acquisition target due diligence and mobile technology strategy.

On May 24, 2010, Hamer's wife Danielle Hamer announced that she was pregnant. Although overjoyed with news of the upcoming birth of his first child, Hamer was concerned that being a father would impact on his career and that focusing on his career would affect his impending duties as a father. "How am I going to be on a plane three to four nights a week with a pregnant wife at home?," he wondered. Becoming a parent meant Hamer would be in the minority at his level in the firm. Many of the other parents within the GTA consulting practice at Deloitte were at higher positions. In an effort to calm his nerves, Hamer turned to his trusted senior manager, Rob Galaski, for advice.

"Is there any way you could make this advantageous to your career?," was the question Galaski asked. Their conversation quickly turned into a brainstorming session. With the Career Moms network already in place, Galaski suggested that Hamer develop a parallel organization for fathers. Career Moms had been successful in expanding beyond the GTA to include four chapters across Canada. Galaski emphasized the fact that due to Hamer's position at the consultant level within the organization, it would be ideal to launch the program as a grassroots initiative. Hamer knew he wanted to be a top 10 decile performer at the firm – but not at the cost of his family. Perhaps this would be his opportunity to lead the way for fathers at the firm with the same goals in mind.

### THE INITIAL IDEA FOR THE DELOITTE DADS

After reaching out to Alison Weyland and Anushka Grant, the co-founders of Deloitte's Career Moms, and studying the preparatory materials and process they developed to launch their initiative, Hamer became more focused in his own efforts to launch

Deloitte Dads. As a management consultant, he knew that in order to build momentum for the project, it would be best to acquire market research regarding fathers balancing careers and family life and to present this data in a concise PowerPoint presentation (as any good consultant would do). He hoped that through this initial development of his pitch he could address the questions: Why? Who? What? and How?

## Why?

Hamer knew that he had to prove an inherent need for the program. He wanted to show that fathers needed their own inclusion and diversity group for support and advice. This group had to be distinctly separate from other parenting initiatives already in place at the firm. Hamer did feel that there was paternal support already embedded informally within the culture at the firm. For newcomers to the firm who weren't yet assimilated into the culture, however, a more formally structured support system would be beneficial.

The research and data also spoke volumes in terms of career-driven men and their desire to be great parents. In 2010, British Prime Minister David Cameron took a paternal leave, indicating a cultural shift in the thinking of career fathers balancing parenting and work. U.S. President Barack Obama was also quoted with saying, on Father's Day in 2009, "I know I have been an imperfect father. I know I have made mistakes. I have lost count of all the times, over the years, when the demands of work have taken me from the duties of fatherhood."[3] Additionally, 60 per cent of working men polled in 2008 believed that they were experiencing a work/life conflict, compared to 48 per cent of working mothers.[4] Hamer believed that this data demonstrated an opportunity for Deloitte to evolve as a firm and offer support for those whom the data showed needed and wanted it the most.

## Who?

The initiative would be directly targeted towards fathers working in Deloitte's management consulting practice in the GTA. This would include expecting fathers, new fathers and seasoned fathers who were married to professionals, single or with partners not in the workforce. With lack of a human resources database to quantify or to keep track of the number of fathers in the practice, Hamer wasn't able to determine initially how large a reach the organization would have. Therefore, he left the target audience broad.

## What?

Hamer's initial idea for the group was to hold one event per quarter across four different categories including fun, education, philanthropy and advancing the mission of supporting working fathers within the firm.

## How

The initiative would be aligned with the four quadrants of Deloitte's scorecard, which included:

1 Quality: "One Deloitte, One Person"
2 Talent: "High Performance and Career-Life Fit"
3 Marketplace: "Living the Deloitte Brand"
4 Financial: "Well-coached Players Win"

Hamer would need to get buy-in from senior leadership; he also knew he would have to build a team willing to work on the initiative on top of their already demanding workloads.

## PITCHING THE IDEA TO SENIOR LEADERSHIP

With the tagline "The Fraternity of Paternity," Hamer pitched his idea for the Deloitte Dads group to senior management. With no formal group yet established, he knew it would be crucial to get senior leadership buy-in before he could coordinate the remaining strategies for the group. With his pitch perfected, his "ask" included three main features:

1 Overall feedback on the initiative: Did senior management believe this was a valuable initiative? Did they have any suggestions on how to improve the proposal? Who else should he seek feedback from?
2 The commitment: Were they willing to be an executive sponsor of the initiative? Could they help gain broader levels of management's commitment for the Deloitte Dads initiative? Could they help put the governance in place required to make the initiative work?
3 The funding: A budget in order to plan events, guest speakers and develop a resource library.[5]

## THE INITIAL REACTIONS

### Rob Lanoue, Partner, Monitor Deloitte

In 2007, Lanoue was asked to sit on the board for Deloitte's Career Moms in its early development stage. Through that experience, he knew that many people in his group appreciated the network for mothers but saw a need for a similar but separate organization for fathers. Therefore, he became an early advocate of the Deloitte Dads initiative. He also felt comfortable giving support based on the fact that Hamer was taking the lead. In Lanoue's opinion, Hamer was a go-getter and had performed well at the firm to that point in time.

### Tim Christmann, Managing Partner, GTA Consulting

Christmann believed that there was already a large focus on inclusion and diversity at the firm; however, to have a group that focused on a segment that hadn't received a lot of attention historically (see Exhibit 1) appealed to him. He believed that the Deloitte Dads group was a good reminder of initiatives that addressed segments of the population generally believed to be "just fine" and that diversity could come in many different ways and not necessarily through traditional aspects. It was also a positive sign that men were coming forward to support other men, something that they may not have been comfortable doing previously. It was a sign of a new generation of leaders feeling empowered to make a difference and take on challenges.

The grassroots nature of the program was also important for Christmann in his decision to be a leader in sponsoring the program. He felt that people had a greater interest in the development of the program at the staff level and would be more passionate about advancing the cause.

### Stephen Cryer, Partner, Monitor Deloitte

As his performance coach, Cryer had heard early on of Hamer's desire to launch Deloitte Dads. He challenged Hamer on his plan and was a critical questioner of the initiative, asking "What is this, some sort of club?" For Cryer, Deloitte Dads was a complete paradigm shift in thinking about the culture at the firm. He had begun working at Deloitte in the consultant role 18 years earlier. At the time of his career launch, the face time environment was the organizational norm. This meant showing up to work early and leaving late, and those who did were rewarded for doing so. In the consulting business, managers and partners picked staff for their client teams. How could Cryer justify picking someone who left work earlier versus the employee who was in the office all day long and made working his or her number one priority? Cryer was supportive of the concept of a more inclusive work environment that itself enhanced Deloitte's performance culture. What he wanted to avoid was a "club" that paid lip service to the topic but had no accountability to improve the firm's culture. As a result, Hamer had work to do in order to convince Cryer that the program made sense for the current generation of practitioners and for the firm.

### THE LAUNCH

After receiving top-level buy-in and sponsorship, Hamer realized that the group had become "top heavy" and reached out to fellow practitioners to become executive members of Deloitte Dads. Although the majority of fathers in the firm were in higher roles than himself, he successfully attracted Daniel Beach

(Schulich MBA) and Alan Hale (Ivey HBA/MBA) to join his team, which effectively became a stretch opportunity for him as he was able to take a leadership role with others senior to him in the firm. Now with the partner sponsorship, an approved budget and an executive team of three (including Hamer himself), it was time to build a network base. The team created a pamphlet and communication plan to solicit participation for the kickoff event (see Exhibit 2).

Planned for September 2010, this event was a way to build awareness and a membership base and to introduce the idea of Deloitte Dads within the consulting practice. Hamer wondered how he could best position the launch as a way to get people interested. Given the fact that most staff were already working an average of 60 hours per week, holding the event after work hours would not be appropriate as it would go against the main goal of the organization – helping fathers succeed at work and at home. Instead, a lunchtime slot on a Friday afternoon was booked, with an incentive of the chance to win a $100 Visa gift card. The result of the launch event was positive in Hamer's opinion, as it not only drew young fathers in the consulting practice as attendees but also older fathers, men not fathers yet and women.

## DEVELOPMENT OF DELOITTE DADS

Four elements that Deloitte Dads tried to continue through its initial phases included:

1  A firm-sponsored employee program,
2  A mentorship network,
3  Straight talk resources, and
4  A support system.

The launch was followed by events such as a "fireside chat" in November, which gave staff-level consultants the chance to chat with partners in a candid environment on the challenges of being a father and a top performer at the firm.

## FEEDBACK AFTER FIRST YEAR

Lanoue believed that the evolution of paternity benefits aligned with the purpose of Deloitte Dads. When he started at the firm 15 years earlier, three days off for paternity leave was the norm. However, Deloitte's policy evolved to include paternity leave for six weeks that could be taken over a six-month period after the birth of the child (as mandated by Canadian law). Not only did the development of the policy make a clear impact on the firm, but it was also the start of a change in culture for fathers to believe it would be acceptable for them to take advantage of the benefits available to them. Since Deloitte Dads began, fathers were taking the full six-week benefit. Looking back on the impact of Deloitte Dads after the first year, Lanoue stated: "Deloitte Dads is another evolution in the way the firm is trying to manage talent. In professional services, our business is our people. You will be a better firm if you are able to find ways to help them manage flexibility in their lives. Who knows, this might become a service line!"

The launch of Deloitte Dads showed that the firm was forward thinking and that innovation was bred within its culture. The positive press the initiative received was especially helpful for the company in the recruiting process for new talent, considering this people-based market. Whether it was with clients, potential new recruits or charitable organizations, connections built within the marketplace were an important aspect of Deloitte Dads. Additionally, connections with clients on a personal level, by living through shared values and building bonds, were essential to the success of the consulting practice as a whole.

Deloitte Dads was also the cause for heightened awareness in the firm regarding work/life balance. The cultural shift noticed by Lanoue and Cryer was around flexibility in the workplace and replacing work/life balance with the term flexibility. According to Cryer, the real question was: How much of your time do you owe to Deloitte? "Can we discriminate against staff who want to leave at 5 p.m. to play softball with friends versus the father who has to pick his child up from daycare?" Cryer asked. Did it really matter to the firm what a person did when the work was finished? For Cryer, Deloitte Dads led the way for the leadership in the firm to say it's okay to set boundaries around work time, regardless of the reason. However, it was also necessary to institute flexibility and substitution so that the consulting team could arrange alternatives to continue to meet client deadlines. Instead of always picking the staff that may work the longest hours onsite, Cryer's mindset shifted to building a team based on matching people's priorities and expectations, building a collaborative team best suited to meet commitments and timelines. "It's the 'abandon ship mentality' that doesn't work, but if you manage expectations and coordinate, it can be successful," he stated. However, he felt that after its first year the goals of the Deloitte Dads program needed to be articulated more effectively. Was it started to change the culture, to change the work environment or to change Deloitte's operating model? Additionally, how did Deloitte Dads integrate into the other diversity initiatives already in place at the firm? Hamer had this to consider in his future plans for the organization.

Discussions of flexibility were starting to come through more frequently within staff performance evaluations. However, within Deloitte's performance management practices, providing flexibility was not integrated into the evaluation process. How could performance be compared between individuals who worked from early to late with those who sought to work flexibly in order to be present for their families, friends or community activities? Would face time always be a factor, albeit unstated, when appraising employees? How could Deloitte expect staff members to be comfortable using flexibility options if that meant sacrificing incentives on a human resources level? How could Deloitte become more understanding to the changing needs of becoming a leader and providing those with leadership potential to become adaptable, versatile and effective in a dynamic environment?

For Managing Partner Christmann, the initial success of Deloitte Dads in the GTA could be attributed to how the idea was received at the staff level and that it wasn't driven from a top-down approach. However, despite the positive feedback Hamer received about Deloitte Dads, two of his founding executives on the team had left the firm by early 2013. Was this a matter of Deloitte Dads failing in its initiatives and not being able to help fathers achieve their career and home goals, or was this just a nature of the consulting business?

## THE FUTURE FOR DELOITTE DADS

Hamer had many questions regarding the future of the Deloitte Dads program. His concerns included:

- How could it be ensured that Deloitte Dads was not just a phase and instead became embedded long-term in the culture of the consulting practice at the firm? Was this a realistic goal? How could this metric possibly be measured?
- Could Deloitte Dads be rolled out into other Deloitte service lines, which included audit and assurance, tax and advisory?
- Should human resources take the lead for this initiative in order to take the workload off Hamer and his team?
- Could this initiative be scaled in order for an eventual rollout in other Deloitte practices across the country and/or around the world? (Interest from Deloitte's China and Japan offices had already been noted.)
- How could Deloitte Dads be integrated with the firm's other diversity initiatives?
- How could the flexibility advocated by Deloitte Dads be integrated into discussions of performance management?
- Could the program join with Career Moms to create one "Deloitte Parents" program?

After becoming a little jaded with all the media attention, Hamer admittedly became tired of people patting him on the back for helping fathers do what mothers have been doing. He wanted to do more with the network – he had the initial success and had received a lot of attention, but what had he really done? Hamer had mastered the quarterly events within the GTA consulting practice office, but how could he create a formal governance model? Already working 80 to 90 hours per week, with no end in sight, how was he going to make Deloitte Dads sustainable and successful?

## Notes

1 The big four professional services firms were Deloitte, Ernst & Young, PricewaterhouseCoopers and KPMG.

2  Company website. www.deloitte.com/view/en_CA/ca/about-Deloitte/diversity/index.htm, accessed September 28, 2013.

3  www.parade.com/104895/presidentbarackobama/barack-obama-we-need-fathers-to-step-up/, accessed September 30, 2013.

4  www.businessweek.com/articles/2013-05-30/alpha-dads-men-get-serious-about-work-life-balance, accessed September 30, 2013

5  Andrew Hamer, "Deloitte Dads Initiative: The Fraternity of Paternity," 2010.

## EXHIBIT 1  DELOITTE CANADA'S DIVERSITY ANNUAL REPORT WEBPAGE

# Our journey to inclusion

### Deloitte's annual Diversity report for 2013

Since developing our diversity strategy, we have made significant inroads on the journey to making our firm more inclusive. Our leadership numbers certainly attest to the fact that we are making progress:

- over the past two years, close to half of new leadership appointments were women or visible minorities
- 25% of our Board of Directors are women
- 23% of our Canadian Executive and Extended Leadership Team are women
- Two of our five service lines are led by women.

**⤓ Download**

In 2012/2013 the following initiatives internally and externally contributed to our reputation as a diversity leader. Here are just a few of those activities.

- We partnered with **The Humphrey Group** to co-develop a unique, learning program called **Proud to lead** which develops the leadership capabilities of our Lesbian, Gay, Bisexual, Transgendered, Queer (LGBTQ) employees.
- We launched our third annual Dialogue on Diversity report entitled **Widening the circle: Increasing opportunities for Aboriginal people in the workforce.**
- In partnership with Carleton University's Centre for Women in Politics & Public Leadership, we published a benchmark study of women's leadership entitled **Progress in Inches, Miles to Go.**

We also revamped our Diversity and Inclusion Strategy and included bold innovative steps to make diversity and inclusion a way of life at Deloitte. Our renewed strategy will set us on a course to realize the benefits of a truly inclusive workplace.

*Source*:  www.deloitte.com/view/en_CA/ca/about-Deloitte/diversity/b8aaf6f1cce61410VgnVCM 1000003256f 70aRCRD.htm, accessed September 30, 2013.

# EXHIBIT 2 DELOITTE DADS' LAUNCH PAMPHLET

**Deloitte.**

### Thank you

Deloitte Dads would like to thank several individuals who have helped bring this initiative to life. The firm leaders who have supported us, your guidance and support is deeply appreciated. To our Advisory Team, Tim Christmann, Rob Lanoue, and Ross Kerr, thank you for making time to be part of our team. Finally, to the Career Moms leads (past and present), Anushka Grant, Alison Weyland, and Parul Goel, your advice has been invaluable.

To everyone who has shown interest in Deloitte Dads, thanks. We are happy to be your arms and legs, but the community needs your ideas! Please share what you want to get out of Deloitte Dads with us.

### We need your ideas! Share them and win a $100 VISA gift card

The Deloitte Dads community will succeed only if we deliver relevant support in a manner that is accessible to our members. We have developed an online survey seeking answers to the following:

- What resources or elements would you find valuable as part of Deloitte Dads?
- What topic areas are you interested in learning about/discussing?
- Which time(s) of day would be most convenient for meetings/events?
- Which day(s) during the week are most convenient for scheduling meetings or events?

The survey is located at:
http://catoamien/DeloitteDads/default.aspx. Please fill in the survey. All completed surveys are entered into a draw for a $100 gift card.

**For further information, please contact:**

**Andrew Hamer**
Founder, Deloitte Dads
ahamer@deloitte.ca

**Allan Hale**
Co-Leader, Deloitte Dads
alhale@deloitte.ca

**Dan Beach**
Co-Leader, Deloitte Dads
dbeach@deloitte.ca

© Deloitte & Touche LLP and affiliated entities.

# Welcome to Deloitte Dads
### The fraternity of paternity

As the role of the modern father evolves, balancing full co-parenting responsibilities with a rewarding career is becoming increasingly challenging.

Fathers today are choosing to be increasingly involved in the lives of their children. This can create challenges for fathers seeking both career success and an active parenting role. Deloitte Dads intends to help fathers at the firm meet these challenges. Our goal is to ensure that practitioners who want to excel at work and at home have the tools to do so.

### So, what is Deloitte Dads?

**A firm sponsored employee program**
Intended to help fathers achieve success at home and in the workplace. Our initial scope is to support GTA consulting. We hope that in the future we will be able to successfully expand the initiative to include a broader group of Deloitte employees.

**A mentorship network**
To connect expectant fathers, new fathers, and veteran fathers at all stages of child rearing. We can all learn from those who have walked the path before us. If you have a question or if you have advice to share, this is the forum.

**A straight talk resource**
To help career-oriented Dads succeed in an active parent/partner role. We intend to provide an environment where fathers can get useful and practical advice.

**A support system**
To help navigate specific life events and milestones that can impact a father at the firm. Whether it is a question submitted to the virtual community or a coffee with a dad who has been there, Deloitte Dads will provide the opportunity to ask questions and receive answers.

### Community and events

Deloitte Dads plans to make an impact through quarterly events and the creation of a virtual community.
Each stage of fatherhood is accompanied by significant life changes; the impact of these changes can be minimized with the help of a strong support network. From the fundamental life change of becoming a parent for the first time to milestones in the life of your family, Deloitte Dads wants to be a resource to help you navigate your path.

**The Deloitte Dads virtual community**
This resource will be both a source of information and a forum for discussion. The virtual community will allow members to share experiences, ask questions, and help define the direction of Deloitte Dads. It will also provide a repository of useful information that members can leverage and contribute to.

**Quarterly events**
These gatherings will focus on relevant topics for fathers at the firm. Through guest speakers, 'town hall' discussions, and 'partner panel' forums, Deloitte Dads will facilitate an environment of learning and straight-forward communication within the firm.

"I know I have been an imperfect father. I know I have made mistakes. I have lost count of all the times, over the years, when the demands of work have taken me from the duties of fatherhood."

US President Barack Obama, Father's Day, 2009

*Source*: Company files.

9B17M153

# ERGONOMICA CONSULTING AND SOLLTRAM HOTELS: AN ETHICAL DILEMMA

*Christopher Williams wrote this case solely to provide material for class discussion. The author does not intend to illustrate either effective or ineffective handling of a managerial situation. The author may have disguised certain names and other identifying information to protect confidentiality.*

In April 2017, Kawun O'Hara, senior manager at Ergonomica Consulting (Ergonomica), was under pressure to demonstrate within the next month, to her employer, as well as to key account Solltram Hotels (Solltram), that Solltram's investment in high-frequency (HF) fluorescent lighting would meet or exceed the expected payback for the client. A lot depended on her being able to do this: winning an extension of the contract with Solltram, developing a new specialist practice area within Ergonomica, improving her chances of promotion, and cementing her reputation. Besides this, she was passionate about helping businesses with their environmental strategies.

However, at a critical moment, O'Hara had discovered that a previously hidden error in her main spreadsheet, which contained over two million data points, had resulted in her overestimating the cost savings for the client. The error would be virtually impossible for the client to discover. Should O'Hara conceal the mistake and win the important contract, improving her chances of promotion? After all, there could be other errors in the data or in the spreadsheet, and the client would still achieve cost savings and other positive outcomes from the project, including great publicity. Or should she own up to the mistake and risk losing the account, her promotion, and her reputation?

## SOLLTRAM HOTELS GROUP

Solltram was founded in 1947 in Tacoma, Washington State, by Antony Solltram. The first hotel was a budget 40-bedroom motel off the main route between Tacoma and Seattle. The business grew steadily, and by the time Solltram handed it over to his son in 1974, it had 17 motels across Washington State. Antony Solltram Jr. took the brand upmarket, expanding into executive downtown hotels, as well as into California. The 1980s and 1990s was a period of tremendous growth for the company, with a new hotel opening practically every other month. By 2005, Solltram had 210 hotels in operation.

It was at that point that Solltram Jr. decided to sell the business to the executive through a US$320[1] million leveraged management buyout (MBO). The lender's conditions stipulated that each of the five directors had to personally contribute $1 million. The balance came through a $315 million loan note payable in 2020. The executive included Andy Levitt, who had become chief executive officer (CEO) after having served as finance director, and Tom Chaparro, who was chief operating officer.

Levitt was a corporate finance high flyer who had made enough money on Wall Street to be able to retire by age 35. However, he found that playing golf every day became rather boring; he needed something to keep his mind occupied but without the 18-hour days he had worked on Wall Street. Through a friend, Levitt was introduced to Solltram Jr. in 2002. Solltram Jr. persuaded Levitt to take up the role of finance director with a view to leading the MBO. Levitt had no problems finding the $1 million to invest in Solltram.

Levitt's colleagues described him as a wolf in sheep's clothing: Most of the time, he came across as a benign but optimistic leader who let his team make decisions without appearing to care what they did. But if anything went wrong, Levitt quickly become intolerant and unforgiving.

Chaparro had started his career as an engineering apprentice in the aviation sector. After 10 years, he became a team leader and eventually moved into production management. In 1987, at age 30, he responded to a job advertisement for regional maintenance manager with Solltram. By that time, he had a young family and needed the extra $3,000 per year. Chaparro did not regret his decision, and over the next 15 years, he rose steadily in the ranks until he became chief operating officer in 2002.

Chaparro's colleagues described him as a methodical and cautious person by nature. He would double-check anything and everything before making a decision. Although colleagues would criticize him for his slow and cautious decision making, he would counter by saying, "Look where I've gotten to; I think I've done alright, so why change?"

Not surprisingly then, it was a big deal for Chaparro when in 2005 he had to decide whether to invest $1 million in the MBO or leave Solltram and find a new job. After agonizing over the decision for weeks, Chaparro, with the support of his wife, decided to make the investment. This meant borrowing $1 million from the bank, a loan that was secured against his house. If it all went wrong, he would have to sell his family home.

Following the MBO in 2005, and under the guidance of Levitt, Solltram continued to grow. It opened 14 new hotels in 2006 and 16 in 2007. However, the global financial crash of 2008 hit the market hard. Either business travel was cut, or business travellers' accommodation was downgraded to lower-cost accommodation. This forced Solltram to cut its prices and operating margin. Consequently, profits collapsed and Solltram had to sell or close 36 of its least profitable hotels through 2008 and 2009. This was a time of huge stress for Chaparro, who was all too aware of the consequences of the business failing.

By mid-2010, the business was stable once again, but there was little appetite for taking the risk of investing in new hotels. Instead, between 2010 and 2015, Levitt and his team focused on improving the profitability of Solltram's existing hotels by cutting costs and increasing occupancy rates. They turned to outside help for advice on this. One of the advisory companies they engaged to support their cost-saving initiatives was Ergonomica, led by George Speed. Speed quickly became "a trusted adviser" to Chaparro on how to reduce energy costs through the design and specifications of the hotels' heating, ventilation, and cooling systems. This advisory work resulted in a steady income for Ergonomica of around $95,000 per year.

At the start of 2015, Solltram had gross revenue of $800 million from 204 hotels. The average occupancy rate was 60 per cent, and the average hotel size was 125 bedrooms. The average revenue per occupied room per night was $100 from accommodation and $42 from food and drink. The company had done all it could to cut costs and now needed a new strategy.

A strategic review identified that increasing occupancy levels together with increasing the average revenue per night per room would be the most cost-efficient and lowest-risk route for returning to growth. To achieve this, Solltram needed to upgrade the standard of the accommodation by refurbishing the hotel's portfolio. The average age of the company's hotels was 25 years, and most were looking "tired" and in desperate need of a facelift. The company started on this new strategic path by borrowing $20 million to improve 39 hotels in Washington State. Solltram's bank agreed to lend it the money to fund the program, which was given the name Project Jewel.

Project Jewel started in late 2015 with two pilot hotels that were completed by the end of that year. The change was impressive, and Solltram saw an immediate increase in occupancy, enabling it to start raising prices. In January 2016, Solltram held a Project Jewel Strategy Day that brought together its key suppliers, including Ergonomica, to review the two completed hotels and agree on a plan for rolling out refurbishments to the remaining hotels in Washington State. At the end of the meeting, Levitt approached Chaparro.

"Hey Tom," Levitt said. "I've just had a very interesting conversation with Kawun O'Hara from Ergonomica about high-frequency lighting."

"Oh, yeah?" replied Chaparro.

"Yeah, and I asked her to come along to our next board meeting with a proposal."

## ERGONOMICA CONSULTING

Speed had thought he was taking a risk when he started Ergonomica in 2002, but it was one with which he had felt comfortable. After all, having majored in engineering at Princeton University and accumulated 10 years' experience in the automotive industry, an MBA, and 10 years working for a major engineering consultancy firm, if he could not make it, who could?

Speed considered there to be a gap in the market for a consultancy firm that could identify and deliver pragmatic and cost-effective environmental programs for businesses. He believed that the big consultancy firms that claimed to assist with environmental programs were composed of either accountants with no practical engineering skills, engineers with no communication skills, or environmentalists with no commercial skills. Ergonomica was going to fill that gap. Moreover, Speed felt passionately that, as well as having technical skills, Ergonomica would be a consultancy firm with a reputation for honesty – it would genuinely put the client first.

Speed quickly found a winning formula, and Ergonomica grew steadily between 2002 and 2007. This growth was in no small part because of Speed's personality and charisma. He was a natural leader and a larger-than-life character; he was always smiling, always positive, and always reassuringly confident. People knew they could trust Speed. Clients liked engaging him, and his employees liked working for him. In the firm's first six years, Speed employed two junior partners, six directors, 15 senior managers, and 24 managers – all who worked along the West Coast. The remaining employees were consultants and support staff.

In the fall of 2007, disaster struck. Financial markets crashed. Within weeks, Ergonomica had lost some of its longest-standing clients. Although the type of projects Ergonomica specialized in offered very good returns, cash flow was suddenly at the top of clients' agendas. Capital investment abruptly stopped.

Up to that point, Speed had given his employees only good news, such as "positive sales growth," "new projects," "new clients," and "bonuses." Now there was no good news. He decided to try to ride out the storm and shield his employees from the reality of the situation. Speed hoped the crash was simply a short-term overreaction in the stock market and that the economy would be back to normal within a few months.

However, by spring 2008, there had been no uplift, and Ergonomica experienced a loss for the first time. Speed realized that if things did not improve by mid-year, he would be forced to let staff go. Until then, he wanted to keep a positive front for his employees.

"We're nearly through this – there's lots of new projects just around the corner," he would tell his team.

To his partners, he would justify his approach to employees by explaining, "There's no point in dishing out the bad news until it is absolutely necessary, otherwise people will start looking for new jobs. Unfortunately, it'll be our best employees who find new jobs first, the ones we really want to keep. So let's try to keep things positive."

By summer of that year, things had not improved. Despite Speed's best efforts to remain positive, rumours were rife within Ergonomica that there were going to be cuts. Morale dropped, and absenteeism increased through sickness and one-day holidays, which Speed suspected were used for job interviews. At the end of August, Speed and his partners decided to cut Ergonomica's workforce by 35 per cent. Forty-eight non-billable and underutilized staff were let go, including a large portion of a program management and quality assurance office that had only been set up in 2006. Speed figured these job cuts might have been more than what was necessary, but he wanted to do only one round of cuts. As for the employees left behind, Speed wanted them to be utilized as much as possible on billable projects, and to "be really, really busy with clients, generating cash flow."

Although the redundancy program was painful, Speed noted that it had the desired effect. Ergonomica returned to breakeven at the end of the year. During 2009, the Federal Reserve System's quantitative easing started to take the pressure off corporate cash flow, and Ergonomica's clients began to invest in new projects again. By the end of 2009, Speed felt positive about the company's prospects, and at the company's February 2010 board meeting, he and his partners decided to start recruiting again (see Exhibit 1). One of the partners asked Speed, "Have you thought of approaching Kawun O'Hara at the [California] Department of Public Health?"

## KAWUN O'HARA

As O'Hara's flight came in for a landing at the Los Angeles International Airport after a family holiday in Canada in 1990, she stared in amazement at the smog covering the great city. The family had just spent a week in the fresh air of the Canadian Rockies.

"Why have the clouds fallen on the ground?" she asked her father, who sat next to her. Despite his uncertainty, her father did his best to explain air pollution and exhaust emissions to his 11-year-old daughter. O'Hara never forgot her feeling of apprehension that day as the plane dipped into the grey–blue fog, nor the acrid air when the plane doors opened and the drive home through gloomy streets.

That day sparked in O'Hara, although she was young, an interest in the causes and effects of pollution that she pursued throughout high school. She was particularly inspired by Erin Brockovich, a woman who, despite a lack of formal education in law, was instrumental in building a successful lawsuit against the Pacific Gas and Electric Company of California in 1993 for contaminating drinking water. O'Hara subsequently became a supporter of the Erin Brockovich Foundation, and a lifetime member of Greenpeace.

At university, O'Hara majored in biology, after which she undertook research that involved developing a mathematical model to describe the relationship between fertilizer-intensive farming and freshwater algae blooms. Algae blooms occurred when algae grew out of control. This process produced toxins that were harmful to people, marine life, and birds, and was often related to the pollution caused by fertilizer runoff from intensive crop farming.

O'Hara could have happily spent the rest of her life working in the fascinating and stimulating – though poorly paid – world of environmental research. However, at age 27, she unexpectedly became a single mother, and reality hit. She wanted to get a better-paying job and earn more money to be able to support herself and her daughter Jasmine, and to afford a live-in nanny so that she could stay active in her career.

In 2006, O'Hara got a job with the California Department of Public Health. Her role was to promote an understanding of climate change and advise the public and local businesses on what they could do to prevent it; for example, she promoted the use of public transit and investing in renewable energy. O'Hara rose quickly through the ranks as she showed real talent, persuading people to change through a combination of her positive and engaging personality and her use of robust facts and data analysis to support her case.

By 2010, O'Hara had built an excellent local reputation as someone who could make a difference – someone who could help businesses to deliver environmental improvements without compromising their strategy for growth and shareholder returns. So it was no surprise when she received a call from Speed at Ergonomica.

O'Hara had heard of Ergonomica from some of the local CEOs she had advised. The company appeared to have a good reputation for guiding businesses on how to invest in new energy-saving technologies.

Over lunch in downtown Seattle, O'Hara was quickly persuaded by Speed to join Ergonomica as a manager. She liked Speed's honest and pragmatic approach. Although the salary was slightly lower, the package from Ergonomica included a performance-related component and sales bonus, which meant she should be able to earn significantly more than she did in the state sector. This, she hoped, would be enough to allow her to afford the beach condominium she wanted for her growing daughter.

After O'Hara joined Ergonomica, she enjoyed a successful honeymoon period, when everything seemed to go her way. She was assigned to receptive clients with interesting projects, which she delivered on time and on budget. She also began to sell some small pieces of repeat business to existing clients, which helped raise her income above the income she had enjoyed at the California Department of Public Health. By

2012, O'Hara felt she had the best job ever. She was working hard, was well paid, had been promoted to the position of senior manager, and was helping to save the environment – her passion for the past 20 years. How could it get any better?

However, 2013 got off to a bad start. First, O'Hara's live-in nanny, who had worked for her for seven years, notified O'Hara of her intention to leave the job, as she would be getting married and moving to the East Coast. Although O'Hara was able to get another nanny, Jasmine reacted badly to the change. She became more demanding and more intolerant of O'Hara working late at the office. This meant O'Hara had to cut back on her hours, and cut back on client and company social events. After six months, she noticed that her sales started to drop. Her income then started to drop, and she was worried she was no longer the rising star she had once been.

## A LUCKY BREAK

In November 2013, Speed introduced O'Hara to Chaparro at Solltram. In a bid to expand Ergonomica's business with Solltram, O'Hara was tasked by Speed to sell to Solltram an energy-saving, HF fluorescent lighting project. For the first time at Ergonomica, she felt she had a client who was going to be difficult.

O'Hara's hunch was right. For two years, she made regular presentations to Chaparro on the case for investing in HF lighting, and Chaparro rejected these proposals every time on the basis of having limited capital expenditure (capex). He thought that the capex he did have available should be spent on replacing heating, ventilation, and cooling systems, because the failure of these systems meant having to close the whole hotel until they were fixed. He did not face this problem with lights.

HF lighting used high-frequency, solid-state electronic circuitry, called "ballast," to start and run a standard fluorescent tube, and it replaced the original electromagnetic ballast. HF ballast had a number of benefits over electromagnetic ballast.

The tangible benefits of HF ballast were that it lowered electricity consumption, and therefore reduced carbon footprints. It also lowered maintenance costs by extending the ballast's life.

The intangible benefits of HF ballast were its production of a higher light output from a standard florescent tube and its improved ambiance due to reduced flickering and noise (electromagnetic ballast was prone to producing light flickering and a humming noise, both of which could induce tiredness and headaches).

HF ballast had become the standard in new light fittings, but its initial high cost meant that it was not cost-effective for retrofitting to existing fluorescent lights. However, lower-cost imports from China and rising electricity prices made retrofitting an increasingly cost-effective option.

By October 2015, having conspicuously failed for two years to sell the low-energy lighting project to Solltram, and having failed to close a decent sale to any client for 30 months, O'Hara was starting to feel the pressure. Nothing had been said openly, but she was getting the impression that the promotion she was after had slipped from Speed's agenda. He had started taking some of the other, less experienced senior managers to sales meetings instead of her. She needed a big win, and she needed it quickly.

In January 2016, O'Hara had a lucky break. During the Project Jewel Strategy Day with the Solltram board, she managed to briefly discuss her idea for low-energy lighting over coffee with CEO Levitt.

"Sounds interesting, Kawun," he said. "Why don't you put a proposal together for us to trial it in our Washington State portfolio, and come and present to the board? Let's see what they think."

## EVENTS LEADING UP TO APRIL 2017

In February 2016, O'Hara commissioned several HF lighting suppliers to survey the existing lighting systems and tender costs for Solltram's 39 hotels in Washington State. As the survey data started to come in, O'Hara began to build an asset register comprising 15,000 light fittings across the 39 hotels. She then added data on current levels of electricity consumption and costs, the material and labour costs for converting the lights to HF, and finally some assumptions around how many times each light was switched on and off and what the maintenance costs were likely to be. After a week of intense analysis with a large and complex spreadsheet, O'Hara finally had the headline numbers for the Washington State business case:

- Capex:   $1.1 million.
- Savings:   $440,000 per year electricity savings + $100,000 per year maintenance savings
- Payback:   Two years

Included in the $1.1 million was Ergonomica's fee for project managing the delivery of the work, which was $120,000. Speed was delighted. "This'll double our income from Solltram if they buy it!" he beamed.

In March 2016, following two weeks of preparation, O'Hara presented her proposal for investing $1.1 million in low energy lighting for the 39 hotels in Washington State. It was a very compelling case:

- Two-year payback from lower electricity and maintenance costs
- Improved ambiance in the "front of house" (guest areas) from the new lights
- Improved environmental credibility from a lower carbon footprint

"So what do you think?" Levitt asked the rest of the Solltram board after O'Hara's presentation. Most looked at Levitt with glazed eyes – lighting was something they simply could not get excited about. They wanted to discuss the presentations on revenue, growth, acquisitions, and stock prices.

"To be honest, Andy," piped up Chaparro, "I've heard this sort of pitch from a hundred salespeople, and the bottom line is that the savings never come through." He continued, "With respect to Kawun, this is all smoke and mirrors, and even if it does deliver what's promised, it is a drop in the ocean compared to our electricity bill – something like 4 per cent. In my opinion, we'll never see these savings, but if you give me that $1.1 million I could facelift four hotels, and that's where we should be spending our money."

O'Hara's heart sank upon hearing this, although she tried not to show it.

"Tom, you're absolutely right," Levitt said as he focused his gaze on Chaparro. He continued, "But as you know, we do precious little to support the green agenda: we talk the talk but never walk the walk. Now I'm not a tree-hugger, but equally I do think we need to do something for our environment, and this is a tree-hugging investment with a two-year payback. Kawun says so, and to be honest I'm inclined to believe her. The stuff you're doing, Tom, is critical to the future of our business but the paybacks are all around three years."

"But Andy," pleaded Chaparro, "you've seen the figures; we're hardly making a profit, cash is really tight, and more than anything we committed to the bank to focus our capex solely on the business strategy we presented to them last year. This pitch is way off-track; we need to put every cent into refurbishing our hotels, not on a pet 'environmental' project."

"Fair point, Tom," said Levitt. "Anyone else got a view?"

"I'd give this project my support," responded Anna Frost, head of corporate social responsibility. "We could get some good PR out of this – perhaps some articles in the local papers, and we know our colleagues like to see us doing stuff for the local environment. I'd say $1 million is within our means."

Levitt leaned back, paused, and summed up his thoughts: "We're only talking 5 per cent of the capex budget for this year – and I'm sure if we went to the bank they would support an investment with a two-year payback, but if I did go to the bank we would get wrapped up in red tape amending the strategy, and before you know it the opportunity has gone. Having heard all points of view, I suggest we go with this project. It sounds like the right thing to do from so many points of view – except Tom's." He smiled as he winked at Chaparro. "Washington will be a trial, Phase 1 if you like, and if it goes to plan we can look at Phase 2, the California portfolio."

Hearing this, Chaparro knew he was beaten.

Having received the green light to deliver the project, O'Hara appointed the contractor who had won the tender to install the lights, Lite-U-Like Inc. She worked hard with them to ensure the right lights were installed in the right place, at the right time, and at the right cost. As the project progressed, she was rewarded with positive feedback from the hotel managers and staff:

"These lights have transformed the place."
"It is so much brighter – almost as if the place has been redecorated."
"The engineers from Lite-U-Like were very good, really kept the place clean and tidy as they worked."
"Good to see someone cares about our environment so much they've put their hand in their pocket."

By November 2016, all 39 hotels had been converted to HF, on time and on budget. All O'Hara had to do then was to measure the reduced electricity consumption, and demonstrate that the savings were in line with the plan. Demonstrating this would be crucial to cementing the relationship with Solltram and winning the deal for Phase 2 in California.

"I'll give it another month," she thought, "before I download and analyze the data. That'll mean all the hotels will have been operating with the new lights for at least two months."

One evening in December 2016, after her daughter had gone to bed, O'Hara sat down with her laptop. "Time to concentrate," she thought, as she downloaded the electricity consumption of each hotel from the supplier's web portal.

O'Hara had always been a good mathematician, and she truly enjoyed analyzing complex data. She had seen in the past how it could reveal very powerful business insights. Analyzing electricity savings was a great example of this. The electricity meters fitted to each hotel measured consumption in half-hourly intervals and transmitted the data to a web portal for downloading and analysis. As the consumption varied on an hourly, daily, monthly, and yearly basis (see Exhibits 2, 3, and 4) by considerably more than the 4 per cent savings she was looking for, the analysis was going to be quite complex. A variation in consumption was caused by dependencies such as occupancy levels, outside temperature, hours of sunlight per day, and events in the hotels such as conferences and discos. O'Hara knew from experience that the strongest correlation would be with the outside temperature; the warmer it was outside, the less electricity was used to heat a hotel, until it became so warm that the air conditioning kicked in and the electricity consumption started to rise again (see Exhibit 5).

O'Hara decided to calculate the savings by looking over a long period – three years – to smooth out variables that had a limited correlation with consumption. These included, for instance, levels of hotel occupancy. She used linear regression to account for a range of control variables – other factors that could explain electricity consumption. She had used this approach many times over the years and it had always given very good results. This time, however, it was not so easy to analyze the data. Over three years, 39 hotels would produce around 2,000,000 data points (48 points per day × 365 days × 3 years × 39 hotels). She knew she had to take great care with her analysis. O'Hara had done this sort of analysis dozens of times before, and she took a great sense of satisfaction in knowing that she was one of the few people in Ergonomica who was able to do it. Indeed, since the re-organization in 2008, only two people in the company did this particular type of analysis on hotel data.

After four hours of careful and detailed work, O'Hara finally had her first insight into the actual savings that were being delivered for Phase 1, based on two months of data:

- forecast annual savings of $540,000 per year, and
- actual savings run-rate of $580,000 per year.

"Amazing!" she thought, hardly daring to believe what she saw. "We're above target!"

Just to make sure of this, she spent the next half an hour going through her calculations and spreadsheet formulas again. She arrived at the same result, and thought, "Excellent. I can't wait to tell Tom!"

She was so keen to share the good news that she immediately sent an e-mail, time-stamped at 1:15 a.m., to Speed, Chaparro, Levitt, and Frost, and then went to bed smiling.

The next morning, Speed replied with, "Excellent news." A couple of hours later, Levitt replied, "Good start."

"Please, could you continue to monitor and issue an update after Christmas?" came the reply from Chaparro – three days later.

In February 2017, after a fantastic Christmas break, O'Hara relished the idea of sitting down once again in her home office to crunch another two months of data for Phase 1. Once again, she was delighted:

- forecast annual savings of $540,000 per year, and
- actual savings run-rate of $590,000 per year.

This was marginally up from the previous calculation, and O'Hara was very pleased. The savings were nearly 10 per cent ahead of plan based on four months of data. She was starting to become very comfortable with the results. Once again, she was keen to share the good news in a late-night email.

"Excellent," Speed replied the next morning. "This really does look promising," replied Levitt, a couple of hours later.

"Dear Kawun," began Chaparro's reply, "I have to confess that I may have been wrong – these savings really are good, much better than I would have thought. I have to also report that I have had some excellent feedback from our colleagues in terms of the improvement to the look of the hotels. I'm thinking that we should look at including this upgrade in my Hotel Refurbishment Program. Perhaps you could put some thought into that?"

"Hi all," replied Frost. "Just to say the local newspaper has just done a nice little page-three article on this project. We tied it into a press release on the 'Annual Litter Pick' that a few of our managers do each year. I'm talking to a couple of TV stations later as well. We got some good feedback from our colleagues too – it seems they like to be associated with a business that does more than just think about the bottom line."

On April 27, 2017, back at the office in Seattle, Speed approached O'Hara.

"Great news, Kawun: Tom wants us to deliver Phase 2 of the energy-saving lighting project in the California portfolio as part of his refurbishment program. That's 165 hotels!" he beamed. "He's been really impressed with the improved ambiance for residents as well, and you've convinced him that the savings are coming through. He wants you to put together a proposal by tomorrow; is that okay?"

"Wow," replied O'Hara. "I imagine that's going to be at least a $4 million project."

"Well, with around 10 per cent for us that sure will help your case for promotion!" said Speed.

Later that evening, O'Hara made a coffee, and sat down to put together the business case for the investment. She had been anticipating this and so had most of the information ready to use. By 7:00 p.m., it was complete. All she had really done was conduct pro-rata calculations of the costs from the Washington portfolio, used the savings she had calculated back in February, and cut and pasted the text.

O'Hara was just about to e-mail the proposal to Speed for his approval when she thought, "It's only 7 o'clock; I've actually got time to update the actual savings calculation for the Washington portfolio and put that in the business case instead of February's calculation. It's possible that the savings might be even better now, which would make the case even more compelling." With renewed energy, she sat down to update the energy savings calculation. O'Hara was feeling very pleased; she was close to winning an important contract for Ergonomica, but more importantly for her, she had won over Chaparros's skepticism and put herself back in contention for a promotion.

Everything was looking very rosy until O'Hara looked as the spreadsheet on her laptop a second time. She could not believe what she was seeing. Her heart rate increased and she shifted uneasily in her chair.

"How could I have been so dumb?" she asked herself.

She had just realized that the savings numbers for Phase 1 of the project, which she had presented to Levitt and Chaparro eight weeks earlier, were wrong – and they were wrong because of a simple error O'Hara had made linking cells from different sheets within her spreadsheet. This meant that, once corrected, the $1.1 million capex she had convinced Levitt to invest in HF lighting would take four years to payback, not the two years she had assured him. O'Hara winced as she remembered using phrases such as "low risk" and "predictable savings" in her business case, and the skepticism with which Chaparro had received it.

## OPTIONS FOR O'HARA

O'Hara looked again at the error. She checked previous versions of the spreadsheet and found the error had always been there. She put her head in her hands. It was getting late and she could see only two options.

### Option 1

Ignore the error and do not tell anyone about it. Issue the business case with the (incorrect) savings and secure a major piece of work and a promotion, and achieve something positive for the environment.

### Option 2

Own up to the mistake and to the fact that the savings were only half of what was reported previously.

This could jeopardize everything – the firm's relationship with Solltram, O'Hara's promotion, and, perhaps more than anything, her reputation.

## Note

1  All currency amounts in the case are in U.S. dollars.

## EXHIBIT 1  GROWTH OF ERGONOMICA CONSULTING (2002–2010)

|      | Number of Employees at Year End | Utilization Rate of Billable Staff (%) |
|------|---------------------------------|----------------------------------------|
| 2002 | 2                               | 60                                     |
| 2003 | 18                              | 74                                     |
| 2004 | 33                              | 73                                     |
| 2005 | 64                              | 81                                     |
| 2006 | 78                              | 88                                     |
| 2007 | 138                             | 56                                     |
| 2008 | 93                              | 34                                     |
| 2009 | 89                              | 61                                     |
| 2010 | 95                              | 72                                     |

*Source*: Created by case authors.

## EXHIBIT 2  VARIATION IN ELECTRICITY CONSUMPTION, HOUR-TO-HOUR

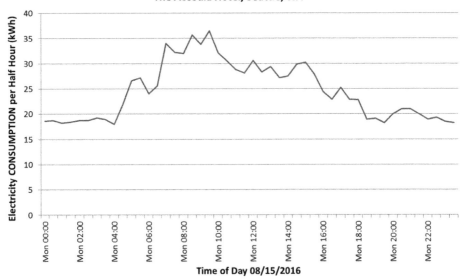

*Note*: WA = Washington State; kWh = kilowatt hours.

*Source*: Created by case authors.

## EXHIBIT 3  VARIATION IN ELECTRICITY CONSUMPTION, DAY-TO-DAY

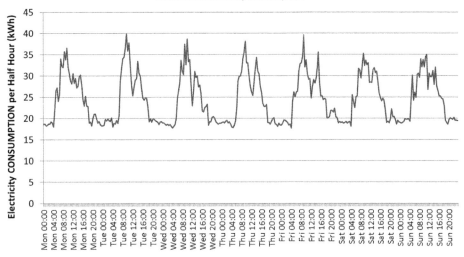

**Electricity Consumption Variation During the Day**
**The Accodia Hotel, Seattle, WA**

*Note*: WA = Washington State; kWh = kilowatt hours.

*Source*: Created by case authors.

## EXHIBIT 4  VARIATION IN ELECTRICITY CONSUMPTION AND OUTSIDE TEMPERATURE

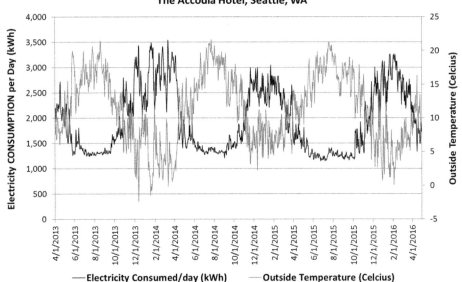

**Electricity Consumption and Outside Temperature**
**The Accodia Hotel, Seattle, WA**

—— Electricity Consumed/day (kWh)       —— Outside Temperature (Celcius)

*Note*: WA = Washington State; kWh = kilowatt hours.

*Source*: Created by case authors.

## EXHIBIT 5 RELATIONSHIP BETWEEN ELECTRICITY CONSUMPTION AND OUTSIDE TEMPERATURE

**Electricity Consumption versus Outside Temperature**
**The Accodia Hotel, Seattle, WA**

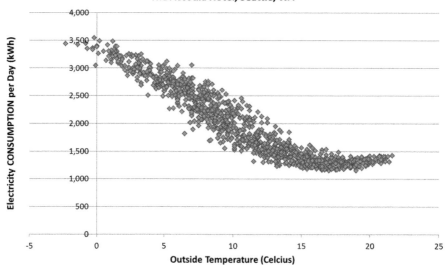

*Note*: WA = Washington State; kWh = kilowatt hours.

*Source*: Created by case authors.

9B18M159

# INNOGY CONSULTING GMBH: COMPETING AWAY FROM HOME

In September 2016, Dr. Klaus Grellmann, managing director of innogy Consulting GmbH (iCon), had many reasons to be delighted. iCon had risen to second place in an annual ranking of internal consultancies and had successfully expanded into four different countries.[1] Sitting in his office overlooking a leafy district of Essen in Germany's otherwise-industrial skyline, he pondered new challenges and directions he might take iCon.

Grellmann originally took the helm of RWE Consulting – the predecessor to iCon – in 2007. As an internal consulting department within the RWE Group (RWE) in Germany, iCon mainly conducted information technology (IT) implementation and project management on behalf of entities within RWE. While the newly formed iCon could rely on this safe home for internal projects, Grellmann was well aware of the tough competition in the external management-consultancy market. How could iCon take steps to compete away from home?

## RWE GROUP

RWE was founded in Essen, Germany, in 1898 as *Rheinisch-Westfälisches Elektrizitätswerk Aktiengesellschaft* ("Rhine-Westphalian Power Station Stock Company"). The company had won a contract from the city of Essen to build its first power plant, which was operational by 1900. By the early 2010s, the company had grown to be one of the world's largest energy giants, spanning Europe with a business focused on the generation, distribution, trading, and retail of power. In 2015, the company had an earnings before interest, tax, depreciation, and amortization (EBITDA) of €7 billion[2] from a revenue of €48.6 billion and with a total workforce of 60,000 employees.[3]

RWE was firmly positioned in the "old world" of energy generation – 32 per cent of electricity-generation capacity was based on gas, 23 per cent on lignite (mined by the company), 22 per cent on hard coal, 8 per cent on nuclear, and only 9 per cent on renewables.[4] The distribution business was in a dominant position in Germany and Eastern Europe, with over 570,000 kilometres of grid network and approximately 3,000 electricity- and 800 gas-network licences.[5] Long-term contracts provided a stable cash flow with high predictability. Barriers to entry in this sector were high, owing to the complex tendering process for each subsection of the grid and the presence of long-standing incumbents. By the time the decision was made in 2016 to separate the renewables, grid, and retail segments from RWE (i.e., to create innogy), the "grid" segment was expected to provide almost two-thirds of innogy's EBITDA.[6]

In 2015, RWE's customer-facing business ("retail") grew to 16 million electricity customers and seven million gas customers across 11 European countries.[7] The company ranked first or second in market position in Germany, the Netherlands, and the Czech Republic. Nevertheless, continuous deregulation posed a challenge, and RWE had to deal with increased competition, thinning margins, and IT-related issues in its United Kingdom subsidiary that were causing high customer turnover.

Apart from the three core segments (generation, grid, and retail), RWE also ran its own energy-trading activities in the global commodity markets. Additionally, since 2013, RWE had seen a rapid expansion into the renewables-generation sector. Focusing primarily on wind power, RWE became the third-largest offshore wind farm operator in the world. The push behind entry into this relatively nascent field was Germany's *Energiewende* ("energy transition").

### GERMANY'S ENERGIEWENDE[8]

At the turn of the 21st century, the German government embarked on a new Energiewende, which culminated in 2010 with legislation that aimed to reduce greenhouse gas emissions by 80–95 per cent and meet a renewable energy target of 60 per cent by 2050. In response to fears surrounding climate change, this policy shifted Germany's generation profile toward renewable energy. In 2000, feed-in tariffs had already been introduced.[9] These tariffs paid guaranteed above-the-market rates for 20-year periods to suppliers of solar and wind power; yet, it was the 2010 legislative bill that truly led to a boom in the capacity of installed renewables within the country. By 2016, renewables accounted for 32 per cent of overall electricity generation – up from 14.3 per cent just nine years earlier.[10]

Energiewende called for a phase-out of nuclear power, and efforts to denuclearize reached a peak in 2011, following the 9.0-magnitude earthquake that occurred off the coast of Japan and caused the Fukushima Daiichi nuclear disaster. Fifty minutes after the initial quake, a 13-metre-high tsunami reached the power plant and overwhelmed the seawall defences, disabling the primary emergency diesel generators, and causing coolant water in the plant to stop circulating. A day later, the battery-powered secondary emergency generators ran out of energy, causing the reactor to begin overheating and to eventually melt down. In Germany, reaction to this strengthened anti-nuclear feeling, and Chancellor Angela Merkel announced the immediate shutdown of the country's oldest nuclear reactors and a total cessation of nuclear power by the year 2022.[11] German energy companies were to be responsible for funding the cleanup of the nuclear plants, which was estimated to cost up to €70 billion for the entire industry, with RWE's share more than €10 billion.[12]

## INNOGY'S CARVING OUT AND ITS INITIAL PUBLIC OFFERING

These events put significant pressure on RWE's business model. Over 90 per cent of RWE's generation capacity was in forms that the government was actively moving the country away from. The glut in electricity added by renewables had destroyed margins in the company's relatively high-cost plants, and the company's share price had dropped drastically from a high of €100 per share in December 2007 to around €9 per share by September 2015.[13] The company realized that it needed to act strategically in changing markets and to fund long-term liabilities such as nuclear decommissioning and pensions. In reaction to a similar announcement by RWE's main domestic competitor, E.ON, the company decided to spin off a new entity to deal with the nuclear liabilities. Unlike E.ON, RWE decided to place its profitable power grid, renewable-energy generation, and retail operations into innogy SE, a new corporate entity that would be offered to the market in an initial public offering (IPO). RWE would retain a 76.8 per cent stake of the new company but act as a financial investor while retaining the old generation facilities. As a result, the IPO in October 2016 issued 129 million shares and generated proceeds of €4.6 billion. innogy SE was injected with €2 billion, and the remainder was left to RWE. It was the largest IPO in Germany in the new millennium.[14]

## INNOGY CONSULTING GMBH (ICON)

The roots of iCon were established in 1981, when RWE bundled its internal-consulting department with shared services such as accounting, IT, and process support into a subsidiary called RWE Systems Consulting. Small teams within the consulting arm were tasked with ad hoc projects referred to as "body leasing."[15] In the early 2000s, the unit became an independent legal entity under the name RWE Systems Consulting. Its work pipeline relied heavily on the implementation of IT projects within RWE.

Reaching a staff of 50 by 2005, RWE Systems Consulting opened up its first satellite office in Berlin to seek external clients for the first time. The company believed there were external clients that faced implementation challenges similar to those faced by RWE. Dropping "Systems" from its name in the same year, RWE Consulting became heavily reliant on freelancers.

In 2016, RWE Consulting was rebranded as innogy Consulting (iCon) and placed under innogy, the newly formed publicly traded company. iCon maintained strong relations with its clients within the former RWE Group in spite of the consultancy's frequent name and structural changes (see Exhibit 1).

iCon grew to be one of Germany's largest in-house management consultancies. It advised innogy and the RWE Group in strategic and operational areas linked to project implementation and process improvement. By 2016, iCon had offices in Germany, the Netherlands, the United Kingdom, the Czech Republic, and the United Arab Emirates. iCon consisted of 140 consultants who offered various advisory services and projects that spanned the entire value chain of the energy market: from energy generation to electricity and gas retail.

With growing numbers of projects within the parent company, as well as some initial external clients, iCon recruited a new wave of consultants from different backgrounds but with a unified passion for energy. iCon successfully delivered over 100 projects yearly, spanning across its various practices. The firm's general management practice accounted for the largest share of revenue, while newer practices such as "change" and "operations" also made important revenue contributions (see Exhibit 2).

## IN-HOUSE CONSULTANCIES IN THE GERMAN CONSULTING INDUSTRY

In Germany, the presence of in-house consultancy units (ICUs) at large corporations was more common. Two-thirds of the 30 DAX companies had an ICU in 2015.[16] These units were similar to external consultants in that they were used by the organization to solve a wide range of challenging problems. ICUs also were more active in implementing solutions – something that external consultancies did not always do. A benefit to the parent organization was that it was cheaper to perform a project with internal consultants rather than use an external firm. Additionally, knowledge was retained in-house, which aided future problem solving and guarded know-how from competitors. Internal consultants also had a better understanding of the underlying business model and were typically able to ramp up quickly on a project due to the familiarity with the business and stakeholders. They were also ideally suited to advise on softer aspects of change, such as the company culture and internal dynamics. However, there were also disadvantages, such as being seen as less impartial – and conflicts of interest occasionally arose.

Since 2010, the German consulting landscape had undergone a series of changes. Until then, only the top-tier external management-consulting companies were involved in high-profile strategic engagements. In 2007, the German government removed the strict separation of consultants and auditors.[17] Consequently, the top auditing companies decided to acquire a number of advisory boutiques to build up their management-consulting capabilities. A driving factor behind the rise of auditing firms was their focus on operations consulting compared with the focus on strategy presented by traditional management-consulting companies. This trend coincided with a shift in client expectation toward measurable indicators for the success of strategy implementation and also contributed to the rise of in-house consultancies; their inherent closeness to management and involvement in implementation made ICUs uniquely suited to fulfill the need for operational consulting and monitoring of strategy implementation.

ICUs entered the mainstream in the mid-1990s. Siemens Management Consulting (Siemens) and Porsche Consulting pioneered the model. These consultancies were expected not only to realize complex strategic and operative transformation processes but also to serve as a talent pool and train future managers for the company. Since 2010, these internal units had become the fourth pillar of consulting in Germany. The country's advisory industry consisted of traditional management consultancies, which were often subsidiaries of overseas firms (e.g., McKinsey & Company, Boston Consulting Group, Bain & Company, and A.T. Kearney), the "Big Four" auditing companies (i.e., PwC, KPMG, Deloitte, and Ernst & Young), smaller boutique consulting firms, and the ICUs. According to a study by German magazine *WirtschaftsWoche*, 43 per cent of consulting mandates from DAX 30 companies were given to their own internal consultants by 2014.[18]

ICUs acquired projects in three different ways: (1) they could be delegated an assignment directly from management, (2) they could compete for projects with external consultancies, or (3) they could proactively identify current issues and initialize a project. Traditional project profiles for ICUs included strategy development, end-to-end process management, customer-journey analysis, and change management. DAX 30 companies had also been hiring many different large external consulting firms. These companies often worked on projects in collaboration with ICUs, taking advantage of company-specific knowledge. This model was common in Germany; an internal consultant's specialist knowledge was integrated with new ideas and insights from external consultants to great effect.

Due to the fact that the DAX 30 companies increasingly conducted their business abroad, ICUs had to adapt to their global client base and set up offices in key foreign locations. Siemens, for instance, operated regional offices in Beijing and Mumbai, alongside its Munich headquarters.

## GRELLMANN'S NEW STRATEGY

Based on his experience from PwC and later at RWE, Grellmann recognized the need to professionalize the organization. Changes were made to turn the company into a competitive management consultancy that charged daily rates comparable to those of the top external consultancies.

One of the longest-serving partners in the company described the changes as follows:

> The new vision wanted to put us on an eye-level with top external strategy consultancies in the industry. We suddenly wanted to move away from the previous business model of long-term operational assistance and body leasing. We now wanted to participate every year in top-10 projects with high strategic importance and visibility to the RWE board. We, however, did not have the people to deliver such services, as [the] core of RWE Consulting staff, including parts of leadership, consisted of long-timers with a mindset fitting usual corporate functions, rather than management consulting. As we already had 100 staff in 2008, it became apparent we had to accept a high turnover of personnel to get the right people on board.

Following an initial assessment, Grellmann focused on the RWE Group and cut all external project work. Freelancers were cut, and job titles were changed to match industry standards. Roles became more clearly defined. The hiring process became more rigorous, job requirements were aligned with those in other consulting companies, and assessment centres were set up to include case interviews during the recruiting process. Senior managers were hired from, among others, companies such as McKinsey & Company, the Boston Consulting Group, and Accenture. Grellmann introduced policies aimed at capability building through formal training and encouraging co-operation within teams. He also changed the culture by establishing continuous feedback and coaching as the centrepiece of people development.

Grellmann also initiated a significant shift from seniority-based promotions and compensation to a performance-based system. Regular performance evaluations and feedback after every project enabled employees to clearly see where they stood. This approach made the promotion process transparent and tied to individuals' development. Partners started working toward overarching financial goals rather than focusing on their individual targets. As one partner noted, RWE Consulting started transitioning from a "single-fighter" mentality to an environment where a "team result is of paramount importance."

Back-office activities such as IT support were outsourced to increase efficiency and achieve a better service level. RWE Consulting also became a separate legal entity with its own profit and loss. Even though it was still a fully owned subsidiary of RWE, RWE Consulting was able to operate independently of the mother company and make strategic decisions without requiring prior consultation with RWE.

This strategic change resulted in a major makeover of RWE Consulting staff. Within one and a half years of Grellmann's arrival, approximately 80 per cent of the leadership team had been replaced, and within four years, approximately 80 per cent of

RWE Consulting's employees had been hired under his leadership, replacing a large number of staff that did not want to, or were unable to, make the transition. One year after Grellmann's arrival, in 2008, RWE Consulting won its first high-profile project working directly for RWE's new chief strategy officer. With this project, the transformed consultancy unit was now seen as a trusted advisor on both strategic and tactical questions within RWE.

## INTERNATIONAL EXPANSION

The other pivotal change that Grellmann led was RWE Consulting/iCon's international expansion. As the parent company, RWE pursued an aggressive international expansion strategy throughout the 2000s; consulting opportunities within the group started appearing all over Europe – and eventually beyond.

RWE Consulting's first venture outside of Germany was in the United Kingdom, where it established the London office in 2007. Primarily serving npower – RWE's retail arm, acquired in 2002 – the U.K. branch also supported RWE Generation with its eight power plants in the United Kingdom. npower had been among the United Kingdom's six-largest utilities, with more than five million electricity and gas customers. A similar situation happened in the Netherlands, where RWE acquired the country's largest energy supplier, Essent, in 2009. Absorbing Essent's consulting department as a result, RWE Consulting added a branch in Den Bosch that mostly focused on Essent's core retail business that served electricity and gas customers. Moreover, RWE Generation's gas-fired power plants presented further project opportunities. The Prague office was founded in 2010. Originally designed to serve RWE's business in Eastern Europe, the Prague office grew to advise the group's retail and grid businesses in the Czech Republic, Slovakia, Poland, and the Balkans, with a focus on the gas business.

All three offices (in the United Kingdom, Netherlands, and the Czech Republic) operated a hybrid model, officially reporting to the consulting head while being hosted by local retail branches. In practice, this meant that consultants outside of Germany were officially employees of npower (United Kingdom), Essent (Netherlands), and RWE CZ (Czech Republic), respectively.

Another important strategic decision for RWE Consulting was its expansion into external consulting in 2014 through the establishment of its Dubai office. While RWE had previously attempted to launch operations in the Middle East, it was ultimately unsuccessful. Grellmann decided to seize the chance, seeing the need for energy transformation in the Gulf region. He successfully transformed an ongoing technical co-operation with a local partner into a springboard for the launch of iCon's management-consulting services. A new office in Dubai was established, winning high-profile strategy projects within the first two years. This success was partly due to forming a joint venture with the Dubai Electricity and

Water Authority. The Dubai office pioneered RWE Consulting's renewed venture into external consulting, competing with top-tier consultancies in the region.

## PROJECTS AND GOVERNANCE AT THE NEWLY FORMED ICON

With RWE Consulting being recast as iCon, the firm needed to continue building on its capabilities and international presence (see Exhibit 3). iCon's strengths included energy expertise, organizational-design skills, capability building, and strategy development. The firm had delivered a number of highly successful projects within RWE/innogy throughout the 2010s, including grid strategy development, renewables market analysis, creating customer journeys in retail, and setting up innogy's Innovation Hub. iCon tended to do well on projects that required heavy client interaction, as its consultants were seen as highly collaborative and serving the group's interests. As a result, the project teams had unprecedented access to data and information that clients would have been hesitant to share with external consultants. iCon also managed change projects, coaching RWE/innogy managers to help them handle the disruptive transformation of their business due to the Energiewende (see Exhibit 4). In 2016, iCon was the sole management consultancy to manage innogy's IPO from idea to execution. This project lasted nine months and gave iCon unprecedented access and exposure to the top management of RWE/innogy.

On the other hand, iCon lacked external client experience, which made it difficult to compete in certain areas. For instance, the firm faced challenges in projects that required organizational health[19] analysis, non-energy industry knowledge, or external benchmarking.[20] iCon was also not considered completely impartial in projects that were more sensitive in nature. Concerns regarding a lack of impartiality would lead to a client preferring to work with other external consultancies on certain projects.

iCon's culture was different from the culture at larger management-consulting firms in a number of ways. Most within innogy saw iCon as part of their own company. While communication and analytical skills were essential traits of every consultant, iCon consultants differed through focus and shared passion for the energy industry – something not found in consulting companies that dealt with a wide range of industries. The firm put a strong emphasis on interpersonal skills during the recruiting process, underlining iCon's core value of co-creation through collaborative partnership with clients. Consultants were expected to build their own client network, cementing iCon's trusted advisor role (see Exhibit 5).

Consultants regularly worked with colleagues from within innogy, accessing an expert network of more than 40,000 employees. Socializing and developing one's personal network within the client company was common and encouraged. Additionally, iCon's culture and governance relied on all consulting staff contributing to its internal development. The consultants also often cited an emphasis on work–life balance that was offered by the firm as a reason for joining. This focus on work–life balance was, in part, attributed to the vast majority of iCon's projects being conducted in the Essen area, where most professional staff were based. Recent internationalization of the firm also increased importance of biannual "Consulting Days": company-wide, all-hands meetings that offered opportunities to meet colleagues from other offices.

There had been some changes in the culture over time that encouraged new approaches, and led to more independent operations, which enabled consultants to take a more critical viewpoint on client problems. Independence also had practical implications, allowing iCon to operate outside of the usual German works council[21] framework that was common at large corporates. In practice, this approach allowed the firm to mimic external consultancies in areas such as compensation, promotion policy, working hours, and travel policy. This way, iCon also managed to steadily increase its revenues (see Exhibit 6).

## GRELLMANN'S CHALLENGES GOING FORWARD

### Revenue Growth

The leadership team set a revenue-growth target of 45 per cent within five years. The company contemplated entering industries such as telecommunications, transportation, or manufacturing. Additionally, further countries beyond the existing network were also debated. With an expectation to showcase iCon's experience of dealing with the Energiewende, potential energy markets needed to be ripe for innovation and at the right stage of maturity to benefit from iCon's expertise.

### New Capabilities for New Niches

An altered client base required iCon to reconsider its offering. Digitization had become the word on the street, with competing consultancies moving toward engagements that were not fixed term, were not traditional consulting, and involved a continuous, data-driven approach. Being able to drive innovation for the client also turned out to be a service in high demand. Another new trend was pushing consultancies towards a more specific, tangible service offering, such as focusing on cross-selling retail products to end consumers. iCon would have to find new niches without spreading its capabilities too thin.

### Managing People

Longer-tenured employees saw a distinct iCon culture emerge. However, this culture was now at risk due to employee turnover. While many new employees had joined, the overall number of consulting staff had remained at between 120 and 140 personnel for the past few years. One consultant commented as follows:

> Back in 2013, we would add four or five new faces every quarter. Now we had that number of new employees joining every month. We all used to know each

other very well, which made teams more close-knit and created [a] better environment for mentorship. As we grow, we need to make sure we do not forget about our culture.

Rapid international growth also put a strain on the firm's internal administration and support services. As the company was poised to grow, its human resources, financial, and IT also needed to expand. The hybrid model at the international offices made this growth potentially more complicated. Another consultant observed:

It is rather difficult to get staffed on projects of choice and receive appropriate support, as that requires spending more time in the HQ [headquarters]. This is of course tricky for those of us based out of satellite offices.

Grellmann pondered these three challenges as he sat in his office in Essen in September 2016. The external management consultancy market was extremely competitive and most of iCon's strong ties were within its internal market. But iCon did have a platform on which to expand? The key question was: How could iCon take further steps to compete away from home?

## Notes

1  "innogy Consulting (in German)," squeaker.net, 2016, accessed April 19, 2018, www.squeaker. net/de/Inhouse-Consulting-Ranking/p/15/t/Platz-2.
2  All currency amounts are in euros unless otherwise stated; US$1 = €0.83 on January 1, 2015.
3  RWE, Annual Report 2015, March 8, 2016, www.rwe.com/web/cms/mediablob/en/2974774/ data/2705502/7/rwe/investor-relations/reports/2015/RWE-Annual-Report-2015.pdf.
4  Ibid.
5  innogy, "Further Steps towards the Planned IPO," September 12, 2016, accessed April 19, 2018, https://iam.innogy.com/-/media/innogy/documents/ueber-innogy/Investor-Relations/ipo/ ipo-2016-09-12-en.pdf.
6  RWE operated major distribution grids in Germany, Poland, the Czech Republic, Hungary, and Slovakia.
7  RWE, op. cit.
8  German for "energy transition" – the pivotal shift in German politics away from fossil fuels and toward renewable energy generation.
9  Feed-in tariffs were a regulatory mechanism that provided compensation above retail or wholesale electricity prices to operators of generation facilities, intended to increase investments in renewable energy.
10  Frauenhofer Institute for Solar Energy Systems ISE, "Power Generation in Germany – Assessment of 2016," February 7, 2017, accessed April 19, 2018, www.ise.fraunhofer.de/content/dam/ise/en/ documents/publications/studies/power-generation-from-renewable-energies-2016.pdf.
11  Rebecca Staudenmaier, "Germany's Nuclear Phase-Out Explained," Deutsche Welle, June 15, 2017, accessed April 19, 2018, www.dw.com/en/germanys-nuclear-phase-out-explained/a-39171204.
12  Christian von Hirschhausen, Clemens Gerbaulet, Claudia Kemfert, Felix Reitz, and Cornelia Ziehm, "German Nuclear Phase-Out Enters the Next Stage: Electricity Supply Remains Secure – Major Challenges and High Costs for Dismantling and Final Waste Disposal," DIW Economic Bulletin no. 22/23 (2015): 293–301, www.diw.de/documents/publikationen/73/diw_01.c.506840. de/diw_econ_bull_2015-22-1.pdf.

13  RWE, "RWE Share Price Information," 2016, accessed April 27, 2018, www.rwe.com/web/cms/en/109536/rwe/investor-relations/shares/share-prices/.

14  innogy, "Annual Report 2016," March 13, 2017, accessed April 27, 2018, https://iam.innogy.com/-/media/innogy/documents/ueber-innogy/Investor-Relations/q4-2016/annual-report-2016.pdf.

15  Individual consultants were leased by RWE to work on-site for a set amount of time – generally, a couple of months. These consultants would usually perform ordinary business functions rather than advise clients.

16  The DAX was a blue-chip stock market index that consisted of the 30 major German companies trading on the Frankfurt Stock Exchange. Horst J. Kayser, *Inhouse Consulting* (Frankfurt: Frankfurter Allgemeine Buch, 2015), 16.

17  Ibid.

18  Ibid., 23.

19  Organizational health was a quality that signified an organization's ability to grasp strategic priorities and follow through with their execution. The concept included intangible measures such as culture, innovation, and leadership.

20  External benchmarking was a tool used to compare the client's statistical data with other organizations within the industry. It helped companies assess their relative performance compared with the market average.

21  Germany's *Works Council Constitution* Act formulated the way in which employers interacted with their employees. The council's "co-determination" rights empowered elected employees to be involved in any decisions pertaining to areas such as rules of operation, wages, working hours and holidays, or workforce development.

## EXHIBIT 1 HISTORY OF INNOGY CONSULTING, 1981–2016

| | 1981 Org-consult | 1999 MIT & OC consult | 2002 RWE Systems | 2007 RWE Syst. Consulting | 2010 RWE Consulting | 2016 innogy Consulting |
|---|---|---|---|---|---|---|
| **Sectors** | • General<br>• Waste/disposal industry (from 1986) | • General | | | | |
| **Sectors** | | | • Energy<br>• Telecommunications | • Energy | • Energy | • Energy<br>• Public Sector |
| **Clients** | • Chemical industry<br>• Ministries, authorities<br>• RWE Entsorgung. AG | • RWE Group<br>• Other industries | • RWE Group<br>• Other industries | • RWE Group | • RWE Group | • innogy & RWE<br>• Partially externals – e.g. Dubai |
| **Focus** | • Organisation<br>• IT | • Procedural/ structural enhancement<br>• IT | • Project management<br>• IT | • Strategy<br>• Management advisory | • Strategy<br>• Management advisory | • Strategy<br>• Change<br>• Lean<br>• Reorganisation |
| **Staff** | 4 – 25 | ~100 | ~50 | ~120 | ~128 | ~165 (including Support Staff) |
| **Location** | Essen | Essen, Berlin, Mainz | Essen, Berlin, Mainz | Essen, Berlin, Frankfurt, London | Essen, Berlin, Frankfurt, Den Bosch, London, Prague | Essen, Berlin, Frankfurt, Den Bosch, London, Prague, Munich, Dubai |

*Note*: IT = information technology.

*Source*: Company documents.

## EXHIBIT 2 CONSULTING SERVICES OFFERED AT INNOGY CONSULTING IN 2016

| Groups | Services | | | | |
|---|---|---|---|---|---|
| **1 Strategy & Corporate Development** | Corporate strategy | Business unit strategy | Product & market strategy | Digital strategy | |
| **2 Operations** | Operational diagnostics | Operational excellence | Lean management & transformation | E2E process redesign | |
| **3 Systemic Change** | Leadership coaching & capability development | Systemic team & organisational development | Large group interventions and process facilitation | Design and facilitation of communication processes | |
| **4 Efficiency Programmes** | Organisational re-design | | Restructuring/cost-cutting | | |
| **5 Enterprise PMO** | Active project/programme management | | | | |
| **6 Digital Empowerment** | Digital transformation | | Digital customer Journey Design | | |
| **7 Start-up Support** | Business modelling/prototyping | Business case & financial planning | Business setup | Market introduction and stabilization | |

*Note:* E2E = end-to-end; PMO = project management office.

*Source:* Company documents.

## EXHIBIT 3 INNOGY CONSULTING'S INTERNATIONAL OFFICES AND HEADCOUNTS IN 2016

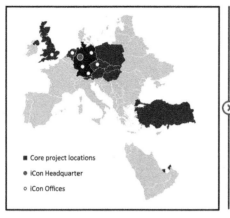

■ Core project locations
● iCon Headquarter
○ iCon Offices

| Country | Office Location | Headcount in 2016 |
|---|---|---|
| Germany | Essen (HQ), Berlin, Frankfurt, Munich | 107 |
| United Kingdom | London | 10 |
| Netherlands | Den Bosch | 8 |
| Czech Republic | Prague | 7 |
| UAE | Dubai | 8 |

*Note*: iCon = innogy Consulting; HQ = headquarters; UAE = United Arab Emirates.
*Source*: Company documents.

## EXHIBIT 4 INNOGY CONSULTING'S REPRESENTATIVE SAMPLE OF PROJECTS IN 2015/16

| Project Location | Sample Project Description |
|---|---|
| Germany | **Project Lux**: Development of innogy's steering model for grid, renewables, retail, and support functions |
| | **B2C TOM**: Set-up of a target operating model for innogy's B2C segment |
| United Kingdom | **NWoW@Pembroke**: Diagnostics phase of process-transformation project in gas power station aimed at enhancing effectiveness and performance |
| | **Future of Functions**: Definition of organizational design and set-up of support functions for innogy's retail arm |
| Netherlands | **NWoW@Eemshaven**: Diagnostic phase of a process-transformation project for a coal-powered plant |
| Czech Republic | **R&D@RWE ČR**: Technology-based scenario analysis, including strategic implications for the future development of the Czech energy sector |
| Slovakia | **Set-up RWE Slovensko**: Set-up of a new governance structure for RWE's operations in Slovakia |
| Poland | **IT assessment@RWE**: IT assessment of processes and organizational set-up at RWE Polska and RWE IT Poland |
| Belgium | **Project Silver**: Creation of an external spend reduction target |
| United Arab Emirates (UAE) | **Mobile Workforce**: Development of a mobile workforce-management system for UAE's key utilities |

*Notes*: B2C = business to consumer; TOM = target operating model; NWoW = new way of working; R&D = research and development; IT = information technology.
*Source*: Company documents.

## EXHIBIT 5  INNOGY CONSULTING'S EMPLOYEE STRUCTURE IN 2016

| innogy Consulting – Consulting & Support Staff | |
| --- | --- |
| Managing Director and Partners | 13 |
| Principals | 23 |
| Project Leads | 26 |
| Senior Consultants | 36 |
| Consultants | 42 |
| Support Staff | 25 |

*Source*: Company documents.

## EXHIBIT 6  INNOGY CONSULTING REVENUES, 2011–2016 (IN € MILLION)

| Year | Revenue |
| --- | --- |
| 2011 | 23.0 |
| 2012 | 24.5 |
| 2013 | 29.3 |
| 2014 | 29.0 |
| 2015 | 28.5 |
| 2016 | 32.8 |

*Note*: US$1 = €0.83 on January 1, 2015; 2016 = forecast for 2016 from Q3/2016.

*Source*: Company documents.

**Ivey** | Publishing

SCHOOL OF MANAGEMENT, XIAMEN UNIVERSITY

9B14M113

# HONGXIN ENTREPRENEUR INCUBATOR: EXPANDING THE CLOUD

*Professors Xiaosong Lin, Christopher Williams and Zhirong Mu wrote this case solely to provide material for class discussion. The authors do not intend to illustrate either effective or ineffective handling of a managerial situation. The authors may have disguised certain names and other identifying information to protect confidentiality.*

In June 2014, Qiang Li, founder and president of the Hongxin Entrepreneur Incubator, was reflecting on the success of his entrepreneurial efforts over the course of 13 years since 2001. He had established an entrepreneur incubator in Xiamen, Fujian Province that had become one of the most successful in China and had built high-level relationships with banks, government departments and leading companies in a range of industries. More than 100 companies, both start-ups and more developed enterprises, had joined and benefited from participation in the Hongxin Entrepreneur Incubator.

For the next phase of growth, Li intended to develop the incubator further by providing an online platform in which prospective member companies could register and share information about their ideas, strategies and business needs. Hongxin Entrepreneur Incubator would become a platform that would connect and support an alliance of entrepreneurs on a scale never seen before in China. As Li looked forward to taking the incubator in this new direction, he wondered how he could ensure continued success and maintain his philosophy of providing the best service to entrepreneurs.

## QIANG LI

Li was born in 1969 in Xiamen in the Fujian Province of China. Xiamen, also known as Amoy, was a port city of four million people in southeastern China. The Taiwan Strait separated Xiamen from the island of Taiwan. Xiamen had a natural harbour with deep water that was ice-free all year round. Thus, the city had been an important seaport for foreign trade on the southeast coast since ancient times. It had been one of the first four special economic zones designated by the national government in 1980 and had grown to be a vibrant manufacturing and trading hub with one of the best standards of living in China. It had attracted large amounts of investment from Hong Kong, Macao and Taiwan as well as from foreign countries and overseas Chinese.[1]

After earning a first degree in computing science, Li graduated with an MBA from Xiamen University in 2006. He later earned a PhD in management from Wuhan University of Technology. His thesis topic was in the field of micro-economics, with a specific focus on entrepreneur incubator business models. Before setting up his first business in 2001, he had worked for a state-owned enterprise (SOE), the Xiamen Port Authority, and had become the youngest member of its middle management team.

However, Li always considered himself to be an entrepreneur, albeit one who was motivated not only by financial gain, but also by being a "helping hand" to others. This trait was guided by his Taoist background and philosophy. Li emphasized a sense of belonging to community in his business affairs. He believed that when one is willing to put in effort to helping others, one will in turn be rewarded with help from others. He noted that "it is the same way by which people run a successful business."[2] His eventual success as an entrepreneur brought him accolades. He was awarded a Top-Ten Young Entrepreneurs prize by the Xiamen government in 2006. Since 2006, he had been an entrepreneurship mentor for MBA students at Xiamen University. Li was the largest shareholder of Hongxin Entrepreneur Incubator and had been its chief executive officer (CEO) since he set it up in 2001.

## HONGXIN ENTREPRENEUR INCUBATOR, 2001 TO 2010

Li's first entrepreneurial venture was set up in July 2001 in container leasing. Being a port city at a time of unprecedented economic growth in China, Xiamen was experiencing a boom in the logistics industry. Li's container leasing business was a simple idea in the right place and at the right time. The business soon took off.

The next venture materialized in late 2003. Li had majored in computing during his first degree at university and had always been interested in information technology (IT). His new venture came about because a high school classmate had experienced a failure in his own IT business that manufactured flexible printed circuit boards (FPCBs). Li felt he needed to help his friend. He invested in the business, establishing it as a joint venture ( JV), and helped to turn it around. The company – Hong-Flex – eventually became one of the top manufacturers of FPCBs in China.

By 2006, Li's businesses were growing fast and gaining capital. He decided to take a big step forward in the transportation business by purchasing one used bulk cargo ship and running an international shipping business. In 2010, he ordered two ships to be built to his specifications in the Xiamen shipyard, a stone's throw from his office. The ships, called *Honyworld* and *Honyfuture*, were delivered in 2012.

In 2008, Li entered the investment banking arena for the first time. A PhD classmate from the Wuhan University of Technology had approached him in July for financial advice and guidance. The classmate's own business in the security equipment manufacturing industry was experiencing severe financial difficulties. He wanted to sell it. Although he did not make any investment in his classmate's business, Li provided consulting on improving the company's operational efficiency in preparation for the sale and then helped orchestrate the sale to Swiss engineering conglomerate ABB, which had had operations in Xiamen for many years. The sale price in July 2009 was over 10 times what Li's friend had expected.

ABB was a big investor in Xiamen and was very well-known to the provincial government, which heard about the deal struck by Li between ABB and his friend's business. The provincial government then approached Li to help with a seemingly intractable problem it was facing. One of its SOEs was a mobile phone manufacturer called Amoisonic, which provided mobile phones to the Chinese market and, while originally profitable, had experienced severe financial difficulties between 2007 and 2009. In fact, the company had made a cumulative loss of $500 million over the three-year period. The provincial government approached Li for his help in avoiding bankruptcy, which would have been a disaster for the government and would have resulted in a delisting of the company from the Chinese stock exchange. As the license to be a listed company on the Chinese stock exchange was valuable, the government faced potential damage to its reputation. At that time, Amoisonic had 4,000 creditors, 70,000 shareholders (in addition to the provincial government) and 20,000 employees all over China.

Li provided a route map for restructuring Amoisonic's debt, as well as business consulting to improve operating efficiency. The result was a successful turnaround, with the company split into two parts, one SOE – Xiangyu Company Limited – in which most debt resided, and the other a retail mobile phone company. In 2011, the Amoisonic case was nominated as one of the best in class for merger and restructuring by the Shanghai Stock Exchange.[3] Stakeholders were satisfied with the outcome, and Li received widespread praise.

During this period of time (2009 to 2010), Li became involved in real estate and set up a new investment business, investing capital in real estate opportunities in and around the Xiamen area. He had previously given advice on real estate transactions, but was now actively investing.

Over the 10 years from 2001 to 2010, Li had provided a range of consulting services to local private and public sector organizations and had established wholly owned business units within the Hongxin Entrepreneur Incubator that had all been very successful. At the beginning of 2011, he began to write his PhD dissertation at Wuhan University of Technology.[4] It was at this time that he felt the success of Hongxin Entrepreneur Incubator was not by chance but by a unique business model he had developed. He labeled this "Hongxin Cloud Entrepreneurship." He wanted more people to know about this business model and felt the need to expand into new geographies and industries and to open up his incubator to external companies to join. Li recalled: "I felt I was doing well, but I wanted to give something back to society and help smaller businesses realize their potential."

## HONGXIN CLOUD ENTREPRENEURSHIP, 2010 TO 2013

The Hongxin Cloud Entrepreneurship model meant that external companies in Xiamen (either in start-up mode or more established local companies that were facing some kind of crisis) would contact the Hongxin Entrepreneur Incubator in pursuit of a range of potential outcomes. These could be financial resources, access to government, industry information or other opportunities to do business with leading companies. In return, the incubator would take an equity stake in the business. The external companies joining the incubator would normally build their relationships over time through personal contact with Li.

Li saw that many small companies in the Xiamen area at the time were run by owners who lacked financial expertise and core knowledge in how to run a business. He had observed how their knowledge was gained by doing, rather than through formal education. Start-up failure rates in Xiamen were high as it was difficult for many of these companies to get financial support and human capital, as well as the basic information and market intelligence needed to have a successful start. For a long time, the Chinese provincial and national governments were powerful and controlled a lot of the resources that small businesses required. As such, entrepreneurs had little opportunity to connect with government officials in order to secure land (cheaper land was more difficult to obtain), funds (government loads were often free of interest), favourable tax rates and procurement opportunities in government.

Based on its financial resources, industry experiences, management skills and strong relationships with industry and government, the Hongxin Entrepreneur Incubator assessed the qualifications, competency and potential of the start-up or developing companies and then linked these companies with banks, government and leading companies in a range of industries. The Hongxin Entrepreneur Incubator not only provided resources and support to the start-up or developing companies but also played a role as a risk assessor and endorser between them and banks, government and other leading companies.

Starting in 2012, the Hongxin Entrepreneur Incubator collaborated with some provincial governments to build industrial parks. Five industrial parks – located in Xiamen and four other cities in different provinces outside of Fujian Province – had been built or were in the process of being built by 2014. Playing the lead role in a company's network of alliances, the Hongxin Entrepreneur Incubator had strong bargaining power and was able to get very favourable conditions from provincial governments. The incubator could lease land or factories to members at a lower price, attract the leading companies in a range of industries to locate their factories in the industrial park by facilitating their business and then link members to these leading companies, help them get supporting policies from governments and so on. By actually building industrial parks, Hongxin Entrepreneur Incubator expected to develop high-level relationships with provincial governments, leading companies and its members while making profit for itself.

Since 2007, the Hongxin Entrepreneur Incubator had organized and hosted the Hongxin Annual Forum of Economic Situation Analysis.[5] The main objective of this forum was to analyze how macro-economic situational changes would affect small businesses and suggest how small business people could adapt to new situations. This forum was made open to the public in 2013. Not only Li but also distinguished scholars from Xiamen University, top managers of banks in Xiamen and senior Xiamen government officers gave speeches. Most of the forecasts given in the forum turned out to be correct. In the 2013 forum, Li suggested that companies should be ready for an upcoming economic crisis, focus on their core businesses and maintain a strong financial position and liquidity. In this way, Hongxin Entrepreneur Incubator provided advice to current and prospective members while enhancing its reputation.

By 2012, Li had built a management team of about 100 full-time employees to help him manage the incubator. He felt that environmental change was becoming ever faster and that small companies were finding it increasingly difficult to make sense of and adapt to the environment. Building an effective organization to run the incubator was key to his expansion vision for it. Exhibit 1 shows the organizational chart.

Two examples of companies that sought assistance from the incubator were Hengkun New Material Technology and Hongxin Health Industry Investment.

### Hengkun New Material Technology

Hengkun New Material Technology (Hengkun) was established in 1996 and joined the Hongxin Cloud Entrepreneurship program in 2013. Hengkun supplied electronic information products, such as nameplate and LCD screens, to leading electronic information companies such as Sony, Apple and Samsung. Key clients in 2014 are shown in Exhibit 2. Although the company had been moderately successful, it found it increasingly difficult to develop high-level connections within client organizations; top level managers would simply not see them.

Rong-Kun Yi (Kerry) was Hengkun's CEO and largest shareholder. He was enrolled in the EMBA program at Xiamen University and had been a friend of Li for several years, having originally met him at a social event a decade previously. Joining the Hongxin Entrepreneur Incubator had a number of benefits for Kerry and Hengkun. First and foremost, the incubator enabled him to obtain more face-to-face time with senior managers in potential client organizations within China. The subsequent sales pitches resulted in an immediate improvement in sales of existing product lines. Secondly, both the incubator and client organizations provided new product development requests and presented Hengkun with ideas for product enhancements that it had not previously considered. Kerry noted how creativity within Hengkun increased as a result of joining the incubator.

However, as a condition of joining and receiving financial support, Hongxin Entrepreneur Incubator required Hengkun to undergo certain improvements in its management practices, mainly around core functions such as human resources (HR), finance and production. These changes increased management costs and initially presented a challenge for managers during implementation. Hengkun had previously sought strategy advice from Chinese consulting companies, but Kerry noted that the consultants' advice was seen by Hengkun's managers as rather superficial and not that practical. The incubator, by contrast, provided suggestions and helped with implementation. Said Kerry: "Mr. Li's team of professional managers has helped . . . there was more follow through. Before we were fighting on our own . . . now we are part of a team."

Like many others in the business community in Xiamen, Kerry saw Li as a role model and someone who provided a boost to his confidence by providing management expertise as well as financial support.

By mid-2014, Hengkun had entered a growth phase and had plans to set up three new factories across China. The company had started to prepare for an initial public offering (IPO) for 2015 and Hongxin Entrepreneur Incubator, having taken an equity stake, was intricately involved in preparing the IPO. Kerry was willing to help other companies in the Hongxin Entrepreneur Incubator. He shared Li's philosophy and approach. For example, Hengkun was a majority partner in a JV with a Japanese electronics company for a manufacturing plant in China. Kerry was willing to introduce other members of the incubator to the Japanese company. He was willing to use his company's resources to help others – particularly smaller companies – in the incubator.

### Hongxin Health Industry Investment

Hongxin Health Industry Investment was a brand new start-up with a fresh entrepreneurial idea and proposition. The entrepreneur in question was Xiaodong Mao. Mao graduated in 1996 with a degree in international politics. He worked for an SOE for 17 years in the power generation industry. He then decided to start his own business. His idea, formed in May 2013, was to build a business that supplied health-related and wellness services to entrepreneurs and their families, such as supplying healthy food from local and international markets, sending clients abroad for medical service and organizing social events for clients to build relationships with each other. Mao had observed how entrepreneurs in small businesses were often so caught up in their enterprises that they tended to neglect their own well-being. In July 2013, Mao's younger brother, who had known Li for over five years and whose company had joined the Hongxin Cloud Entrepreneurship program, introduced Mao to Li.

As a consequence of their conversation, Mao put together a formal proposal to form Hongxin Health Industry Investment, a start-up that would deliver health-related services to other entrepreneurs within the Hongxin cloud. Mao held 20 per cent share of Hongxin Health Industry Investment while the Hongxin Entrepreneur Incubator held the majority stake of the company. Mao was worried about the potential risks of failure, but these were diminished by setting up within the Hongxin cloud and accepting an equity investment from it. He felt that Hongxin Entrepreneur Incubator helped his business model to become sound. By June 2014, his business was generating sales to about 150 entrepreneurs and their families. In total, the company looked after around 600 people.

Mao had 10 full-time employees and two additional companies under his control. One of these companies was responsible for running a hospitality space in downtown Xiamen, where members from companies within the incubator could meet over traditional Fujian tea and meals to discuss business (a layout of one of the meeting rooms is shown in Exhibit 3). Hongxin Entrepreneur Incubator also provided a regular micro-economic analysis of Mao's company and other forms of help such as a monthly review to monitor performance and provide guidance as needed.

Following the steady development within the first year of operation, Mao wondered how he could expand his business by offering high quality health and well-being services to entrepreneurs in other cities in China. He had heard about Li's plans to extend the Hongxin cloud across the whole of China and considered the prospect of potentially thousands of entrepreneur clients and family members. But his service delivery model was very personalized, and service delivery would always need to be localized. He did not know how to explore and pursue this possible direction for his company.

Mao also wondered how he could tap into international markets to boost his business. Although Hongxin Entrepreneur Incubator did not have a specific plan to extend to the international market, Mao was aware of a vast amount of health and well-being information in other countries, particularly developed countries. Such information could help him make informed decisions about how to develop his own services in China. There were many international conferences and seminars that he and his team could attend and many health and well-being providers around the world, but he had not made any specific plans to go on any fact-finding missions abroad. He was aware of the global medical devices industry but had not yet tapped into it. He also wondered whether there was a lucrative opportunity to connect his clients within China to international markets, for example, by sending them abroad as part of their personalized care program.

## EXTENDING THE CLOUD TO A NATIONAL ONLINE ALLIANCE

Following the initial success of the Hongxin Cloud Entrepreneurship program, Li set in motion plans for a new phase for the incubator in 2014. The new vision was to develop the program as an on-line alliance across the whole of China, not just in Fujian Province. The idea was that any start-up or, for that matter, established company such as Hengkun, could apply for membership online. The online platform would allow a company to specify what kind of support it needed from the incubator as well as provide a range of information about its own goals and strategies. By opening up in this way, the Hongxin Entrepreneur Incubator would multiply the number of potential members, connecting together an increasingly wide net of companies and developing the alliance in new geographies and industries. Exhibit 4 shows organizational descriptive data for the period 2001 to 2014, as well as the anticipated growth in the year following the start of the national online alliance.

In May 2014, Li organized a meeting to discuss how to extend the cloud as an online alliance. Some of the Hongxin Entrepreneur Incubator management team members, as well as representatives from Hongxin Cloud Entrepreneurship member companies, attended this meeting. There were so many people that they needed to sit as two circles around the table. Delegates needed to consider which circle was suitable for themselves by considering their status. When Li entered, he suggested people in the inner circle move away from the table and form a bigger circle so that people seating in the outer circle could join in one big circle. People applauded Li for his suggestion. One said, "Brother Qiang is always able to have a good idea and make everybody feel happy." Li smiled.

As of June 2014, Li had deployed an internal team to work on the design of the online platform. No development had actually started, and Li envisaged that development work would be carried out by an external agency.

## ISSUES BEFORE LI IN JUNE 2014

### Scaling the incubator nationally

Li was concerned that it would become more difficult for the Hongxin Entrepreneur Incubator to act effectively in its role as a risk assessor and endorser between new companies and banks, government and other established companies. He wondered how the Hongxin Entrepreneur Incubator could get to know new members as well as it did in the past with local companies. How could he ensure that long-term relationships could still be established if the incubator was scaled nationally through the online platform? How could the local personal contact approach be maintained and risks be managed on a national basis?

With an anticipated growth in companies joining the incubator, Li wondered how their needs could be met. Companies such as Hongxin Health Industry Investment had already indicated an international mindset and a willingness to engage in international markets. The online platform was also likely to attract more companies with different capabilities and problems to solve. How could Li ensure that diversity within the alliance would not be a threat but an opportunity for Hongxin Entrepreneur Incubator?

## Protecting the philosophy

In Li's view, one of the incubator's main strengths was that it was not just a profit-seeking business, it was also a mechanism to provide support to new companies and to establish a community within society. With change occurring faster and faster, the incubator was a place where small business people could come to make sense of trends in the business environment. With increasing numbers of companies joining the incubator, and with ventures in new geographies and industries, how could Li maintain the central philosophy of being a helping hand to small business people?

## Entering new industries

With the growing number of members and more diversity in industries represented within the Hongxin Entrepreneur Incubator, Li felt it was the right time to enter a new business domain. He believed that the emerging mobile Internet industry was promising. How could he reorganize the incubator's businesses and resources to support members in this new segment? How could he select and lead the members to focus on the mobile Internet industry?

## Notes

1   Xiamen Government website, http://english.xm.gov.cn/, accessed July 16, 2014.
2   Interview with case authors, June 30, 2014.
3   Shanghai Stock Exchange, www.sse.com.cn/, accessed July 16, 2014.
4   The title of Qiang Li's PhD thesis was "Research on Cloud Entrepreneurial Platforms."
5   www.xmhx.com/newsview.aspx?mid=8&childid=44&linkid=511, accessed July 19, 2014.

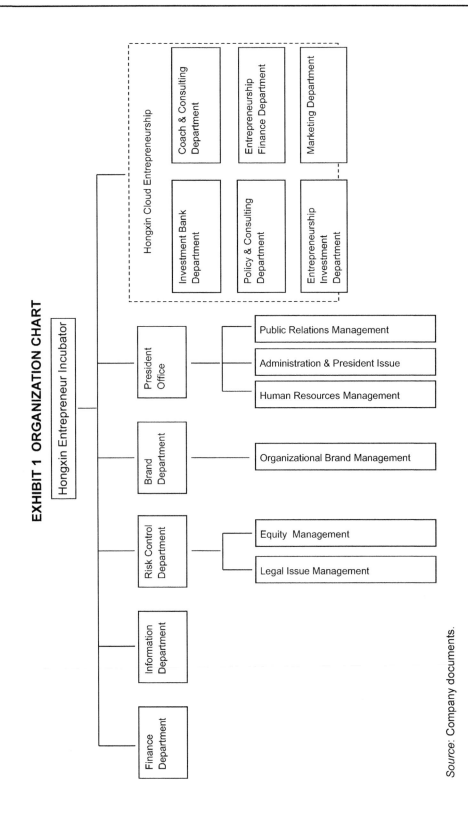

## EXHIBIT 1 ORGANIZATION CHART

**Hongxin Entrepreneur Incubator**

- Finance Department
- Information Department
- Risk Control Department
  - Equity Management
  - Legal Issue Management
- Brand Department
  - Organizational Brand Management
- President Office
  - Public Relations Management
  - Administration & President Issue
  - Human Resources Management
- Hongxin Cloud Entrepreneurship
  - Investment Bank Department
  - Policy & Consulting Department
  - Entrepreneurship Investment Department
  - Coach & Consulting Department
  - Entrepreneurship Finance Department
  - Marketing Department

*Source:* Company documents.

## EXHIBIT 2  KEY CLIENTS OF HENGKUN NEW MATERIALS TECHNOLOGY

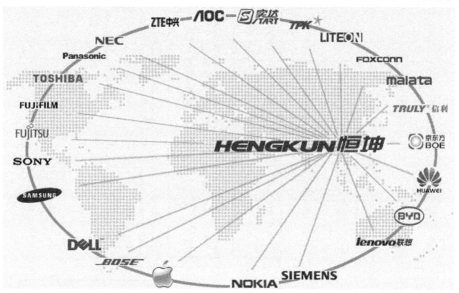

*Source*: Company documents.

## EXHIBIT 3  INCUBATOR MEETING ROOM RUN BY HONGXIN HEALTH INDUSTRY INVESTMENT

*Source*: Case authors.

## EXHIBIT 4  KEY CHARACTERISTICS OF HONGXIN ENTREPRENEUR INCUBATOR

| Characteristic | Initial Phase 2001–2010 | Cloud Phase 2010–2013 | Cloud Expansion Phase 2014–2015 (Predicted) |
|---|---|---|---|
| # employees in the incubator | 12–50 | 50–100 | 100–150 |
| Range of industries of incubator's own business | container leasing, equipment leasing, electronics, logistics, shipping | container leasing, equipment leasing, financial lease, electronics, logistics, shipping, real estate | container leasing, equipment leasing, financial lease, electronics, logistics, shipping, real estate, mobile Internet |
| # companies in incubator's own business | 1–9 | 9–21 | +21 |
| # companies in which incubator has investment | 0 | 8 | 20 |
| Type of member company | principally owned by Hongxin Entrepreneur Incubator | fully owned + shared ownership (equity stake) | fully owned + shared ownership (equity stake) + no stake |
| # companies in the incubator | 0 | 16 | 50 |
| # companies with international business | 0 | 4 | 20 |
| Range of industries | 0 | 3 | +3 |
| Range of provinces | 0 | 3 | +6 |
| Gross turnover of all member companies in the incubator | 0 | $0.25 billion | $1.67 billion |
| Total employees of all member companies in the incubator | 0 | +8,000 | +20,000 |

Source: Company documents and interviews with company managers on June 30, 2014.

# References

Abernathy, W.J. and Clark, K.B., 1985. Innovation: Mapping the winds of creative destruction. *Research Policy*, *14*(1), pp. 3–22.

Accenture, 2017. Retrieved from www.accenture.com/t00010101T000000Z__w__/gb-en/_acnmedia/PDF-75/Accenture-2017-Corporate-Citizenship-Report.pdf accessed 16 January 2019.

Acs, Z.J. and Audretsch, D.B., 1987. Innovation in large and small firms. *Economics Letters*, *23*(1), pp. 109–112.

Acs, Z.J. and Fitzroy, F.R., 1989. Inside the firm and organizational capital: A review article. *International Journal of Industrial Organization*, 7(2), pp. 309–314.

Adler, P.S. and Kwon, S.W., 2002. Social capital: Prospects for a new concept. *Academy of Management Review*, *27*(1), pp. 17–40.

Afsarmanesh, H. and Camarinha-Matos, L.M., 2005, September. A framework for management of virtual organization breeding environments. In *Working conference on virtual enterprises* (pp. 35–48). Springer, Boston, MA.

Ahmed, P.K., 1998. Culture and climate for innovation. *European Journal of Innovation Management*, *1*(1), pp. 30–43.

Ahuja, G., 2000. Collaboration networks, structural holes, and innovation: A longitudinal study. *Administrative Science Quarterly*, *45*(3), pp. 425–455.

Allard, G., Martinez, C.A. and Williams, C., 2012. Political instability, pro-business market reforms and their impacts on national systems of innovation. *Research Policy*, *41*(3), pp. 638–651.

Amara, N. and Landry, R., 2005. Sources of information as determinants of novelty of innovation in manufacturing firms: Evidence from the 1999 statistics Canada innovation survey. *Technovation*, *25*(3), pp. 245–259.

Amara, N., Landry, R. and Doloreux, D., 2009. Patterns of innovation in knowledge-intensive business services. *The Service Industries Journal*, *29*(4), pp. 407–430.

Anand, N., Gardner, H.K. and Morris, T., 2007. Knowledge-based innovation: Emergence and embedding of new practice areas in management consulting firms. *Academy of Management Journal*, *50*(2), pp. 406–428.

Andreu, R., Lara, E. and Sieber, S., 2004. 'Knowledge management at CAP Gemini, Ernst & Young', *IESE Publishing* (product number: IES133).

Atkeson, A. and Kehoe, P.J., 2005. Modeling and measuring organization capital. *Journal of Political Economy*, *113*(5), pp. 1026–1053.

Back, Y., Parboteeah, K.P. and Nam, D.I., 2014. Innovation in emerging markets: The role of management consulting firms. *Journal of International Management*, 20(4), pp. 390–405.

Baldwin, J. and Johnson, J., 1995. *Business strategies in innovative and non-innovative firms in Canada* (No. 73). Statistics Canada, Ottawa.

Baptista, A., Santos, F., Páscoa, J. and Sändig, N., 2016. Project management methodologies as main tool for current challenges in global economy driving historical changes. *Journal of Advanced Management Science*, 4(2), pp. 146–151.

Baregheh, A., Rowley, J. and Sambrook, S., 2009. Towards a multidisciplinary definition of innovation. *Management Decision*, 47(8), pp. 1323–1339.

Barker, M. and Neailey, K., 1999. From individual learning to project team learning and innovation: A structured approach. *Journal of Workplace Learning*, 11(2), pp. 60–67.

Barney, J.B., 1996. The resource-based theory of the firm. *Organization Science*, 7(5), pp. 469–469.

Bartlett, C., 1996. 'McKinsey & Company: Managing knowledge and learning', *Harvard Business School* (product number: 9-396-357).

Bartlett, C.A. and Ghoshal, S., 2002. *Managing across borders: The transnational solution*. Harvard Business Press, Boston, MA.

Batra, S. and Puri, S., 2015. 'GCS consulting: Should corporate or personal interests come first?', Ivey Publishing (product number: 9B15M042).

Becker, G.S., 1962. Investment in human capital: A theoretical analysis. *Journal of Political Economy*, 70(5, Part 2), pp. 9–49.

Bell, B.S. and Kozlowski, S.W., 2002. A typology of virtual teams: Implications for effective leadership. *Group & Organization Management*, 27(1), pp. 14–49.

Bergiel, B.J., Bergiel, E.B. and Balsmeier, P.W., 2008. Nature of virtual teams: A summary of their advantages and disadvantages. *Management Research News*, 31(2), pp. 99–110.

Besner, C. and Hobbs, B., 2008. Discriminating contexts and project management best practices on innovative and noninnovative projects. *Project Management Journal*, 39(1_suppl), pp. S123–S134.

Bessant, J. and Davies, A., 2007. Managing service innovation. *Innovation in Services*, DTI Occasional Paper No. 9, pp. 61–96.

Bessant, J. and Rush, H., 1995. Building bridges for innovation: The role of consultants in technology transfer. *Research Policy*, 24(1), pp. 97–114.

Blaug, M., 1976. The empirical status of human capital theory: A slightly jaundiced survey. *Journal of Economic Literature*, 14(3), pp. 827–855.

Bloom, N., Kretschmer, T. and Van Reenan, J., 2009. Work-life balance, management practices and productivity. In *International differences in the business practices and productivity of firms* (pp. 15–54). University of Chicago Press, Chicago.

Bolino, M.C., Turnley, W.H. and Bloodgood, J.M., 2002. Citizenship behavior and the creation of social capital in organizations. *Academy of Management Review*, 27(4), pp. 505–522.

Bontis, N. and Fitz-Enz, J., 2002. Intellectual capital ROI: A causal map of human capital antecedents and consequents. *Journal of Intellectual Capital*, 3(3), pp. 223–247.

Booth, A.L. and Bryan, M.L., 2005. Testing some predictions of human capital theory: New training evidence from Britain. *Review of Economics and Statistics*, 87(2), pp. 391–394.

Bornay-Barrachina, M., la Rosa-Navarro, D., López-Cabrales, A. and Valle-Cabrera, R., 2012. Employment relationships and firm innovation: The double role of human capital. *British Journal of Management, 23*(2), pp. 223–240.

Boudreau, M.C., Loch, K.D., Robey, D. and Straud, D., 1998. Going global: Using information technology to advance the competitiveness of the virtual transnational organization. *Academy of Management Perspectives, 12*(4), pp. 120–128.

Bourdieu, P., 1989. Social space and symbolic power. *Sociological Theory, 7*(1), pp. 14–25.

Boxall, P. and Steeneveld, M., 1999. Human resource strategy and competitive advantage: A longitudinal study of engineering consultancies. *Journal of Management studies, 36*(4), pp. 443–463.

Bozeman, B., Dietz, J.S. and Gaughan, M., 2001. Scientific and technical human capital: An alternative model for research evaluation. *International Journal of Technology Management, 22*(7–8), pp. 716–740.

Braun Jr, J.A. and Crumpler, T.P., 2004. The social memoir: An analysis of developing reflective ability in a pre-service methods course. *Teaching and Teacher Education, 20*(1), pp. 59–75.

Brescia, R.H., McCarthy, W., McDonald, A., Potts, K. and Rivais, C., 2014. Embracing disruption: How technological change in the delivery of legal services can improve access to justice. *Albany Law Review, 78*, pp. 553–621.

Brown, J.S. and Duguid, P., 1991. Organizational learning and communities-of-practice: Toward a unified view of working, learning, and innovation. *Organization Science, 2*(1), pp. 40–57.

Buckler, B., 1996. A learning process model to achieve continuous improvement and innovation. *The Learning Organization, 3*(3), pp. 31–39.

Buday, R., 2003. 'A consultant's comeuppance', *Harvard Business Review Case Study* (product number: R0302X).

Buganza, T. and Verganti, R., 2006. Life-cycle flexibility: How to measure and improve the innovative capability in turbulent environments. *Journal of Product Innovation Management, 23*(5), pp. 393–407.

Bunderson, J.S. and Sutcliffe, K.M., 2003. Management team learning orientation and business unit performance. *Journal of Applied Psychology, 88*(3), pp. 552–560.

Burns, T. and Stalker, G.M., 1961. *The management of innovation.* Tavistock, London.

Burt, R.S., 2000. The network structure of social capital. *Research in Organizational Behavior, 22*, pp. 345–423.

Burt R.S., 2001. Structural holes versus network closure as social capital. In Lin, N., Cook, K., and Burt, R.S. (eds.) *Social capital: Theory and research* (pp. 31–56). Aldine de Gruyter, Chicago, IL.

Camarinha-Matos, L.M., Afsarmanesh, H., Galeano, N. and Molina, A., 2009. Collaborative networked organizations – Concepts and practice in manufacturing enterprises. *Computers & Industrial Engineering, 57*(1), pp. 46–60.

Canato, A. and Giangreco, A., 2011. Gurus or wizards? A review of the role of management consultants. *European Management Review, 8*(4), pp. 231–244.

Chen, C.J. and Huang, J.W., 2009. Strategic human resource practices and innovation performance – The mediating role of knowledge management capacity. *Journal of Business Research, 62*(1), pp. 104–114.

Chen, J., Tran, T.S. and Williams, C., 2018. 'innogy Consulting: Competing away from home', *Ivey Publishing* (product ID: 9B18M159).

Cheng, G. and Chau, J., 2013. A study of the effects of goal orientation on the reflective ability of electronic portfolio users. *The Internet and Higher Education, 16*, pp. 51–56.

Chesbrough, H.W. and Teece, D.J., 1996. Organizing for innovation. *Harvard Business Review, 74*(1), pp. 65–73.

Choi, S.B. and Williams, C., 2016. Entrepreneurial orientation and performance: Mediating effects of technology and marketing action across industry types. *Industry and Innovation, 23*(8), pp. 673–693.

Christensen, C.M., 1997. *The innovator's dilemma*. Harvard Business School Press, Cambridge, MA.

Christensen, C.M., Wang, D. and Van Bever, D., 2013. Consulting on the cusp of disruption. *Harvard Business Review, 91*(10), pp. 106–114.

Cicmil, S. and Hodgson, D., 2006. New possibilities for project management theory: A critical engagement. *Project Management Journal, 37*(3), pp. 111–122.

Cohen, S.G. and Mankin, D., 1999. Collaboration in the virtual organization. *Journal of Organizational Behavior, 6*, pp. 105–120.

Coleman, J.S., 1988. Social capital in the creation of human capital. *American Journal of Sociology, 94*, pp. S95–S120.

Collyer, S., Warren, C., Hemsley, B. and Stevens, C., 2010. Aim, fire, aim – Project planning styles in dynamic environments. *Project Management Journal, 41*(4), pp. 108–121.

Cooke, P. and Wills, D., 1999. Small firms, social capital and the enhancement of business performance through innovation programmes. *Small Business Economics, 13*(3), pp. 219–234.

Costanza, R., d'Arge, R., de Groot, R., Farber, S., Grasso, M., Hannon, B., Limburg, K., Naeem, S., O'Neill, R.V., Paruelo, J., Raskin, R.G., Sutton, P. and van den Belt, M., 1997. The value of the world's ecosystem services and natural capital. *Nature, 387*(6630), pp. 253–260.

Crawford, L., 2006. Developing organizational project management capability: Theory and practice. *Project Management Journal, 37*(3), pp. 74–86.

Creplet, F., Dupouet, O., Kern, F., Mehmanpazir, B. and Munier, F., 2001. Consultants and experts in management consulting firms. *Research Policy, 30*(9), pp. 1517–1535.

Crevani, L., Palm, K. and Schilling, A., 2011. Innovation management in service firms: A research agenda. *Service Business, 5*(2), pp. 177–193.

Cunha, J.A. and Moura, H., 2014. Project management office: The state of the art based on a systematic review. In *European conference on management, leadership & governance* (pp. 41–49). Academic Conferences International Limited, Zagreb.

Czarnitzki, D. and Spielkamp, A., 2003. Business services in Germany: Bridges for innovation. *The Service Industries Journal, 23*(2), pp. 1–30.

Daft, R.L., 1978. A dual-core model of organizational innovation. *Academy of Management Journal, 21*(2), pp. 193–210.

Damanpour, F., 1991. Organizational innovation: A meta-analysis of effects of determinants and moderators. *Academy of Management Journal, 34*(3), pp. 555–590.

Damanpour, F. and Aravind, D., 2012. Managerial innovation: Conceptions, processes and antecedents. *Management and Organization Review, 8*(2), pp. 423–454.

Darling, E.J. and Whitty, S.J., 2016. The project management office: It's just not what it used to be. *International Journal of Managing Projects in Business*, *9*(2), pp. 282–308.

Dauda, R.S., 2012. The scourge of HIV/AIDS pandemic and economic performance: The case of Nigeria. *Global Journal of Human-Social Science Research*, *12*(1). Retrieved from https://socialscienceresearch.org/index.php/GJHSS/article/view/255 accessed 25 January 2019.

Davidsson, P. and Honig, B., 2003. The role of social and human capital among nascent entrepreneurs. *Journal of Business Venturing*, *18*(3), pp. 301–331.

DeSanctis, G. and Monge, P., 1999. Introduction to the special issue: Communication processes for virtual organizations. *Organization Science*, *10*(6), pp. 693–703.

D'Este, P., Rentocchini, F. and Vega-Jurado, J., 2014. The role of human capital in lowering the barriers to engaging in innovation: Evidence from the Spanish innovation survey. *Industry and Innovation*, *21*(1), pp. 1–19.

De Vries, E.J., 2006. Innovation in services in networks of organizations and in the distribution of services. *Research Policy*, *35*(7), pp. 1037–1051.

Dewar, R.D. and Dutton, J.E., 1986. The adoption of radical and incremental innovations: An empirical analysis. *Management Science*, *32*(11), pp. 1422–1433.

Dewey, J., 1922. *Human nature and conduct*. Holt, New York.

De Winne, S. and Sels, L., 2010. Interrelationships between human capital, HRM and innovation in Belgian start-ups aiming at an innovation strategy. *The International Journal of Human Resource Management*, *21*(11), pp. 1863–1883.

Dittrich, K., Duysters, G. and de Man, A.P., 2007. Strategic repositioning by means of alliance networks: The case of IBM. *Research Policy*, *36*(10), pp. 1496–1511.

Drach-Zahavy, A. and Somech, A., 2001. Understanding team innovation: The role of team processes and structures. *Group Dynamics: Theory, Research, and Practice*, *5*(2), pp. 111–123.

Eccles, R.G., Narayandas, D. and Rossano, P., 2013. 'Innovation at the Boston Consulting Group', *Harvard Business School* (product number: 9-313-137).

Edmondson, A.C., 1999. Psychological safety and learning behavior in work teams. *Administrative Science Quarterly*, *44*(2), pp. 350–383.

Edmondson, A.C., Bohmer, R.M. and Pisano, G.P., 2001. Disrupted routines: Team learning and new technology implementation in hospitals. *Administrative Science Quarterly*, *46*(4), pp. 685–716.

Eisenhardt, K.M. and Santos, F.M., 2002. Knowledge-based view: A new theory of strategy. *Handbook of Strategy and Management*, *1*(1), pp. 139–164.

Engeström, Y., 1999. Innovative learning in work teams: Analyzing cycles of knowledge creation in practice. *Perspectives on Activity Theory*, pp. 377–404.

Erskine, J.A. and Cruji, C., 2010. 'Campbell management consulting', *Ivey Publishing* (product number: 9A99D003).

Evan, W.M., 1966. Organizational lag. *Human Organization*, *25*(1), pp. 51–53.

Flap, H., 2002. No man is an Island: The research programme of a social capital theory. In Favereau, O. and Lazega, E. (eds.) *Conventions and structures in economic organisations: Markets and hierarchies*, Chapter 1. Edward Elgar, Cheltenham.

Florin, J., Lubatkin, M. and Schulze, W., 2003. A social capital model of high-growth ventures. *Academy of Management Journal*, *46*(3), pp. 374–384.

Furst, S.A., Reeves, M., Rosen, B. and Blackburn, R.S., 2004. Managing the life cycle of virtual teams. *Academy of Management Perspectives, 18*(2), pp. 6–20.

Gallié, E.P. and Legros, D., 2012. Firms' human capital, R&D and innovation: A study on French firms. *Empirical Economics, 43*(2), pp. 581–596.

Gallivan, M.J., 2001. Striking a balance between trust and control in a virtual organization: A content analysis of open source software case studies. *Information Systems Journal, 11*(4), pp. 277–304.

Gallouj, F. and Weinstein, O., 1997. Innovation in services. *Research Policy, 26*(4–5), pp. 537–556.

Gibson, C.B. and Birkinshaw, J., 2004. The antecedents, consequences, and mediating role of organizational ambidexterity. *Academy of Management Journal, 47*(2), pp. 209–226.

Gibson, C.B. and Gibbs, J.L., 2006. Unpacking the concept of virtuality: The effects of geographic dispersion, electronic dependence, dynamic structure, and national diversity on team innovation. *Administrative Science Quarterly, 51*(3), pp. 451–495.

Gibson, C. and Vermeulen, F., 2003. A healthy divide: Subgroups as a stimulus for team learning behavior. *Administrative Science Quarterly, 48*(2), pp. 202–239.

Glynn, M.A., 1996. Innovative genius: A framework for relating individual and organizational intelligences to innovation. *Academy of Management Review, 21*(4), pp. 1081–1111.

Goyal, A. and Akhilesh, K.B., 2007. Interplay among innovativeness, cognitive intelligence, emotional intelligence and social capital of work teams. *Team Performance Management: An International Journal, 13*(7–8), pp. 206–226.

Granovetter, M., 1983. The strength of weak ties: A network theory revisited. *Sociological Theory, 1*, pp. 201–233.

Grant, A., Kinnersley, P., Metcalf, E., Pill, R. and Houston, H., 2006. Students' views of reflective learning techniques: An efficacy study at a UK medical school. *Medical Education, 40*(4), pp. 379–388.

Grant, R.M., 1996. Toward a knowledge-based theory of the firm. *Strategic Management Journal, 17*(S2), pp. 109–122.

Harary, F., Norman, R. and Cartwright, D., 1965. *Structural models: An introduction to the theory of directed graphs.* Wiley, New York.

Hargadon, A. and Sutton, R.I., 1997. Technology brokering and innovation in a product development firm. *Administrative Science Quarterly*, pp. 716–749.

Harvey, M.G. and Griffith, D.A., 2007. The role of globalization, time acceleration, and virtual global teams in fostering successful global product launches. *Journal of Product Innovation Management, 24*(5), pp. 486–501.

Hatch, N.W. and Dyer, J.H., 2004. Human capital and learning as a source of sustainable competitive advantage. *Strategic Management Journal, 25*(12), pp. 1155–1178.

Hays, R. and Gay, S., 2011. Reflection or 'pre-reflection': What are we actually measuring in reflective practice? *Medical Education, 45*(2), pp. 116–118.

Hertog, den P., 2000. Knowledge-intensive business services as co-producers of innovation. *International Journal of Innovation Management, 4*(04), pp. 491–528.

Hicks, J. and Lehmberg, D., 2012. 'Collision course: Selling European high performance motorcycles in Japan', *Ivey Publishing* (product number: 9B12M025).

Hidalgo, A. and Albors, J., 2008. Innovation management techniques and tools: A review from theory and practice. *R&D Management, 38*(2), pp. 113–127.

Hilhorst, T., van Liere, M., Ode, A.V. and de Koning, K., 2006. Impact of AIDS on rural livelihoods in Benue State, Nigeria. *SAHARA-J: Journal of Social Aspects of HIV/AIDS, 3*(1), pp. 382–393.

Hipp, C. and Grupp, H., 2005. Innovation in the service sector: The demand for service-specific innovation measurement concepts and typologies. *Research Policy, 34*(4), pp. 517–535.

Hirst, G., Van Knippenberg, D. and Zhou, J., 2009. A cross-level perspective on employee creativity: Goal orientation, team learning behavior, and individual creativity. *Academy of Management Journal, 52*(2), pp. 280–293.

Hislop, D., 2002. The client role in consultancy relations during the appropriation of technological innovations. *Research Policy, 31*(5), pp. 657–671.

Hitt, M.A., Bierman, L., Shimizu, K. and Kochhar, R., 2001. Direct and moderating effects of human capital on strategy and performance in professional service firms: A resource-based perspective. *Academy of Management Journal, 44*(1), pp. 13–28.

Hodges, J., 2017. *Consultancy, organizational development and change: A practical guide to delivering value.* Kogan Page Publishers, London.

Huang, J.C. and Newell, S., 2003. Knowledge integration processes and dynamics within the context of cross-functional projects. *International Journal of Project Management, 21*(3), pp. 167–176.

Huber, G., 1999. Facilitating project team learning and contributions to organizational knowledge. *Creativity and Innovation Management, 8*(2), pp. 70–76.

Huchzermeier, A. and Loch, C.H., 1996. Project management under risk: Using the real options approach to evaluate flexibility in R&D. *Management Science, 47*(1), pp. 100–113.

Hughes, M., Ireland, R.D. and Morgan, R.E., 2007. Stimulating dynamic value: Social capital and business incubation as a pathway to competitive success. *Long Range Planning, 40*(2), pp. 154–177.

Jack, S.L. and Anderson, A.R., 1999. Entrepreneurship education within the enterprise culture: Producing reflective practitioners. *International Journal of Entrepreneurial Behavior & Research, 5*(3), pp. 110–125.

Jansen, J.J., Van Den Bosch, F.A. and Volberda, H.W., 2006. Exploratory innovation, exploitative innovation, and performance: Effects of organizational antecedents and environmental moderators. *Management Science, 52*(11), pp. 1661–1674.

Jarle Gressgård, L., 2011. Virtual team collaboration and innovation in organizations. *Team Performance Management: An International Journal, 17*(1–2), pp. 102–119.

Jarvenpaa, S.L. and Leidner, D.E., 1999. Communication and trust in global virtual teams. *Organization Science, 10*(6), pp. 791–815.

Jones, G.G. and Lefort, A., 2005. 'McKinsey and the globalization of consultancy', *Harvard Business School* (product number: 9-806-035).

Julian, J., 2008. How project management office leaders facilitate cross-project learning and continuous improvement. *Project Management Journal, 39*(3), pp. 43–58.

Jünemann, E. and Lloyd, B., 2003. Consulting for virtual excellence: Virtual teamwork as a task for consultants. *Team Performance Management: An International Journal, 9*(7–8), pp. 182–189.

Kapsali, M., 2011. Systems thinking in innovation project management: A match that works. *International Journal of Project Management, 29*(4), pp. 396–407.

Kasper-Fuehrer, E.C. and Ashkanasy, N.M., 2003. The interorganizational virtual organization: Defining a Weberian ideal. *International Studies of Management & Organization, 33*(4), pp. 34–64.

Kato, M., Okamuro, H. and Honjo, Y., 2015. Does founders' human capital matter for innovation? Evidence from Japanese Start-ups. *Journal of Small Business Management, 53*(1), pp. 114–128.

Kemmis, S. and McTaggart, R., 2005. Participatory action research: Communicative action and the public sphere. In Denzin, N. and Lincoln, Y. (eds.) *The Sage handbook of qualitative research*, 3rd Edition (pp. 559–603). Sage, Thousand Oaks.

Kipping, M. and Clark, T., eds., 2012. *The Oxford handbook of management consulting*. Oxford University Press, Oxford.

Kirkman, B.L., Rosen, B., Gibson, C.B., Tesluk, P.E. and McPherson, S.O., 2002. Five challenges to virtual team success: Lessons from Sabre, Inc. *Academy of Management Perspectives, 16*(3), pp. 67–79.

Konrad, A. and Shuh, A., 2013. 'Deloitte Consulting GTA: The Deloitte Dads initiative', *Ivey Publishing* (product number: 9B13C046).

Koria, M., 2009. Managing for innovation in large and complex recovery programmes: Tsunami lessons from Sri Lanka. *International Journal of Project Management, 27*(2), pp. 123–130.

Koskela, L.J. and Howell, G., 2002. The underlying theory of project management is obsolete. In *Proceedings of the PMI research conference* (pp. 293–302). PMI, Seattle.

Kransdorff, A., 1996. Using the benefits of hindsight-the role of post-project analysis. *The Learning Organization, 3*(1), pp. 11–15.

Kraus, S., Rigtering, J.C., Hughes, M. and Hosman, V., 2012. Entrepreneurial orientation and the business performance of SMEs: A quantitative study from the Netherlands. *Review of Managerial Science, 6*(2), pp. 161–182.

Kuhn, T., 1962. *The structure of scientific revolutions*. Chicago University Press, Chicago.

Kurland, N.B. and Egan, T.D., 1999. Telecommuting: Justice and control in the virtual organization. *Organization Science, 10*(4), pp. 500–513.

Landry, R., Amara, N. and Lamari, M., 2002. Does social capital determine innovation? To what extent? *Technological Forecasting and Social Change, 69*(7), pp. 681–701.

Larsen, K.R. and McInerney, C.R., 2002. Preparing to work in the virtual organization. *Information & Management, 39*(6), pp. 445–456.

Laursen, K., Masciarelli, F. and Prencipe, A., 2012. Regions matter: How localized social capital affects innovation and external knowledge acquisition. *Organization Science, 23*(1), pp. 177–193.

Lawrence, P.R. and Lorsch, J.W., 1967. *Organization and environment*. Harvard Business School Press, Boston, MA.

Lee, S.H. and Williams, C., 2007. Dispersed entrepreneurship within multinational corporations: A community perspective. *Journal of World Business, 42*(4), pp. 505–519.

Lepak, D.P. and Snell, S.A., 1999. The human resource architecture: Toward a theory of human capital allocation and development. *Academy of Management Review*, *24*(1), pp. 31–48.

Lévárdy, V. and Browning, T.R., 2009. An adaptive process model to support product development project management. *IEEE Transactions on Engineering Management*, *56*(4), pp. 600–620.

Li, X., Williams, C. and Mu, Z., 2014. 'Hongxin Entrepreneur Incubator: Expanding the cloud', *Ivey Publishing* (product ID: 9B14M113).

Lin, L.H., 2011. Electronic human resource management and organizational innovation: The roles of information technology and virtual organizational structure. *The International Journal of Human Resource Management*, *22*(02), pp. 235–257.

Lin, N., 2008. A network theory of social capital. *The Handbook of Social Capital*, *50*(1), p. 69.

Love, J.H., Roper, S. and Bryson, J.R., 2011. Openness, knowledge, innovation and growth in UK business services. *Research Policy*, *40*(10), pp. 1438–1452.

Lumpkin, G.T. and Dess, G.G., 1996. Clarifying the entrepreneurial orientation construct and linking it to performance. *Academy of Management Review*, *21*(1), pp. 135–172.

Lycett, M., Macredie, R.D., Patel, C. and Paul, R.J., 2003. Migrating agile methods to standardized development practice. *Computer*, *36*(6), pp. 79–85.

Lynn, G.S., Skov, R.B. and Abel, K.D., 1999. Practices that support team learning and their impact on speed to market and new product success. *Journal of Product Innovation Management*, *16*(5), pp. 439–454.

Ma, P. and Saigaonkar, P., 2010. 'Robertson and Davies Management Consultants – Toronto Office', *Ivey Publishing* (product number: 9A94C010).

Maister, D.H., 2003. *Managing the professional service firm*. Simon and Schuster, London.

Maister, D.H., Green, C.H. and Galford, R.M., 2000. *The trusted advisor*. Simon and Schuster, London.

Malhotra, N., Smets, M. and Morris, T., 2016. Career pathing and innovation in professional service firms. *Academy of Management Perspectives*, *30*(4), pp. 369–383.

Mann, K., Gordon, J. and MacLeod, A., 2009. Reflection and reflective practice in health professions education: A systematic review. *Advances in Health Sciences Education*, *14*(4), pp. 595–621.

March, J.G., 1991. Exploration and exploitation in organizational learning. *Organization Science*, *2*(1), pp. 71–87.

Markus, M.L. and Agres, B.M.C.E., 2000. What makes a virtual organization work? *MIT Sloan Management Review*, *42*(1), pp. 13–26.

Markus, M.L. and Tanis, C., 2000. The enterprise systems experience-from adoption to success. *Framing the Domains of IT Research: Glimpsing the Future Through the Past*, *173*, Chapter 10, pp. 173–207.

Margerison, C.J., 1988. *Managerial consulting skills: A practical guide*. Gower Publishing, Aldershot.

Martinez, L.F., Ferreira, A.I. and Can, A.B., 2016. Consultant – Client relationship and knowledge transfer in small-and medium-sized enterprises change processes. *Psychological Reports*, *118*(2), pp. 608–625.

Martins, L.L., Gilson, L.L. and Maynard, M.T., 2004. Virtual teams: What do we know and where do we go from here? *Journal of Management*, *30*(6), pp. 805–835.

Marvel, M.R. and Lumpkin, G.T., 2007. Technology entrepreneurs' human capital and its effects on innovation radicalness. *Entrepreneurship Theory and Practice, 31*(6), pp. 807–828.

McKee, D., 1992. An organizational learning approach to product innovation. *Journal of Product Innovation Management, 9*(3), pp. 232–245.

McKinlay, A., 2002. The limits of knowledge management. *New Technology, Work and Employment, 17*(2), pp. 76–88.

Mezirow, J., 1991. *Transformative dimensions of adult learning*. Jossey-Bass, San Francisco, CA.

Miles, R.E., Snow, C.C., Meyer, A.D. and Coleman Jr, H.J., 1978. Organizational strategy, structure, and process. *Academy of Management Review, 3*(3), pp. 546–562.

Miller, R. and Floricel, S., 2004. Value creation and games of innovation. *Research-Technology Management, 47*(6), pp. 25–37.

Moran, P., 2005. Structural vs. relational embeddedness: Social capital and managerial performance. *Strategic Management Journal, 26*(12), pp. 1129–1151.

Mors, M.L., 2010. Innovation in a global consulting firm: When the problem is too much diversity. *Strategic Management Journal, 31*(8), pp. 841–872.

Mosey, S. and Wright, M., 2007. From human capital to social capital: A longitudinal study of technology-based academic entrepreneurs. *Entrepreneurship Theory and Practice, 31*(6), pp. 909–935.

Mowshowitz, A., 1997a. On the theory of virtual organization. *Systems Research and Behavioral Science: The Official Journal of the International Federation for Systems Research, 14*(6), pp. 373–384.

Mowshowitz, A., 1997b. Virtual organization. *Communications of the ACM, 40*(9), pp. 30–37.

Munro, M. and Huff, S.L., 2008. 'Pay Zone consulting: A global virtual organization', *Ivey Publishing* (product number: 9B08C004).

Nah, F.F., Lau, J.L.S. and Kuang, J., 2001. Critical factors for successful implementation of enterprise systems. *Business Process Management Journal, 7*(3), pp. 285–296.

Nahapiet, J. and Ghoshal, S., 2000. Social capital, intellectual capital, and the organizational advantage. In Lesser, E. (ed.) *Knowledge and social capital* (pp. 119–157). Butterworth-Heinemann, Oxford.

Naidoo, V., 2010. Firm survival through a crisis: The influence of market orientation, marketing innovation and business strategy. *Industrial Marketing Management, 39*(8), pp. 1311–1320.

National Planning Commission (NPC), 2018. Retrieved from www.vanguardngr.com/2018/04/npc-puts-nigerias-population-198m/ accessed 16 April 2018.

Nielsen, B.B. and Nielsen, S., 2009. Learning and innovation in international strategic alliances: An empirical test of the role of trust and tacitness. *Journal of Management Studies, 46*(6), pp. 1031–1056.

Nikolova, N., Möllering, G. and Reihlen, M., 2015. Trusting as a 'leap of faith': Trust-building practices in client – Consultant relationships. *Scandinavian Journal of Management, 31*(2), pp. 232–245.

Nissen, V. and Seifert, H., 2015. Virtualization of consulting – Benefits, risks and a suggested decision process. In *21st Americas conference on information systems*. Puerto Rico.

Nonaka, I. and Takeuchi, H., 1995. *The knowledge-creating company: How Japanese companies create the dynamics of innovation*. Oxford University Press, Oxford.

Normann, R., 2001. *Reframing business: When the map changes the landscape*. John Wiley & Sons: Chichester.

Obeidat, B.Y., Al-Suradi, M.M., Masa'deh, R.E. and Tarhini, A., 2016. The impact of knowledge management on innovation: An empirical study on Jordanian consultancy firms. *Management Research Review, 39*(10), pp. 1214–1238.

Ojasalo, J., 2008. Management of innovation networks: A case study of different approaches. *European Journal of Innovation Management, 11*(1), pp. 51–86.

Olaniyan, D.A. and Okemakinde, T., 2008. Human capital theory: Implications for educational development. *Pakistan Journal of Social Sciences, 5*(5), pp. 479–483.

O'Leary, T. and Williams, T., 2008. Making a difference? Evaluating an innovative approach to the project management centre of excellence in a UK government department. *International Journal of Project Management, 26*(5), pp. 556–565.

O'Mahoney, J., 2011. *Management innovation in the UK consulting industry*. Chartered Management Institute, London.

O'Mahoney, J., 2013. Managing services: Challenges and innovations. In Haynes, K. and Grugulis, I. (eds.) *Management innovation in the UK consulting industry* (pp. 83–104) Oxford University Press, Oxford.

O'Mahoney, J. and Markham, C., 2013. *Management consultancy*. Oxford University Press, Oxford.

O'Mahoney, J. and Sturdy, A., 2016. Power and the diffusion of management ideas: The case of McKinsey & Co. *Management Learning, 47*(3), pp. 247–265.

O'Reilly III, C.A. and Tushman, M.L., 2008. Ambidexterity as a dynamic capability: Resolving the innovator's dilemma. *Research in Organizational Behavior, 28*, pp. 185–206.

Özesmi, U. and Özesmi, S.L., 2004. Ecological models based on people's knowledge: A multistep Fuzzy Cognitive Mapping approach. *Ecological Modelling, 176*(1–2), pp. 43–64.

Panayides, P.M. and Lun, Y.V., 2009. The impact of trust on innovativeness and supply chain performance. *International Journal of Production Economics, 122*(1), pp. 35–46.

Peteraf, M.A., 1993. The cornerstones of competitive advantage: A resource-based view. *Strategic Management Journal, 14*(3), pp. 179–191.

Pidd, M., 2004. Complementarity in systems modelling. In *Systems modelling: Theory and practice*, Chapter 1 (pp. 1–19). Wiley and Sons, Chichester.

Plattfaut, R., Niehaves, B. and Becker, J., 2012. Capabilities for service innovation: A qualitative case study in the consulting industry. In *Pacific Asia conference on information systems (PACIS) proceedings* (paper 58), Vietnam.

Pollack, J., 2007. The changing paradigms of project management. *International Journal of Project Management, 25*(3), pp. 266–274.

Portes, A., 1998. Social capital: Its origins and applications in modern sociology. *Annual Review of Sociology, 24*(1), pp. 1–24.

Posner, B.Z., 1987. What it takes to be a good project manager. *Project Management Journal, 28*(1), pp. 51–54.

Poulfelt, F., Olson, T.H., Bhambri, A. and Greiner, L., 2017. The changing global consulting industry. In Poulfelt, F. and Olson, T.H. (eds.) *Management consulting today and tomorrow* (pp. 5–36). Routledge, New York.

Prescott, E.C. and Visscher, M., 1980. Organization capital. *Journal of Political Economy, 88*(3), pp. 446–461.

Prusak, L., 2001. Where did knowledge management come from? *IBM Systems Journal, 40*(4), pp. 1002–1007.

Rapoport, R.N., 1970. Three dilemmas in action research: With special reference to the Tavistock experience. *Human Relations, 23*(6), pp. 499–513.

Ross, D.D., 1989. First steps in developing a reflective approach. *Journal of Teacher Education, 40*(2), pp. 22–30.

Rost, K., 2011. The strength of strong ties in the creation of innovation. *Research Policy, 40*(4), pp. 588–604.

Sawhney, M. and Prandelli, E., 2000. Communities of creation: Managing distributed innovation in turbulent markets. *California Management Review, 42*(4), pp. 24–54.

Schön, D.A., 1987. *Educating the reflective practitioner: Toward a new design for teaching and learning in the professions.* The Jossey-Bass Higher Education Series, Jossey-Bass, San Francisco, CA.

Schultz, T.W., 1961. Investment in human capital. *The American Economic Review, 51*(1), pp. 1–17.

Schultz, T.W., 1993. The economic importance of human capital in modernization. *Education Economics, 1*(1), pp. 13–19.

Schweitzer, F., Rau, C., Gassmann, O. and van den Hende, E., 2015. Technologically reflective individuals as enablers of social innovation. *Journal of Product Innovation Management, 32*(6), pp. 847–860.

Seibert, S.E., Kraimer, M.L. and Liden, R.C., 2001. A social capital theory of career success. *Academy of Management Journal, 44*(2), pp. 219–237.

Semadeni, M. and Anderson, B.S., 2010. The follower's dilemma: Innovation and imitation in the professional services industry. *Academy of Management Journal, 53*(5), pp. 1175–1193.

Senge, P., 1990. *The fifth discipline: The art and science of the learning organization.* Doubleday, New York.

Shah, D., Rust, R.T., Parasuraman, A., Staelin, R. and Day, G.S., 2006. The path to customer centricity. *Journal of Service Research, 9*(2), pp. 113–124.

Shane, S. and Venkataraman, S., 2000. The promise of entrepreneurship as a field of research. *Academy of Management Review, 25*(1), pp. 217–226.

Sharma, R.S. and Koh, S., 2008. 'Managing intellectual capital at Tata Consultancy Services', *The Asia Business Case Centre* (product number: ABCC-2008-001).

Simonen, J. and McCann, P., 2008. Firm innovation: The influence of R&D cooperation and the geography of human capital inputs. *Journal of Urban Economics, 64*(1), pp. 146–154.

Söderlund, J., 2011. Pluralism in project management: Navigating the crossroads of specialization and fragmentation. *International Journal of Management Reviews, 13*(2), pp. 153–176.

Sparkes, J.R. and Miyake, M., 2000. Knowledge transfer and human resource development practices: Japanese firms in Brazil and Mexico. *International Business Review, 9*(5), pp. 599–612.

Srinivasan, R., 2014. The management consulting industry: Growth of consulting services in India: Panel discussion. *IIMB Management Review, 26*(4), pp. 257–270.

Stata, R., 1989. Organizational learning: The key to management innovation. *Sloan Management Review, 30*(3), pp. 63–74.

Stough, S., Eom, S. and Buckenmyer, J., 2000. Virtual teaming: A strategy for moving your organization into the new millennium. *Industrial Management & Data Systems, 100*(8), pp. 370–378.

Strader, T.J., Lin, F.R. and Shaw, M.J., 1998. Information infrastructure for electronic virtual organization management. *Decision Support Systems, 23*(1), pp. 75–94.

Strober, M.H., 1990. Human capital theory: Implications for HR managers. *Industrial Relations: A Journal of Economy and Society, 29*(2), pp. 214–239.

Sturdy, A., 2011. Consultancy's consequences? A critical assessment of management consultancy's impact on management. *British Journal of Management, 22*(3), pp. 517–530.

Sturdy, A., Clark, T., Fincham, R. and Handley, K., 2009. Between innovation and legitimation – Boundaries and knowledge flow in management consultancy. *Organization, 16*(5), pp. 627–653.

Su, N. and Pirani, N., 2014. 'Transforming the business service portfolio at Global Consultancy', *Ivey Publishing* (product number: 9B14E001).

Subramaniam, M. and Youndt, M.A., 2005. The influence of intellectual capital on the types of innovative capabilities. *Academy of Management journal, 48*(3), pp. 450–463.

Sundbo, J., 1997. Management of innovation in services. *Service Industries Journal, 17*(3), pp. 432–455.

Svejvig, P. and Andersen, P., 2015. Rethinking project management: A structured literature review with a critical look at the brave new world. *International Journal of Project Management, 33*(2), pp. 278–290.

Swan, J., Newell, S., Scarbrough, H. and Hislop, D., 1999. Knowledge management and innovation: Networks and networking. *Journal of Knowledge Management, 3*(4), pp. 262–275.

Swart, J., 2006. Intellectual capital: Disentangling an enigmatic concept. *Journal of Intellectual capital, 7*(2), pp. 136–159.

Swart, J. and Kinnie, N., 2003. Sharing knowledge in knowledge-intensive firms. *Human Resource Management Journal, 13*(2), pp. 60–75.

Taminiau, Y., Smit, W. and De Lange, A., 2009. Innovation in management consulting firms through informal knowledge sharing. *Journal of Knowledge Management, 13*(1), pp. 42–55.

Teece, D.J., Pisano, G. and Shuen, A., 1997. Dynamic capabilities and strategic management. *Strategic Management Journal, 18*(7), pp. 509–533.

Tether, B.S. and Tajar, A., 2008. Beyond industry – University links: Sourcing knowledge for innovation from consultants, private research organisations and the public science-base. *Research Policy, 37*(6–7), pp. 1079–1095.

Thompson, J.D., 1967. *Organizations in action.* McGraw-Hill, New York.

Tomenendal, M. and Boyoglu, C., 2014. Gender imbalance in management consulting firms – A story about the construction and effects of organizational identity. *Management and Organizational Studies, 1*(2), pp. 30–43.

Tomer, J.E., 1998. Organizational capital and joining-up: Linking the individual to the organization and to society. *Human Relations, 51*(6), pp. 825–846.

Tsai, W., 2001. Knowledge transfer in intraorganizational networks: Effects of network position and absorptive capacity on business unit innovation and performance. *Academy of Management Journal, 44*(5), pp. 996–1004.

Tsai, W. and Ghoshal, S., 1998. Social capital and value creation: The role of intrafirm networks. *Academy of Management Journal, 41*(4), pp. 464–476.

Tuckman, B. W., 1965. Developmental sequence in small groups. *Psychological Bulletin, 63*(6), pp. 384–399.

Turak, A., 2013. *Business secrets of the trappist monks: One CEO's quest for meaning and authenticity*. Columbia University Press, New York.

UNAIDS, 2010. UNAIDS report on the global AIDS epidemic. Retrieved from www.unaids.org/globalreport/documents/20101123_GlobalReport_full_en.pdf accessed 16 April 2018.

UNGASS, 2010. UNGASS country progress report, Nigeria. Retrieved from http://data.unaids.org/pub/report/2010/nigeria_2010_country_progress_report_en.pdf accessed 16 April 2018.

Utterback, J.M. and Abernathy, W.J., 1975. A dynamic model of process and product innovation. *Omega, 3*(6), pp. 639–656.

Uzzi, B., 1999. Embeddedness in the making of financial capital: How social relations and networks benefit firms seeking financing. *American Sociological Review, 64*(4), pp. 481–505.

Venkataraman, S., 1997. The distinctive domain of entrepreneurship research. *Advances in Entrepreneurship, Firm Emergence and Growth, 3*(1), pp. 119–138.

Verdonschot, S.G., 2006. Methods to enhance reflective behaviour in innovation processes. *Journal of European Industrial Training, 30*(9), pp. 670–686.

Verona, G., Prandelli, E. and Sawhney, M., 2006. Innovation and virtual environments: Towards virtual knowledge brokers. *Organization Studies, 27*(6), pp. 765–788.

Von Nordenflycht, A., 2010. What is a professional service firm? Toward a theory and taxonomy of knowledge-intensive firms. *Academy of Management Review, 35*(1), pp. 155–174.

Von Platen, S., 2015. The communication consultant: An important translator for communication management. *Journal of Communication Management, 19*(2), pp. 150–166.

Werr, A. and Stjernberg, T., 2003. Exploring management consulting firms as knowledge systems. *Organization Studies, 24*(6), pp. 881–908.

Werth, D., Greff, T. and Scheer, A.W., 2016. Consulting 4.0 – Die digitalisierung der unternehmensberatung. *HMD Praxis der Wirtschaftsinformatik, 53*(1), pp. 55–70.

Westerman, G., McFarlan, F.W. and Iansiti, M., 2006. Organization design and effectiveness over the innovation life cycle. *Organization Science, 17*(2), pp. 230–238.

Wi, H., Oh, S. and Jung, M., 2011. Virtual organization for open innovation: Semantic web based inter-organizational team formation. *Expert Systems with Applications, 38*(7), pp. 8466–8476.

Williams, C., 2017. 'Ergonomica Consulting and Solltram Hotels: An ethical dilemma', *Ivey Publishing* (product number: 9B17M153).

Williams, C. and Allard, G., 2018. University – Industry collaboration in R&D: The role of labor market rigidity. *R&D Management, 48*(4), pp. 410–421.

Williams, C., Colovic, A. and Zhu, J., 2016. Foreign market knowledge, country sales breadth and innovative performance of emerging economy firms. *International Journal of Innovation Management, 20*(6).

Williams, C., Colovic, A. and Zhu, J., 2017. Integration-responsiveness, local hires and subsidiary performance amidst turbulence: Insights from a survey of Chinese subsidiaries. *Journal of World Business, 52*(6), pp. 842–853.

Williams, C. and Kumar, M., 2014. Experiential learning and innovation in offshore outsourcing transitions. In Pedersen, T., Venzin, M., Devinney, T.M. and Tihanyi, L. (eds.) *Orchestration of the global network organization* (pp. 433–461). Emerald Group Publishing Limited, Bingley, UK.

Williams, C. and Lee, S.H., 2009. International management, political arena and dispersed entrepreneurship in the MNC. *Journal of World Business, 44*(3), pp. 287–299.

Williams, C. and Lee, S.H., 2016. Knowledge flows in the emerging market MNC: The role of subsidiary HRM practices in Korean MNCs. *International Business Review, 25*(1), pp. 233–243.

Williams, C. and Van Triest, S., 2017. Product launch performance in Hi-Tech SMEs: Newness to the firm and the role of management controls. *International Journal of Innovation Management, 21*(3).

Williams, C. and You, J., 2018. Building resilience in client organizations: The consultant's challenge. *Management Consulting Journal* (2) (December 2018), pp. 10–12.

Williams, R.L. and Cothrel, J., 2000. Four smart ways to run online communities. *MIT Sloan Management Review, 41*(4), p. 81.

Williams, T., 2004. Identifying the hard lessons from projects – Easily. *International Journal of Project Management, 22*(4), pp. 273–279.

Williams, T., 2005. Assessing and moving on from the dominant project management discourse in the light of project overruns. *IEEE Transactions on Engineering Management, 52*(4), pp. 497–508.

Winsborough, D. and Chamorro-Premuzic, T., 2013. Consulting psychology in the digital era: Current trends and future directions. *Consulting Psychology Journal: Practice and Research, 65*(4), pp. 319–324.

Winter, M., Smith, C., Morris, P. and Cicmil, S., 2006. Directions for future research in project management: The main findings of a UK government-funded research network. *International Journal of Project Management, 24*(8), pp. 638–649.

Winter, M. and Szczepanek, T., 2008. Projects and programmes as value creation processes: A new perspective and some practical implications. *International Journal of Project Management, 26*(1), pp. 95–103.

Wood, P., 2002a. *Consultancy and innovation: The business service revolution in Europe.* Routledge, London.

Wood, P., 2002b. How may consultancies be innovative? In Wood, P. (ed.) *Consultancy and innovation: The business service revolution in Europe* (pp. 72–89). Routledge, London.

Woolcock, M. and Narayan, D., 2000. Social capital: Implications for development theory, research, and policy. *The World Bank Research Observer, 15*(2), pp. 225–249.

Wright, C., Sturdy, A. and Wylie, N., 2012. Management innovation through standardization: Consultants as standardizers of organizational practice. *Research Policy, 41*(3), pp. 652–662.

Wu, W.Y., Chang, M.L. and Chen, C.W., 2008. Promoting innovation through the accumulation of intellectual capital, social capital, and entrepreneurial orientation. *R&D Management*, *38*(3), pp. 265–277.

Yli-Renko, H., Autio, E. and Sapienza, H.J., 2001. Social capital, knowledge acquisition, and knowledge exploitation in young technology-based firms. *Strategic Management Journal*, *22*(6–7), pp. 587–613.

Yu, E. and Sangiorgi, D., 2018. Service design as an approach to implement the value cocreation perspective in new service development. *Journal of Service Research*, *21*(1), pp. 40–58.

Zellmer-Bruhn, M. and Gibson, C., 2006. Multinational organization context: Implications for team learning and performance. *Academy of Management Journal*, *49*(3), pp. 501–518.

Zheng, W., 2010. A social capital perspective of innovation from individuals to nations: Where is empirical literature directing us? *International Journal of Management Reviews*, *12*(2), pp. 151–183.

# Index

Note: Page numbers in *italics* indicate figures.

Abel, K.D. 101
Abernathy, W.J. 3–4
academic entrepreneurs 134
Accenture 152
Acs, Z.J. 21
action research 148–149
adaptive product development process
   (APDP) 80
adaptors 10
Adler, P.S. 34
Afsarmanesh, H. 122–123, 131
agile development 75
Agres, B.M.C.E. 56
Agutter, C. 65, 129
Ahmed, P.K. 102
Ahuja, G. 39
Akhilesh, K.B. 119
Albors, J. 44
Allard, G. 21
Al-Suradi, M.M. 1, 26
alternate controls 83
Amara, N. 38
ambidextrous organizations 7
Anand, N. 2, 11, 24, 42, 104–105
Andersen, P. 77
Anderson, A.R. 103
Anderson, B.S. 2, 7, 10
architectural innovation 4
Ashiru, F. 45
asset management 64
Audretsch, D.B. 21
Autio, E. 40
autonomous innovations 58

Back, Y. xi, 42
Bain & Co. 152
Baldwin, J. 22, 25
Balsmeier, P.W. 52, 59, 128

Baptista, A. 81–82
Baregheh, A. 3
Barker, M. 101
Batra, S. 88
Becker, J. 106–107, 114
Behavior School 76
Belgium 22
Bell, B.S. 130–131
Bergiel, B.J. 52, 59, 128
Bergiel, E.B. 52, 59, 128
Besner, C. 78
Bessant, J. 24, 84
Bhambri, A. 2
Bierman, L. 1, 23
Blackburn, R.S. 128
Bloodgood, J.M. 37
Bloom, N. 151–153
Bohmer, R.M. 97
Bolino, M.C. 37
Bontis, N. 119
Bornay-Barrachina, M. 22
Boston Consulting Group (BCG) 111–112,
   122, 152
Boudreau, M.C. 53–54
boundaries 43, 109
Bower, M. 88, 90
Boxall, P. 25
Boyoglu, C. 152
Bozeman, B. 21, 119
Braun, J.A., Jr. 95
Brazil 20
Brescia, R.H. 85
Brown, J.S. 4–5
Browning, T.R. 79–80, 126
Brugman, J. 26
Bryson, J.R. 8–9, 44
Buckler, B. 102
Buday, R. 47

Buganza, T. 82
Bunderson, J.S. 98–99

Camarinha-Matos, L.M. 122–123, 131
Campbell Management Consulting 28, 29
Can, A.B. 108–109
Canada xii–xiii, 22, 28, 66, 89, 160–161, 175
Canato, A. 108–109
Cap Gemini 67
capital: careers and 153, 155; interactions
    between 147, 150–151, 157; natural 151; *see
    also* human capital; organizational capital;
    social capital
careers: diversity and 152–153; firm size and
    153–154; forms of capital and 153, 155;
    gender imbalances and 152; innovative
    consultancy and 151–155; up-or-out
    paradigm 151–152; work-life balance in
    151–153
case studies: Deloitte Dads initiative 160–168;
    Ergonomica Consulting 172–186; Hongxin
    Entrepreneur Incubator 202–213; innogy
    Consulting GmbH (iCon) 187–201
Centres of Excellence (CoEs) 81, 126
Chamorro-Premuzic, T. 84
Chang, M.L. 119
Chau, J. 94–95
Chen, C.J. 22, 121
Chen, C.W. 119
Chen, J. 187
Cheng, G. 94–95
Chesbrough, H.W. 58, 69
China ix–x, xii–xiii, 66–67, 70, 124, 129,
    139–141, 157, 167, 177, 202–204,
    207–209
Christensen, C.M. 24, 84–85
Cicmil, S. 75–76
citizenship 37, 53
Clark, K.B. 3–4
Clark, T. xi, 1, 34, 43
client capital 34
client-consultant relationship: boundaries in
    43, 109; co-production of innovation and
    41; dual value creation in 38; encoding
    in 44; external consultancy firms and
    61–62; human capital and 135; knowledge
    acquisition and 40; knowledge sharing
    in 108–109; life-cycle disruption and
    83; openness in 43; sharing of context in
    109; social interactions and 34–36, 41, 44,
    47–48, 61; socialized listening and 34–35;
    trust and 61–62, 144, 146–147
client managers 144, 147
clients: human capital and 29–30; innovation
    by 8, 25; project management and 80;

relationships with 8, 10; social capital and
    34–36, 38
'Cloud Entrepreneurship' 138–140
codification 58, 98
cognitive skills 21
Cohen, S.G. 54
Coleman, H.J., Jr. 5–6
collaboration 54–55, 60, 81–82
collaborative innovation 39, 60
collective learning 135
Collyer, S. 83
Colovic, A. 38
communication 55–57, 62–64
communication consultants 109
communities-of-entrepreneurship 5
communities-of-practice 4–5
community relations 64
competing experiments 83
complex adaptive systems (CAS) 80, 126
consultants: communication 109; defensible
    turf and 24; differentiated expertise and
    24; emerging markets and 42; enterprise
    resource planning (ERP) and 84; as functional
    specialist 31; as generalist 31; human capital
    and 24, 28–31; informal knowledge sharing
    and 41–42; knowledge and 25–26, 29,
    43–44; organizational support and 24;
    socialized agency and 24; standardizing and
    83; technology transfer and 24–25; virtual
    organization and 52, 62–63; *see also* client-
    consultant relationship
'Consultant's Comeuppance, A' (Buday) 47
contextual skills 21
Contingency School 76–77
contingency theory 78–79, 140–141
contingent project management 78–79, 89–90
conveyors 10
Cooke, P. 40
Cothrel, J., 64
creativity 100
Crevani, L. xii, 9, 106
Crumpler, T.P. 95
Cunha, J.A. 81
Customer Relationship Management (CRM)
    systems 28
Czarnitzki, D. 24–25
Czech Republic 188, 190, 193, *200*

Daft, R.L. 4
Damanpour, F. 4
Darling, E.J. 81
Davidsson, P. 21, 39, 119
Davies, A. 84
Day, G.S. 38
Decision School 76

defensible turf 24, 42
De Lange, A. 2, 10, 41, 107
'Deloitte Consulting GTA' (Konrad and Shuh) 111
Deloitte Dads initiative: annual diversity report 169; case study 159–168; human capital and 122, 136; launch pamphlet 170; Poles of innovation and *136*; reflective ability and 111, 122, 137; work-life balance and 152
de Man, A.P. 6
Denmark 40, 72
DeSanctis, G. 55
D'Este, P. 22
De Vries, E.J. 61
De Winne, S. 22, 121
Dietz, J.S. 21, 119
differentiated expertise 24, 42
disruption *see* life-cycle disruption
Dittrich, K. 6
diversity 152–153
Doloreux, D. 38
Drach-Zahavy, A. 101
dual value creation 38
Dubai 193–194
Duguid, P. 4–5
Duysters, G. 6
Dyer, J.H. 20
dynamic capabilities 106
dynamic value creation 42–43

eConsultancy 65, 85, 129, 132
Edmondson, A.C. 97–98
emergent planning 83
emerging markets 42
encoding 8, 44
enterprise resource planning (ERP) 84, 90
entrepreneurial orientation theory 12
entrepreneurship: academic 134; cloud-based 138–140; education for 103; human capital and 21; innovation and 9, 21, 156–157; reflective ability and 103; social capital and 39, 134
Ergonomica Consulting: case study 171–186; ethics and 144–145; human capital and 28–29, 112, 137; internal organizational innovation in 139; Poles of innovation and *136*; reflective ability and 112, 122, 127; social capital and 135, 137
Ernst & Young 67
ethics: client-consultant relationship and 144–147; consultancy and 143–146; proactive innovation and 145; risks and 145–146; trust and 144, 146–147
European Union (EU) 40, 79
Evan, W.M. 4
experimentation 98

expertise 105
external networking 43
EY/Knowledge Web 67

facilitators 8, 10, 108
Factor School 76–77
Ferreira, A.I. 108–109
Fincham, R. 43
Finland 21
Fitz-Enz, J. 119
Flap, H. 36
Floricel, S. 78
Florin, J. 37, 118–119
France 21
Furst, S.A. 128
Fuzzy Cognitive Mapping (FCM) 149

Galeano, N. 131
Galford, R.M. 146
Gallié, E.P. 21
Gallivan, M.J. 56
Gardner, H.K. 2, 11, 24, 42, 104–105
Gassmann, O. 103–104
Gaughan, M. 21, 119
Gay, S. 95–96
gender imbalances 152
geographic dispersion 58–59
Germany xii–xiii, 25, 106, 156, 187–191, 193
Ghoshal, S. 37, 40
Giangreco, A. 108–109
Gibbs, J.L. 58–59, 69
Gibson, C.B. 58–59, 69, 98–99, 124
Gilson, L.L. 131–132
'Global Consulting Services (GCS) Consulting' (Batra and Puri) 88
Glynn, M.A. 6
Gordon, J. 96
Governance School 76
Goyal, A. 119
Grant, A. 96
Green, C.H. 146
Greff, T. 85
Greiner, L. 2
Grupp, H. 8

Handley, K. 43
Hargadon, A. 44
Hatch, N.W. 20
Hays, R. 95–96
Hemsley, B. 83
Hertog, P. den 25, 41, 107–109
Hidalgo, A. 44
Hipp, C. 8
Hirst, G. 100
Hislop, D. 61–63
Hitt, M.A. 1, 23

HIV/AIDS social enterprise 45–46, 49
Hobbs, B. 78
Hodges, J. 143
Hodgson, D. 76
Hongxin Cloud Entrepreneurship 138–140
Hongxin Entrepreneur Incubator: case study
    202–213; entrepreneurship and 156–157;
    human capital and 138; Poles of innovation
    and *136*, 154; social capital and 124; virtual
    organization and 66–67, 124, 129, 139–140
'Hongxin Entrepreneur Incubator' (Li, Williams
    and Mu) 66–67
Honig, B. 21, 39, 119
Honjo, Y. 22
Houston, H. 96
Howell, G. 74–75
HR *see* Human Resources (HR)
Huang, J.C. 62
Huang, J.W. 22, 121
Huber, G. 102
Huff, S.L. 66
Hughes, M. 42–43
human capital: client engagement and
    29–31; competitive advantage and 20;
    cultural context and 28; defensible turf
    and 24; differentiated expertise and 24;
    entrepreneurial culture and 21; founders
    and 23; HMR and 22, 31, 121, 133–134;
    implications of 29–31; innovation and 21–31;
    intellectual capital and 119; investment
    in 19–20; knowledge management and
    25–26, 121; organizational capital and 147;
    organizational support and 24; potential
    ownership and 26; professional services and
    23–24; radicalness and 23; reflective ability
    and 120–121, *121*, 122, 132–133, *133*,
    134–135; resource-based theory and 13–14;
    scientific/technical skills in 21; social capital
    and 118, *118*, 119–120, 130, 147; socialized
    agency and 24; strategic HR practices 22;
    technology transfer and 24–25; theory
    of 18–19; training and 21–22, 25; virtual
    organization and 129–130, *130*, 131–132
Human Resource Management (HRM) 22, 31,
    121, 133–134
Human Resources (HR): innovative policies
    in 80–81; knowledge management and 121;
    psychological consulting and 84–85; strategic
    practices of 22, 25–26, 102, 121; training
    investment and 22, 25

Iansiti, M. 78–79, 125
*iCon* case *see* innogy Consulting GmbH (iCon)
ICT *see* information and communication
    technology (ICT)
imitation 10

India 2, 54, 88
informal knowledge sharing 10, 41–42, 110
information and communication technology
    (ICT) 52, 54, 56
information sources 10, 38–39, 41, 56
initial public offerings (IPOs) 37
initiators 11
innogy Consulting GmbH (iCon): case study
    187–201; human capital and 120, 138;
    internal consultancy units in 85, 109, 154,
    156; Poles of innovation and *136*; social
    capital and 138; strategic practices of
    138, 140
innovation: architectural 4; autonomous
    58; barriers to 22; client-led 25;
    collaborative 39, 41, 60; communities-of-
    entrepreneurship and 5; communities-
    of-practice and 4–5; creativity and 100;
    defining 3; determinants of 4; disruptive
    xi, 3–4, 77–84, 89–91; forms of 4, 30–31;
    games and 78; human capital and 21;
    imitation and 10; learning process model
    for 102–103; levels of analysis 6; life-
    cycle flexibility in 82; organizational 59;
    paradigmatic 25; processes for 4; project
    management and 77–81; radicalness in 23,
    39; reflective ability and 99–110; research
    in xi, xii, 2–7; scientific/technical skills
    and 21; service industries and 9, 25, 61, 84,
    106–107; social 103–104; social capital and
    34–50; supplier-dominated 25; systemic 58;
    trust and 39–40; uncertainty in 6–7; virtual
    organization and 52, 57–70
innovation radar *15*, 136, *136*, 157
innovative consultancy: as adaptors 10;
    approaches to 11–12; careers and 151–155;
    as conveyors 10; cultural aspects of 113;
    entrepreneurship and 9; ethical implications
    of 143–147; as facilitators 8, 10, 108; human
    capital in 18–32, 140; human resources and
    25, 31; informal knowledge sharing and 10,
    41–42, 110; information sources and 108;
    as initiators 11; knowledge management in
    25–26, 108, 114; leadership aspects of 113;
    Poles of 14–15, *15*, 117–118, 139–142;
    practice areas in 154; reflective ability and
    104–110; research in 7–11, 147–151; social
    capital in 140; standard setting and 108;
    structural aspect of 113–114; technology
    transfer and 24–25; *see also* management
    consultancy
innovative orientation 12, *12*, 13, *13*, 14–15,
    *15*, *16*
intellectual capital 119
internal consultancy units 85, 109–110,
    154, 156

Ireland, R.D. 42–43
Israel 101

Jack, S.L. 103
Japan 22, 28, 30, 167, 189
Jarle Gressgård, L. 59, 123
Jarvenpaa, S.L. 54–55
Java Center Organization 64
Johnson, J. 22, 25
Jones, G.G. 88
Jordan 26
Julian, J. 126
Jünemann, E. 62
Jung, M. 60

Kapsali, M. 79
Kato, M. 22
Kazakhstan 66
Kinnersley, P. 96
Kinnie, N. 133
Kipping, M. xi, 1, 34
Kirkman, B.L. 124
knowledge barriers 22, 133
knowledge creation 107–108
knowledge integration 62, 108
knowledge intensive business services
    (KIBS) 41, 108
knowledge management: informal knowledge
    sharing and 10, 41; innovative consultancy
    and 25–26, 43–44, 108; managerialist
    approaches to 63; power and 105–106;
    processes of 26; reflection and 106, 121;
    virtual knowledge brokers and 60; virtual
    organization and 69
'Knowledge Management at Cap Gemini
    Ernst & Young' (Andreu, Lara and Sieber) 67
knowledge sharing 107
Kochhar, R. 1, 23
Konrad, A. 111, 159
Korea 20, 119
Koria, M. 80
Koskela, L.J. 74–75
Kozlowski, S.W. 130–131
Kraimer, M.L. 37
Kransdorff, A. 101
Kretschmer, T. 151–153
Kuang, J. 84
Kwon, S.W. 34

Lamari, M. 38
Landry, R. 38
Lardi, K. 86, 90
la Rosa-Navarro, D. 22
Larsen, K.R. 55, 57
Lau, J.L.S. 84

Laursen, K. 38
leadership competences 62, 113, 131
learning process model 102–103
learning theory 97
Lee, S.H. 5, 20, 119
Lefort, A. 88
legal services 85–86
Legros, D. 21
Leidner, D.E. 54–55
Lévárdy, V. 79–80, 126
Li, X. 66
Liden, R.C. 37
life-cycle disruption: implications of 89–91;
    innovation and xi, 3–4, 72–73, 77–84,
    89–91; management consultancy and 14,
    72–73, 86–91; as organizational capital
    xii, 14, 72–73; planning strategies for 83;
    reflective ability and 125, 125, 126–127;
    role of technology in 85–86, 90–91; virtual
    organization and 127, 127, 128–129
life-cycle flexibility (LCF) 82
Lin, F.R. 56
Lin, L.H. 59, 128
Lin, X. 202
Lloyd, B. 62
Loch, K.D. 53–54
longitudinal case-based work 148
López-Cabrales, A. 22
Love, J.H. 8–9, 44
Lubatkin, M. 37, 118–119
Lumpkin, G.T. 23
Lun, Y.V. 39
Lycett, M. 75
Lynn, G.S. 101

MacLeod, A. 96
Macredie, R.D. 75
macro organizational context 99
Maister, D. xi, 1, 18, 35, 93, 146
make static 83
Malhotra, N. 2, 133, 152
management consultancy: client assignments
    in 73–74; consultant virtualization 14;
    diversity in 152–153; gender imbalances in
    152; growth in ix; human capital in 13–14,
    24, 140; human resource functions in 20;
    industry-specific trends in 14; innovative
    orientation 12, 12, 13; internal consultancy
    units in 85, 109–110, 154, 156; knowledge
    management and 1, 105–107; life-cycle
    disruption and 14, 72–73, 86–91; Poles of
    innovation and 14–17, 117–118, 139–142;
    reflective ability and 14, 93–99; social capital
    in 14, 140; traditional 65; virtual organization

and 61–63, 66–67; *see also* innovative consultancy
*Managing the Professional Service Firm* (Maister) xi, 93
Mankin, D. 54
Mann, K. 96
March, J.G. 6
Margerison, C.J. 1
market-related barriers 22
Markham, C. 143–145
Markus, M.L. 56, 84
Martinez, L.F. 108–109
Martins, L.L. 131–132
Marvel, M.R. 23
Masa'deh, R.E. 1, 26
Masciarelli, F. 38
Maynard, M.T. 131–132
McCann, P. 21
McCarthy, W. 85
McDonald, A. 85
McFarlan, F.W. 78–79, 125
McInerney, C.R. 55, 57
McKee, D. 120
McKinlay, A. 63
McKinsey & Company x, 24, 88, 90, 105–106, 114, 151–152
'McKinsey and the Globalization of Consultancy' (Jones and Lefort) 88
McKinsey Solutions practice 24
McPherson, S.O. 124
member development 64
Metcalf, E. 96
Mexico 20
Meyer, A.D. 5–6
Mezirow, J. 126
Miles, R.E. 5–6
Miller, R. 78
Miyake, M. 20
modular consulting 86–87
Molina, A. 131
Monge, P. 55
Morgan, R.E. 42–43
Morris, P. 75
Morris, T. 2, 11, 24, 42, 104–105, 133, 152
Mors, M.L. 2, 10, 41
Mosey, S. 134
Moura, H. 81
Mowshowitz, A. 57–58, 61
Mu, Z. 66, 202
multinational corporations (MNCs) 99
Munro, M. 66

Nah, F.F. 84
Nam, D.I. xi, 42
Narayan, D. 37

National Agency for the Control of AIDS (NACA) 45–46
national diversity 58–59
natural capital 151
Neailey, K. 101
Netherlands xiv, 26, 41, 61, 107, 188, 190, 193
network closure 36
Newell, S. 62–63
new product development (NPD) process 101
New Zealand 26
niche creation 4
Niehaves, B. 106–107, 114
Nielsen, B.B. 119, 134–135
Nielsen, S. 119, 134–135
Nigeria xiv, 45–46, 157
Nissen, V. 128
Nonaka, I. 107–108
Normann, R. 80
novelty 3

Obeidat, B.Y. 1, 26
Oh, S. 60
Ojasalo, J. 59
Okamuro, H. 22
O'Leary, T. 81, 126
Olson, T.H. 2
O'Mahoney, J. ix, x, 7, 9, 72, 105–106, 107, 143–145
online communities 64
openness 43
open source software (OSS) 56
Optimization School 76
organizational capital: defining 52–53; human capital and 147; innovation and 73, 141–142; social capital and 147; *see also* life-cycle disruption; reflective ability; virtual organizations
organizational culture 102
organizational support 24, 42
organizations: adaptation in 5; ambidextrous 7; innovation in 5–6, 59; internal consultancy units in 109–110; learning skills and 100, 120; management ideas in 105; typology of 5–6
*Oxford Handbook of Management Consulting* (Kipping and Clark) xi, 34

Palm, K. xii, 9, 106
Panayides, P.M. 39
paradigmatic innovation 25
Parasuraman, A. 38
Parboteeah, K.P. xi, 42
participation assets 38
Páscoa, J. 81–82
Patel, C. 75

Paul, R.J. 75
Pay Zone case 66, 68, 136
'Pay Zone Consulting' (Munro and Huff) 66
phenomenological paradigm 147, 149
Pill, R. 96
Pirani, N. 88
Pisano, G.P. 97
Plattfaut, R. 106–107, 114
PMBOK (Project Management Body of Knowledge) Guide 74
Poland 193, *200*
Pollack, J. 74, 76
Portes, A. 36
positivist paradigm 147, 149
Potts, K. 85
Poulfelt, F. 2
power 105
practice emergence 24, 42, 104–105
Prandelli, E. 60
Prencipe, A. 38
PricewaterhouseCoopers 130
process mining 26–27
product development 59–60
professional services firms: characteristics of 1; human capital in 23–24; innovation in 1–2, 9; new practice areas in 24, 42, 104–105; potential ownership in 26; reflective ability and 97; strategic HR practices 25–26; up-or-out paradigm 151–152; *see also* management consultancy
project management: adaptive 79–80; alternate controls 83; candidature in 82; collaboration and 81–82; competing experiments 83; complex adaptive systems (CAS) and 80, 126; complexity in 75; conceptualization in 75; contingent 78–79, 89–90; deliberation in 82; emergent planning 83; finalization in 82; hard paradigm 74–76, 90; innovation and 77–81; life-cycle disruption and 81–84; make static 83; management system and 78; organizational systems and 81; overruns in 75; practitioner development in 75; reflective ability and 97, 126; re-interpretation in 74; rethinking project management (RPM) and 77; schools of thought in 76–77; social construction of 76; social processes in 75; soft paradigm 74, 76–77, 90; staged releases 83; structural complexity in 75; systems thinking in 79; theory of 74–76; tight time constraints in 75; uncertainty in 75; value creation in 75, 80
project management offices (PMOs) 81
Prusak, L. 26
psychological consulting 84–85
Puri, S. 88

Qiang Li 66–67, 120, 124, 129, 138–140

Rau, C. 103–104
Reeves, M. 128
reflective ability: content 126; defining 93; human capital and 120–121, *121*, 122, 132–133, *133*, 134–135; implications of 112–115; innovation and 99–110; life-cycle disruption and 125, *125*, 126–127; as organizational capital xii, 14, 93; performance outcomes and 97–98; premise 126; process 126; research in 94–99; social capital and 132–133, *133*, 134–135; team learning and 97–99
relational assets 38
Relationship School 76
Rentocchini, F. 22
research: action 148–149; alternative participative approaches in 149; data collecting in 149–150; innovative consultancy and 7–11, 147, 149–151; interactions between capital in 147, 150–151; longitudinal case-based work and 148; phenomenological paradigm 147, 149; positivist paradigm 147, 149; structural equation model and 147–148; sub-components of capital and 148; virtual organization and 54–56
rethinking project management (RPM) 77
reviewing 101
risk management 26
Rivais, C. 85
Robertson and Davies Management Consultants 47
Robey, D. 53–54
Roper, S. 8–9, 44
Rosen, B. 124, 128
Ross, D.D. 96
Rost, K. 39
Rowley, J. 3
Rush, H. 24
Rust, R.T. 38

Sabre, Inc. 124
Sambrook, S. 3
Sändig, N. 81–82
Sangiorgi, D. 99
Santos, F. 81–82
Sapienza, H.J. 40
Sawhney, M. 60
Scarbrough, H. 63
Scheer, A.W. 85
Schilling, A. xii, 9, 106
Schön, D.A. 120
Schulze, W. 37, 118–119

Schweitzer, F. 103–104
scientific/technical knowledge 21
Scopism 55, 65, 129, 132, 136
Seibert, S.E. 37
Seifert, H. 128
Sels, L. 22, 121
Semadeni, M. 2, 7, 10
senior partners 41–42
service innovation 9, 61, 84, 106–107
Shah, D. 38
Shaw, M.J. 56, 128
Shimizu, K. 1, 23
Shuh, A. 111, 159
Simonen, J. 21
Skov, R.B. 101
Slovakia 193, *200*
Smets, M. 2, 133, 152
Smit, W. 2, 10, 41, 107
Smith, C. 75
Snow, C.C. 5–6
social capital: boundaries and 43; citizenship behavior and 37; client relationships and 34–36, 38; cognitive dimension of 40; collaborative networks and 39; competitive advantage and 37; defensible turf and 42; defining 34; differentiated expertise and 42; direct/indirect ties and 39; entrepreneurial culture and 39; external relationships and 14; government policies for 40; human capital and 118, *118*, 119–120, 130, 147; implications of 48–50; information sources and 38; innovation and 34–35, 37–50, 119; knowledge acquisition and 40; network closure and 36; openness and 43; organizational capital and 147; organizational relations and 48; organizational support and 42; outcomes of 36–37; participation assets and 38; performance outcomes and 39; reflective ability and 132–133, *133*, 134–135; relational 40; relational assets and 38; socialized agency and 42; social networks and 36; structural 35–36, 40; theory of 35–37; trust and 39–40; virtual organization and 122–123, *123*, 124, 129–130, *130*, 131–132
social innovations 103–104
socialization-externalization-codification-internalization (SECI) model 107–108
socialized agency 24, 42
socialized listening 34–35
social network analysis 60
social networks 36, 44
Söderlund, J. 76–77
Somech, A. 101

Spain 22
Sparkes, J.R. 20
Spielkamp, A. 24–25
Srinivasan, R. 2
Staelin, R. 38
staged releases 83
standardization 83
Stata, R. 100
Steeneveld, M. 25
Stevens, C. 83
Strader, T.J. 56, 128
Straud, D. 53–54
structural dynamism 58
structural equation model 147–148
structural holes 35–36
Sturdy, A. ix, xi, 43, 83, 105–106, 109–110
Su, N. 88
Subramaniam, M. 22
Sundbo, J. 9
supplier-dominated innovation 25
supply chain relationships 39
support-based pathways 105
Sutcliffe, K.M. 98–99
Sutton, R.I. 44
Svejvig, P. 77
Swan, J. 63
Swart, J. 133
Sweden (Swedish entrepreneurs) 119
swift trust 55, 61
Switzerland xiv, 45, 86
systemic capabilities 106
systemic innovations 58
systems thinking 79
Szczepanek, T. 80

tacit knowledge 135
Tajar, A. 25, 43
Takeuchi, H. 107–108
Taminiau, Y. 2, 10, 41, 107
Tanis, C. 84
Tarhini, A. 1, 26
Tata Consultancy Services 114
team learning 97–102
teams 54, 100–101; *see also* virtual teams
technological reflectiveness 103–104
technology transfer 24–25
Teece, D.J. 58, 69
telecommuting 52
Tesluk, P.E. 124
Tether, B.S. 25, 43
Tomenendal, M. 152
Tommasi Motorcycles 28, 29, 30, 31
'Transforming the Business Service Portfolio at Global Consultancy' (Su and Pirani) 88

trust: assets 38; client-consultant relationship and 61–62, 144; ethics and 146–147; social capital and 39–40; swift 55, 61; virtual teams and 55–56
Tsai, W. 37, 40
Tuan, S.T. 187
Tuckman, B.W. 128
turf-based pathways 105
Turnley, W.H. 37

UK x, xiv, 7, 39–40, 42, 44–45, 55, 65–66, 75, 81, 107, 114, 188, 190, 193
UK Community Innovation Survey (CIS) 44
United Arab Emirates 190, *200*
up-or-out paradigm 151–152
US xii–xiii, 4, 7, 10, 20, 45, 172

Valle-Cabrera, R. 22
Van Bever, D. 24, 85
van den Hende, E. 103–104
Van Knippenberg, D. 100
Van Reenan, J. 151–153
Vega-Jurado, J. 22
Verdonschot, S.G. 102
Verganti, R. 82
Vermeulen, F. 98–99
Verona, G. 60
virtual knowledge brokers 60
virtual organizations: advantages of 57–61; breeding environment for 122–123, 131; characteristics of 54; citizenship efforts and 53; codified knowledge exchange in 58; collaboration and 54–55, 60; communication in 55–57, 62–64; consulting skills for 63; control mechanisms in 56; defining 52; disadvantages of 58–59, 69; duration and 69; electronic dependence of 58–59; geographic dispersion and 58–59; global 66–67; human capital and 129–130, *130*, 131–132; ICT and 52, 54, 56, 69; implications of 68–70; informational needs of 56; innovation and 52, 57–70; knowledge management and 60, 69; learning and 57; life-cycle disruption and 127, *127*, 128–129; life-cycle model of 128; management consultancy and 61–63, 66–67; membership choices in 69; national diversity and 58–59; online

communities and 64; opportunities and 57; as organizational capital xii, 14, 52–53; product development in 59–60; purpose for 69; research in 54–56; shared understanding in 123–124; social capital and 122–123, *123*, 124, 129–130, *130*, 131–132; social processes in 63–64, 69; structural dynamism and 58; tenuous relationships in 55–56; virtual mentality and 69
virtual teams: collaboration and 54–55; communication in 55; global 54; heterogeneity and 128; inputs/outputs of 131; leadership competences for 62, 131; life-cycle disruption and 128–129; managerial interventions for 128; outcomes of 131–132; team processes and 131; trust in 55–56
Von Nordenflycht, A. 1, 9
Von Platen, S. 109

Wang, D. 24, 85
Warren, C. 83
Werth, D. 85
Westerman, G. 78–79, 125
Whitty, S.J. 81
Wi, H. 60
Williams, C. 5, 20–21, 38, 66, 119, 171, 187, 202
Williams, R.L. 64
Williams, T. 75, 81, 126
Wills, D. 40
Winsborough, D. 84
Winter, M. 74, 80
Wood, P. 10
Woolcock, M. 37
work-life balance 151–153
Wright, C. xi, 83
Wright, M. 134
Wu, W.Y. 119
Wylie, N. xi, 83

Yli-Renko, H. 40
Youndt, M.A. 22
Yu, E. 99

Zellmer-Bruhn, M. 99
Zheng, W. 6, 40
Zhou, J. 100
Zhu, J. 38